Just The Facts 101
Textbook Key Facts

Cote D'ivoire Diplomatic Handbook

by Cram101
Textbook NOT Included

Table of Contents

Title Page

Copyright

Foundations of Business

Management

Business law

Finance

Human resource management

Information systems

Marketing

Manufacturing

Commerce

Business ethics

Accounting

Index: Answers

Just The Facts101

Exam Prep for

Cote D'ivoire Diplomatic Handbook

Just The Facts101 Exam Prep is your link from
the textbook and lecture to your exams.

**Just The Facts101 Exam Preps are unauthorized and comprehensive reviews
of your textbooks.**

All material provided by CTI Publications (c) 2019

Textbook publishers and textbook authors do not participate in or contribute to these reviews.

Just The Facts101 Exam Prep

Copyright © 2019 by CTI Publications. All rights reserved.

eAIN 444553

Foundations of Business

A business, also known as an enterprise, agency or a firm, is an entity involved in the provision of goods and/or services to consumers. Businesses are prevalent in capitalist economies, where most of them are privately owned and provide goods and services to customers in exchange for other goods, services, or money.

:: Payments ::

A _____ is the trade of value from one party to another for goods, or services, or to fulfill a legal obligation.

Exam Probability: **Medium**

1. *Answer choices:*

(see index for correct answer)

- a. Tuition payments
- b. KlickEx
- c. Deficiency payments
- d. Payment

Guidance: level 1

:: Organizational behavior ::

_____ is the state or fact of exclusive rights and control over property, which may be an object, land/real estate or intellectual property. _____ involves multiple rights, collectively referred to as title, which may be separated and held by different parties.

Exam Probability: **Low**

2. *Answer choices:*

(see index for correct answer)

- a. Ownership
- b. Collaborative partnerships
- c. Organizational Expedience

- d. Affective events theory

Guidance: level 1

:: Investment ::

In finance, the benefit from an _____ is called a return. The return may consist of a gain realised from the sale of property or an _____ , unrealised capital appreciation , or _____ income such as dividends, interest, rental income etc., or a combination of capital gain and income. The return may also include currency gains or losses due to changes in foreign currency exchange rates.

Exam Probability: **Medium**

3. *Answer choices:*

(see index for correct answer)

- a. Tontine
- b. American Bullion
- c. MarketSmith
- d. Investment

Guidance: level 1

:: Marketing ::

A _____ is a group of customers within a business's serviceable available market at which a business aims its marketing efforts and resources. A _____ is a subset of the total market for a product or service. The _____ typically consists of consumers who exhibit similar characteristics and are considered most likely to buy a business's market offerings or are likely to be the most profitable segments for the business to service.

Exam Probability: **High**

4. *Answer choices:*

(see index for correct answer)

- a. Product naming
- b. Masstige
- c. Customer insight
- d. Target market

Guidance: level 1

:: Actuarial science ::

_____ is the possibility of losing something of value. Values can be gained or lost when taking _____ resulting from a given action or inaction, foreseen or unforeseen. _____ can also be defined as the intentional interaction with uncertainty. Uncertainty is a potential, unpredictable, and uncontrollable outcome; _____ is a consequence of action taken in spite of uncertainty.

Exam Probability: **Low**

5. *Answer choices:*

(see index for correct answer)

- a. Risk
- b. Future interests
- c. Area compatibility factor
- d. CRESTA

Guidance: level 1

:: Business ::

_____ is a trade policy that does not restrict imports or exports; it can also be understood as the free market idea applied to international trade. In government, _____ is predominantly advocated by political parties that hold liberal economic positions while economically left-wing and nationalist political parties generally support protectionism, the opposite of _____ .

Exam Probability: **Low**

6. *Answer choices:*

(see index for correct answer)

- a. Local multiplier effect
- b. Free trade

- c. Westnile Distilling Company Limited
- d. Casengo

Guidance: level 1

:: Real estate valuation ::

> _____ or OMV is the price at which an asset would trade in a competitive auction setting. _____ is often used interchangeably with open _____ , fair value or fair _____ , although these terms have distinct definitions in different standards, and may or may not differ in some circumstances.

Exam Probability: **Medium**

7. *Answer choices:*
(see index for correct answer)

- a. Real estate appraisal
- b. Uniform Standards of Professional Appraisal Practice
- c. Market value
- d. Extraordinary assumptions and hypothetical conditions

Guidance: level 1

:: Competition (economics) ::

_____ arises whenever at least two parties strive for a goal which cannot be shared: where one's gain is the other's loss.

Exam Probability: **Medium**

8. *Answer choices:*

(see index for correct answer)

- a. Blindspots analysis
- b. Level playing field
- c. School choice
- d. Competition

Guidance: level 1

:: Industrial Revolution ::

The _____, now also known as the First _____, was the transition to new manufacturing processes in Europe and the US, in the period from about 1760 to sometime between 1820 and 1840. This transition included going from hand production methods to machines, new chemical manufacturing and iron production processes, the increasing use of steam power and water power, the development of machine tools and the rise of the mechanized factory system. The _____ also led to an unprecedented rise in the rate of population growth.

Exam Probability: **Low**

9. *Answer choices:*

(see index for correct answer)

- a. Industrial Revolution
- b. Masson Mill
- c. Spinning frame
- d. Soho Foundry

Guidance: level 1

:: Budgets ::

A _____ is a financial plan for a defined period, often one year. It may also include planned sales volumes and revenues, resource quantities, costs and expenses, assets, liabilities and cash flows. Companies, governments, families and other organizations use it to express strategic plans of activities or events in measurable terms.

Exam Probability: **Medium**

10. *Answer choices:*

(see index for correct answer)

- a. Budget
- b. Film budgeting
- c. Operating budget
- d. Budget set

Guidance: level 1

:: Data collection ::

A _____ is an utterance which typically functions as a request for information. _____ s can thus be understood as a kind of illocutionary act in the field of pragmatics or as special kinds of propositions in frameworks of formal semantics such as alternative semantics or inquisitive semantics. The information requested is expected to be provided in the form of an answer. _____ s are often conflated with interrogatives, which are the grammatical forms typically used to achieve them. Rhetorical _____ s, for example, are interrogative in form but may not be considered true _____ s as they are not expected to be answered. Conversely, non-interrogative grammatical structures may be considered _____ s as in the case of the imperative sentence "tell me your name".

Exam Probability: **High**

11. *Answer choices:*
(see index for correct answer)

- a. Data farming
- b. Paradata
- c. Synthetic Environment for Analysis and Simulations
- d. Question

Guidance: level 1

:: Money ::

In economics, _____ is money in the physical form of currency, such as banknotes and coins. In bookkeeping and finance, _____ is current assets comprising currency or currency equivalents that can be accessed immediately or near-immediately. _____ is seen either as a reserve for payments, in case of a structural or incidental negative _____ flow or as a way to avoid a downturn on financial markets.

Exam Probability: **Medium**

12. *Answer choices:*

(see index for correct answer)

- a. Purse bid
- b. Constant dollars
- c. Monetization
- d. Coin of account

Guidance: level 1

:: Shareholders ::

A _____ is a payment made by a corporation to its shareholders, usually as a distribution of profits. When a corporation earns a profit or surplus, the corporation is able to re-invest the profit in the business and pay a proportion of the profit as a _____ to shareholders. Distribution to shareholders may be in cash or, if the corporation has a _____ reinvestment plan, the amount can be paid by the issue of further shares or share repurchase. When _____ s are paid, shareholders typically must pay income taxes, and the corporation does not receive a corporate income tax deduction for the _____ payments.

Exam Probability: **High**

13. *Answer choices:*

(see index for correct answer)

- a. Shareholder resolution
- b. UK Individual Shareholders Society
- c. Proxy fight
- d. Shareholder primacy

Guidance: level 1

:: Meetings ::

An _____ is a group of people who participate in a show or encounter a work of art, literature, theatre, music, video games, or academics in any medium. _____ members participate in different ways in different kinds of art; some events invite overt _____ participation and others allowing only modest clapping and criticism and reception.

Exam Probability: **Low**

14. *Answer choices:*

(see index for correct answer)

- a. Speed thinking
- b. Brown bag seminar
- c. Audience
- d. Mighty Men Conference

Guidance: level 1

:: Human resource management ::

_____ are the people who make up the workforce of an organization, business sector, or economy. "Human capital" is sometimes used synonymously with " _____ ", although human capital typically refers to a narrower effect . Likewise, other terms sometimes used include manpower, talent, labor, personnel, or simply people.

Exam Probability: **High**

15. *Answer choices:*

(see index for correct answer)

- a. Co-determination
- b. Adaptive performance

- c. Progress, plans, problems
- d. Administrative services organization

Guidance: level 1

:: Security compliance ::

A _____ is a communicated intent to inflict harm or loss on another person. A _____ is considered an act of coercion. _____ s are widely observed in animal behavior, particularly in a ritualized form, chiefly in order to avoid the unnecessary physical violence that can lead to physical damage or the death of both conflicting parties.

Exam Probability: **Low**

16. *Answer choices:*

(see index for correct answer)

- a. Federal Information Security Management Act of 2002
- b. Information assurance vulnerability alert
- c. Threat
- d. Attack

Guidance: level 1

:: Currency ::

A _____ , in the most specific sense is money in any form when in use or circulation as a medium of exchange, especially circulating banknotes and coins. A more general definition is that a _____ is a system of money in common use, especially for people in a nation. Under this definition, US dollars , pounds sterling , Australian dollars , European euros , Russian rubles and Indian Rupees are examples of currencies. These various currencies are recognized as stores of value and are traded between nations in foreign exchange markets, which determine the relative values of the different currencies. Currencies in this sense are defined by governments, and each type has limited boundaries of acceptance.

Exam Probability: **High**

17. *Answer choices:*

(see index for correct answer)

- a. Demurrage
- b. Commodity currency
- c. Fictional currency
- d. Representative money

Guidance: level 1

:: Majority–minority relations ::

_____ , also known as reservation in India and Nepal, positive discrimination / action in the United Kingdom, and employment equity in Canada and South Africa, is the policy of promoting the education and employment of members of groups that are known to have previously suffered from discrimination. Historically and internationally, support for _____ has sought to achieve goals such as bridging inequalities in employment and pay, increasing access to education, promoting diversity, and redressing apparent past wrongs, harms, or hindrances.

Exam Probability: **Medium**

18. *Answer choices:*

(see index for correct answer)

- a. Affirmative action
- b. cultural dissonance
- c. cultural Relativism

Guidance: level 1

:: Elementary arithmetic ::

In mathematics, a _____ is a number or ratio expressed as a fraction of 100. It is often denoted using the percent sign, "%", or the abbreviations "pct.", "pct"; sometimes the abbreviation "pc" is also used. A _____ is a dimensionless number .

Exam Probability: **Medium**

19. *Answer choices:*

(see index for correct answer)

- a. 0
- b. Subtraction
- c. Fourth power
- d. Percentage

Guidance: level 1

:: Management ::

_____ is the identification, evaluation, and prioritization of risks followed by coordinated and economical application of resources to minimize, monitor, and control the probability or impact of unfortunate events or to maximize the realization of opportunities.

Exam Probability: **High**

20. *Answer choices:*

(see index for correct answer)

- a. Event chain diagram
- b. U-procedure and Theory U
- c. Meeting
- d. Shrinkage

Guidance: level 1

:: Social security ::

_____ is "any government system that provides monetary assistance to people with an inadequate or no income." In the United States, this is usually called welfare or a social safety net, especially when talking about Canada and European countries.

Exam Probability: **Low**

21. *Answer choices:*

(see index for correct answer)

- a. Social security
- b. Total Social Security Accounts
- c. Government Service Insurance System
- d. Social security in Sweden

Guidance: level 1

:: Financial markets ::

A _____ is a financial market in which long-term debt or equity-backed securities are bought and sold. _____ s channel the wealth of savers to those who can put it to long-term productive use, such as companies or governments making long-term investments. Financial regulators like the Bank of England and the U.S. Securities and Exchange Commission oversee _____ s to protect investors against fraud, among other duties.

Exam Probability: **Low**

22. *Answer choices:*

(see index for correct answer)

- a. Real-time economy
- b. Capital market
- c. CUSIP-linked MIP code
- d. Derivatives market

Guidance: level 1

:: Market research ::

A _____ is a small, but demographically diverse group of people and whose reactions are studied especially in market research or political analysis in guided or open discussions about a new product or something else to determine the reactions that can be expected from a larger population. It is a form of qualitative research consisting of interviews in which a group of people are asked about their perceptions, opinions, beliefs, and attitudes towards a product, service, concept, advertisement, idea, or packaging. Questions are asked in an interactive group setting where participants are free to talk with other group members. During this process, the researcher either takes notes or records the vital points he or she is getting from the group. Researchers should select members of the _____ carefully for effective and authoritative responses.

Exam Probability: **Medium**

23. *Answer choices:*

(see index for correct answer)

- a. IModerate
- b. GlobalWebIndex
- c. Cambashi
- d. Sectoral analysis

Guidance: level 1

:: Business law ::

A _____ is a business entity created by two or more parties, generally characterized by shared ownership, shared returns and risks, and shared governance. Companies typically pursue _____ s for one of four reasons: to access a new market, particularly emerging markets; to gain scale efficiencies by combining assets and operations; to share risk for major investments or projects; or to access skills and capabilities.

Exam Probability: **Medium**

24. *Answer choices:*

(see index for correct answer)

- a. Financial Security Law of France
- b. Operating lease
- c. Joint venture
- d. Process agent

Guidance: level 1

:: Labour relations ::

_____ is a field of study that can have different meanings depending on the context in which it is used. In an international context, it is a subfield of labor history that studies the human relations with regard to work – in its broadest sense – and how this connects to questions of social inequality. It explicitly encompasses unregulated, historical, and non-Western forms of labor. Here, _____ define "for or with whom one works and under what rules. These rules determine the type of work, type and amount of remuneration, working hours, degrees of physical and psychological strain, as well as the degree of freedom and autonomy associated with the work."

Exam Probability: **Medium**

25. *Answer choices:*

(see index for correct answer)

- a. Comprehensive campaign
- b. Broad left
- c. Labour council
- d. Open shop

Guidance: level 1

:: Private equity ::

_____ is a type of private equity, a form of financing that is provided by firms or funds to small, early-stage, emerging firms that are deemed to have high growth potential, or which have demonstrated high growth. _____ firms or funds invest in these early-stage companies in exchange for equity, or an ownership stake, in the companies they invest in. _____ists take on the risk of financing risky start-ups in the hopes that some of the firms they support will become successful. Because startups face high uncertainty, VC investments do have high rates of failure. The start-ups are usually based on an innovative technology or business model and they are usually from the high technology industries, such as information technology, clean technology or biotechnology.

Exam Probability: **High**

26. *Answer choices:*

(see index for correct answer)

- a. Club deal
- b. World Business Angels Association
- c. Rollup
- d. Corporate raid

Guidance: level 1

:: Accounting terminology ::

_____ is a legally enforceable claim for payment held by a business for goods supplied and/or services rendered that customers/clients have ordered but not paid for. These are generally in the form of invoices raised by a business and delivered to the customer for payment within an agreed time frame. _____ is shown in a balance sheet as an asset. It is one of a series of accounting transactions dealing with the billing of a customer for goods and services that the customer has ordered. These may be distinguished from notes receivable, which are debts created through formal legal instruments called promissory notes.

Exam Probability: **High**

27. *Answer choices:*

(see index for correct answer)

- a. Accounts receivable
- b. Adjusting entries
- c. revenue recognition principle
- d. Fair value accounting

Guidance: level 1

:: Mereology ::

_____ , in the abstract, is what belongs to or with something, whether as an attribute or as a component of said thing. In the context of this article, it is one or more components , whether physical or incorporeal, of a person's estate; or so belonging to, as in being owned by, a person or jointly a group of people or a legal entity like a corporation or even a society. Depending on the nature of the _____ , an owner of _____ has the right to consume, alter, share, redefine, rent, mortgage, pawn, sell, exchange, transfer, give away or destroy it, or to exclude others from doing these things, as well as to perhaps abandon it; whereas regardless of the nature of the _____ , the owner thereof has the right to properly use it , or at the very least exclusively keep it.

Exam Probability: **Medium**

28. *Answer choices:*

(see index for correct answer)

- a. Mereology
- b. Mereological nihilism
- c. Gunk
- d. Property

Guidance: level 1

:: Business ethics ::

_____ is a type of harassment technique that relates to a sexual nature and the unwelcome or inappropriate promise of rewards in exchange for sexual favors. _____ includes a range of actions from mild transgressions to sexual abuse or assault. Harassment can occur in many different social settings such as the workplace, the home, school, churches, etc. Harassers or victims may be of any gender.

Exam Probability: **Medium**

29. *Answer choices:*

(see index for correct answer)

- a. Philosophy of business
- b. Sexual harassment
- c. CUC International
- d. Society of Corporate Compliance and Ethics

Guidance: level 1

:: Public relations ::

_____ is the public visibility or awareness for any product, service or company. It may also refer to the movement of information from its source to the general public, often but not always via the media. The subjects of _____ include people, goods and services, organizations, and works of art or entertainment.

Exam Probability: **Medium**

30. Answer choices:

(see index for correct answer)

- a. The Centre for Corporate Public Affairs
- b. International
- c. European Public Relations Education and Research Association
- d. Publicity

Guidance: level 1

:: ::

_____ or accountancy is the measurement, processing, and communication of financial information about economic entities such as businesses and corporations. The modern field was established by the Italian mathematician Luca Pacioli in 1494. _____ , which has been called the "language of business", measures the results of an organization's economic activities and conveys this information to a variety of users, including investors, creditors, management, and regulators. Practitioners of _____ are known as accountants. The terms " _____ " and "financial reporting" are often used as synonyms.

Exam Probability: **High**

31. Answer choices:

(see index for correct answer)

- a. personal values
- b. corporate values

- c. Accounting
- d. process perspective

Guidance: level 1

:: Marketing ::

_____ comes from the Latin neg and otsia referring to businessmen who, unlike the patricians, had no leisure time in their industriousness; it held the meaning of business until the 17th century when it took on the diplomatic connotation as a dialogue between two or more people or parties intended to reach a beneficial outcome over one or more issues where a conflict exists with respect to at least one of these issues. Thus, _____ is a process of combining divergent positions into a joint agreement under a decision rule of unanimity.

Exam Probability: **Low**

32. *Answer choices:*

(see index for correct answer)

- a. Movement marketing
- b. Albuquerque Craft Beer Market
- c. Fixed value-added resource
- d. Negotiation

Guidance: level 1

:: Scientific method ::

In the social sciences and life sciences, a _____ is a research method involving an up-close, in-depth, and detailed examination of a subject of study, as well as its related contextual conditions.

Exam Probability: **Medium**

33. *Answer choices:*

(see index for correct answer)

- a. Preference test
- b. Causal research
- c. Case study
- d. explanatory research

Guidance: level 1

:: ::

An _____ is the production of goods or related services within an economy. The major source of revenue of a group or company is the indicator of its relevant _____. When a large group has multiple sources of revenue generation, it is considered to be working in different industries. Manufacturing _____ became a key sector of production and labour in European and North American countries during the Industrial Revolution, upsetting previous mercantile and feudal economies. This came through many successive rapid advances in technology, such as the production of steel and coal.

Exam Probability: **Medium**

34. *Answer choices:*

(see index for correct answer)

- a. functional perspective
- b. cultural
- c. interpersonal communication
- d. hierarchical

Guidance: level 1

:: Decision theory ::

A _____ is a deliberate system of principles to guide decisions and achieve rational outcomes. A _____ is a statement of intent, and is implemented as a procedure or protocol. Policies are generally adopted by a governance body within an organization. Policies can assist in both subjective and objective decision making. Policies to assist in subjective decision making usually assist senior management with decisions that must be based on the relative merits of a number of factors, and as a result are often hard to test objectively, e.g. work-life balance _____ . In contrast policies to assist in objective decision making are usually operational in nature and can be objectively tested, e.g. password _____ .

Exam Probability: **Medium**

35. *Answer choices:*

(see index for correct answer)

- a. Business rules engine
- b. Bulk Dispatch Lapse
- c. Policy
- d. Homothetic preferences

Guidance: level 1

:: Marketing ::

The _____ is a foundation model for businesses. The _____ has been defined as the "set of marketing tools that the firm uses to pursue its marketing objectives in the target market". Thus the _____ refers to four broad levels of marketing decision, namely: product, price, place, and promotion. Marketing practice has been occurring for millennia, but marketing theory emerged in the early twentieth century. The contemporary _____ , or the 4 Ps, which has become the dominant framework for marketing management decisions, was first published in 1960. In services marketing, an extended _____ is used, typically comprising 7 Ps, made up of the original 4 Ps extended by process, people, and physical evidence. Occasionally service marketers will refer to 8 Ps, comprising these 7 Ps plus performance.

Exam Probability: **Medium**

36. *Answer choices:*

(see index for correct answer)

- a. Product naming convention
- b. Place branding
- c. Health marketing
- d. Marketing mix

Guidance: level 1

:: ::

Some scenarios associate "this kind of planning" with learning "life skills". Schedules are necessary, or at least useful, in situations where individuals need to know what time they must be at a specific location to receive a specific service, and where people need to accomplish a set of goals within a set time period.

Exam Probability: **Low**

37. *Answer choices:*

(see index for correct answer)

- a. levels of analysis
- b. process perspective
- c. Scheduling
- d. similarity-attraction theory

Guidance: level 1

:: ::

_____ refers to a business or organization attempting to acquire goods or services to accomplish its goals. Although there are several organizations that attempt to set standards in the _____ process, processes can vary greatly between organizations. Typically the word "_____" is not used interchangeably with the word "procurement", since procurement typically includes expediting, supplier quality, and transportation and logistics in addition to _____ .

Exam Probability: **Low**

38. *Answer choices:*

(see index for correct answer)

- a. empathy
- b. levels of analysis
- c. Purchasing
- d. similarity-attraction theory

Guidance: level 1

:: Retailing ::

_____ is the process of selling consumer goods or services to customers through multiple channels of distribution to earn a profit. _____ ers satisfy demand identified through a supply chain. The term " _____ er" is typically applied where a service provider fills the small orders of a large number of individuals, who are end-users, rather than large orders of a small number of wholesale, corporate or government clientele. Shopping generally refers to the act of buying products. Sometimes this is done to obtain final goods, including necessities such as food and clothing; sometimes it takes place as a recreational activity. Recreational shopping often involves window shopping and browsing: it does not always result in a purchase.

Exam Probability: **Low**

39. *Answer choices:*

(see index for correct answer)

- a. Retail
- b. Cash on Delivery
- c. Bulk bins
- d. Consignment Store

Guidance: level 1

:: Production economics ::

_____ is the joint use of a resource or space. It is also the process of dividing and distributing. In its narrow sense, it refers to joint or alternating use of inherently finite goods, such as a common pasture or a shared residence. Still more loosely, "_____" can actually mean giving something as an outright gift: for example, to "share" one's food really means to give some of it as a gift. _____ is a basic component of human interaction, and is responsible for strengthening social ties and ensuring a person's well-being.

Exam Probability: **Low**

40. *Answer choices:*
(see index for correct answer)

- a. Marginal product of labor
- b. Productivity Alpha
- c. Sharing
- d. Isocost

Guidance: level 1

:: Statistical terminology ::

_____ es can be learned implicitly within cultural contexts. People may develop _____ es toward or against an individual, an ethnic group, a sexual or gender identity, a nation, a religion, a social class, a political party, theoretical paradigms and ideologies within academic domains, or a species. _____ ed means one-sided, lacking a neutral viewpoint, or not having an open mind. _____ can come in many forms and is related to prejudice and intuition.

Exam Probability: **High**

41. *Answer choices:*

(see index for correct answer)

- a. probability function
- b. Collectively exhaustive
- c. Bias
- d. Aggregate data

Guidance: level 1

:: Systems theory ::

A _____ is a group of interacting or interrelated entities that form a unified whole. A _____ is delineated by its spatial and temporal boundaries, surrounded and influenced by its environment, described by its structure and purpose and expressed in its functioning.

Exam Probability: **Medium**

42. *Answer choices:*

(see index for correct answer)

- a. transient state
- b. System
- c. co-design
- d. subsystem

Guidance: level 1

:: Financial statements ::

In financial accounting, a _____ or statement of financial position or statement of financial condition is a summary of the financial balances of an individual or organization, whether it be a sole proprietorship, a business partnership, a corporation, private limited company or other organization such as Government or not-for-profit entity. Assets, liabilities and ownership equity are listed as of a specific date, such as the end of its financial year. A _____ is often described as a "snapshot of a company's financial condition". Of the four basic financial statements, the _____ is the only statement which applies to a single point in time of a business' calendar year.

Exam Probability: **High**

43. *Answer choices:*

(see index for correct answer)

- a. quarterly report
- b. Clean surplus accounting
- c. Emphasis of matter
- d. Consolidated financial statement

Guidance: level 1

:: Management ::

_____ is the practice of initiating, planning, executing, controlling, and closing the work of a team to achieve specific goals and meet specific success criteria at the specified time.

Exam Probability: **High**

44. *Answer choices:*

(see index for correct answer)

- a. Product breakdown structure
- b. Investment control
- c. Supply network
- d. Project management

Guidance: level 1

:: Industrial design ::

In physics and mathematics, the _____ of a mathematical space is informally defined as the minimum number of coordinates needed to specify any point within it. Thus a line has a _____ of one because only one coordinate is needed to specify a point on it for example, the point at 5 on a number line. A surface such as a plane or the surface of a cylinder or sphere has a _____ of two because two coordinates are needed to specify a point on it for example, both a latitude and longitude are required to locate a point on the surface of a sphere. The inside of a cube, a cylinder or a sphere is three-_____ al because three coordinates are needed to locate a point within these spaces.

Exam Probability: **Low**

45. *Answer choices:*

(see index for correct answer)

- a. Flip
- b. Sky-Sailor
- c. Bauhaus
- d. Dimension

Guidance: level 1

:: Auditing ::

_____, as defined by accounting and auditing, is a process for assuring of an organization's objectives in operational effectiveness and efficiency, reliable financial reporting, and compliance with laws, regulations and policies. A broad concept, _____ involves everything that controls risks to an organization.

Exam Probability: **Low**

46. *Answer choices:*

(see index for correct answer)

- a. Audit plan
- b. Internal control
- c. Inherent risk
- d. Sales tax audit

Guidance: level 1

:: ::

_____ is the study and management of exchange relationships. _____ is the business process of creating relationships with and satisfying customers. With its focus on the customer, _____ is one of the premier components of business management.

Exam Probability: **Low**

47. *Answer choices:*

(see index for correct answer)

- a. Sarbanes-Oxley act of 2002
- b. functional perspective
- c. imperative
- d. Marketing

Guidance: level 1

:: International relations ::

A _____ is any event that is going to lead to an unstable and dangerous situation affecting an individual, group, community, or whole society. Crises are deemed to be negative changes in the security, economic, political, societal, or environmental affairs, especially when they occur abruptly, with little or no warning. More loosely, it is a term meaning "a testing time" or an "emergency event".

Exam Probability: **Medium**

48. *Answer choices:*

(see index for correct answer)

- a. Hollings Center
- b. Fragile state
- c. Global Alliance for Peace and Prosperity
- d. International relations

Guidance: level 1

:: Survey methodology ::

An _____ is a conversation where questions are asked and answers are given. In common parlance, the word "_____" refers to a one-on-one conversation between an _____ er and an _____ ee. The _____ er asks questions to which the _____ ee responds, usually so information may be transferred from _____ ee to _____ er. Sometimes, information can be transferred in both directions. It is a communication, unlike a speech, which produces a one-way flow of information.

Exam Probability: **Low**

49. *Answer choices:*

(see index for correct answer)

- a. Survey sampling
- b. Sampling
- c. National Health Interview Survey
- d. Interview

Guidance: level 1

:: Project management ::

Contemporary business and science treat as a _____ any undertaking, carried out individually or collaboratively and possibly involving research or design, that is carefully planned to achieve a particular aim.

Exam Probability: **High**

50. *Answer choices:*

(see index for correct answer)

- a. Enterprise project management
- b. DICE framework
- c. Critical path drag
- d. Project appraisal

Guidance: level 1

:: Industry ::

_____ describes various measures of the efficiency of production. Often , a _____ measure is expressed as the ratio of an aggregate output to a single input or an aggregate input used in a production process, i.e. output per unit of input. Most common example is the labour _____ measure, e.g., such as GDP per worker. There are many different definitions of _____ and the choice among them depends on the purpose of the _____ measurement and/or data availability. The key source of difference between various _____ measures is also usually related to how the outputs and the inputs are aggregated into scalars to obtain such a ratio-type measure of _____ .

Exam Probability: **Medium**

51. *Answer choices:*

(see index for correct answer)

- a. Wedge based mechanical exfoliation
- b. Industrial region
- c. Exposure action value
- d. Productivity

Guidance: level 1

:: Land value taxation ::

_____, sometimes referred to as dry _____, is the solid surface of Earth that is not permanently covered by water. The vast majority of human activity throughout history has occurred in _____ areas that support agriculture, habitat, and various natural resources. Some life forms have developed from predecessor species that lived in bodies of water.

Exam Probability: **High**

52. *Answer choices:*

(see index for correct answer)

- a. Land
- b. Land value tax

- c. Lands Valuation Appeal Court
- d. Georgism

Guidance: level 1

:: Bribery ::

_____ is the act of giving or receiving something of value in exchange for some kind of influence or action in return, that the recipient would otherwise not offer. _____ is defined by Black's Law Dictionary as the offering, giving, receiving, or soliciting of any item of value to influence the actions of an official or other person in charge of a public or legal duty. Essentially, _____ is offering to do something for someone for the expressed purpose of receiving something in exchange. Gifts of money or other items of value which are otherwise available to everyone on an equivalent basis, and not for dishonest purposes, is not _____ . Offering a discount or a refund to all purchasers is a legal rebate and is not _____ . For example, it is legal for an employee of a Public Utilities Commission involved in electric rate regulation to accept a rebate on electric service that reduces their cost for electricity, when the rebate is available to other residential electric customers. Giving the rebate to influence them to look favorably on the electric utility's rate increase applications, however, would be considered _____ .

Exam Probability: **Medium**

53. *Answer choices:*

(see index for correct answer)

- a. Global Corruption Barometer
- b. Kickback

- c. Bribery
- d. GSIS-Meralco bribery case

Guidance: level 1

:: Business law ::

A _____ is an arrangement where parties, known as partners, agree to cooperate to advance their mutual interests. The partners in a _____ may be individuals, businesses, interest-based organizations, schools, governments or combinations. Organizations may partner to increase the likelihood of each achieving their mission and to amplify their reach. A _____ may result in issuing and holding equity or may be only governed by a contract.

Exam Probability: **High**

54. *Answer choices:*

(see index for correct answer)

- a. Ordinary course of business
- b. Companies law
- c. Limited partnership
- d. TRIPS Agreement

Guidance: level 1

:: Casting (manufacturing) ::

A _____ is a regularity in the world, man-made design, or abstract ideas. As such, the elements of a _____ repeat in a predictable manner. A geometric _____ is a kind of _____ formed of geometric shapes and typically repeated like a wallpaper design.

Exam Probability: **High**

55. *Answer choices:*

(see index for correct answer)

- a. Ablation casting
- b. Plano-convex ingot
- c. Die casting
- d. Pattern

Guidance: level 1

:: Systems theory ::

A _____ is a set of policies, processes and procedures used by an organization to ensure that it can fulfill the tasks required to achieve its objectives. These objectives cover many aspects of the organization's operations . For instance, an environmental _____ enables organizations to improve their environmental performance and an occupational health and safety _____ enables an organization to control its occupational health and safety risks, etc.

Exam Probability: **High**

56. *Answer choices:*

(see index for correct answer)

- a. decentralized system
- b. process system
- c. co-design
- d. equifinality

Guidance: level 1

:: Marketing ::

_____ or stock is the goods and materials that a business holds for the ultimate goal of resale.

Exam Probability: **Medium**

57. *Answer choices:*

(see index for correct answer)

- a. Contribution margin-based pricing
- b. Inventory
- c. Aspirational brand
- d. Digital omnivore

Guidance: level 1

:: National accounts ::

_____ is a monetary measure of the market value of all the final goods and services produced in a period of time, often annually. GDP per capita does not, however, reflect differences in the cost of living and the inflation rates of the countries; therefore using a basis of GDP per capita at purchasing power parity is arguably more useful when comparing differences in living standards between nations.

Exam Probability: **Medium**

58. *Answer choices:*

(see index for correct answer)

- a. National Income
- b. Gross domestic product
- c. Fixed capital

Guidance: level 1

:: ::

_____ is the means to see, hear, or become aware of something or someone through our fundamental senses. The term _____ derives from the Latin word perceptio, and is the organization, identification, and interpretation of sensory information in order to represent and understand the presented information, or the environment.

Exam Probability: **Medium**

59. *Answer choices:*

(see index for correct answer)

- a. personal values
- b. empathy
- c. hierarchical
- d. corporate values

Guidance: level 1

Management

Management is the administration of an organization, whether it is a business, a not-for-profit organization, or government body. Management includes the activities of setting the strategy of an organization and coordinating the efforts of its employees (or of volunteers) to accomplish its objectives through the application of available resources, such as financial, natural, technological, and human resources.

:: Project management ::

Some scenarios associate "this kind of planning" with learning "life skills". _____s are necessary, or at least useful, in situations where individuals need to know what time they must be at a specific location to receive a specific service, and where people need to accomplish a set of goals within a set time period.

Exam Probability: **Low**

1. *Answer choices:*

(see index for correct answer)

- a. System anatomy
- b. Agile management
- c. Participatory impact pathways analysis
- d. ISO 31000

Guidance: level 1

:: Marketing ::

_____ or stock control can be broadly defined as "the activity of checking a shop's stock." However, a more focused definition takes into account the more science-based, methodical practice of not only verifying a business' inventory but also focusing on the many related facets of inventory management "within an organisation to meet the demand placed upon that business economically." Other facets of _____ include supply chain management, production control, financial flexibility, and customer satisfaction. At the root of _____, however, is the _____ problem, which involves determining when to order, how much to order, and the logistics of those decisions.

Exam Probability: **Medium**

2. *Answer choices:*

(see index for correct answer)

- a. Impulse purchase
- b. Pitching engine
- c. Inventory control
- d. Landing page

Guidance: level 1

:: Systems theory ::

A _____ is a set of policies, processes and procedures used by an organization to ensure that it can fulfill the tasks required to achieve its objectives. These objectives cover many aspects of the organization's operations . For instance, an environmental _____ enables organizations to improve their environmental performance and an occupational health and safety _____ enables an organization to control its occupational health and safety risks, etc.

Exam Probability: **Medium**

3. *Answer choices:*

(see index for correct answer)

- a. steady state
- b. equifinality
- c. transient state
- d. process system

Guidance: level 1

:: Internet privacy ::

An _____ is a private network accessible only to an organization's staff. Often, a wide range of information and services are available on an organization's internal _____ that are unavailable to the public, unlike the Internet. A company-wide _____ can constitute an important focal point of internal communication and collaboration, and provide a single starting point to access internal and external resources. In its simplest form, an _____ is established with the technologies for local area networks and wide area networks . Many modern _____ s have search engines, user profiles, blogs, mobile apps with notifications, and events planning within their infrastructure.

Exam Probability: **Medium**

4. *Answer choices:*
(see index for correct answer)

- a. Intranet
- b. Web bug
- c. Atdmt
- d. Web storage

Guidance: level 1

:: Game theory ::

_____ is the idea that rationality is limited when individuals make decisions: by the tractability of the decision problem, the cognitive limitations of the mind, and the time available to make the decision. Decision-makers, in this view, act as satisficers, seeking a satisfactory solution rather than an optimal one.

Exam Probability: **Low**

5. *Answer choices:*

(see index for correct answer)

- a. Blotto games
- b. Public goods game
- c. Bounded rationality
- d. Differential game

Guidance: level 1

:: Organizational behavior ::

_____ is the state or fact of exclusive rights and control over property, which may be an object, land/real estate or intellectual property. _____ involves multiple rights, collectively referred to as title, which may be separated and held by different parties.

Exam Probability: **Low**

6. *Answer choices:*

(see index for correct answer)

- a. Ownership
- b. Administrative Behavior
- c. Burnout
- d. Nut Island effect

Guidance: level 1

:: Management occupations ::

_____ ship is the process of designing, launching and running a new business, which is often initially a small business. The people who create these businesses are called _____ s.

Exam Probability: **High**

7. *Answer choices:*

(see index for correct answer)

- a. Councillor
- b. Legislator
- c. City manager
- d. Chief customer officer

Guidance: level 1

:: ::

_____ involves decision making. It can include judging the merits of multiple options and selecting one or more of them. One can make a _____ between imagined options or between real options followed by the corresponding action. For example, a traveler might choose a route for a journey based on the preference of arriving at a given destination as soon as possible. The preferred route can then follow from information such as the length of each of the possible routes, traffic conditions, etc. The arrival at a _____ can include more complex motivators such as cognition, instinct, and feeling.

Exam Probability: **High**

8. *Answer choices:*

(see index for correct answer)

- a. hierarchical perspective
- b. open system
- c. deep-level diversity
- d. Choice

Guidance: level 1

:: ::

_____, known in Europe as research and technological development, refers to innovative activities undertaken by corporations or governments in developing new services or products, or improving existing services or products. _____ constitutes the first stage of development of a potential new service or the production process.

Exam Probability: **Medium**

9. *Answer choices:*
(see index for correct answer)

- a. Research and development
- b. surface-level diversity
- c. open system
- d. deep-level diversity

Guidance: level 1

:: Office administration ::

An _____ is generally a room or other area where an organization's employees perform administrative work in order to support and realize objects and goals of the organization. The word " _____ " may also denote a position within an organization with specific duties attached to it ; the latter is in fact an earlier usage, _____ as place originally referring to the location of one's duty. When used as an adjective, the term " _____ " may refer to business-related tasks. In law, a company or organization has _____ s in any place where it has an official presence, even if that presence consists of a storage silo rather than an establishment with desk-and-chair. An _____ is also an architectural and design phenomenon: ranging from a small _____ such as a bench in the corner of a small business of extremely small size , through entire floors of buildings, up to and including massive buildings dedicated entirely to one company. In modern terms an _____ is usually the location where white-collar workers carry out their functions. As per James Stephenson, " _____ is that part of business enterprise which is devoted to the direction and co-ordination of its various activities."

Exam Probability: **Medium**

10. *Answer choices:*

(see index for correct answer)

- a. Activity management
- b. Inter departmental communication
- c. Office
- d. Fish! Philosophy

Guidance: level 1

:: Problem solving ::

A _____ is a unit or formation established to work on a single defined task or activity. Originally introduced by the United States Navy, the term has now caught on for general usage and is a standard part of NATO terminology. Many non-military organizations now create "_____ s" or task groups for temporary activities that might have once been performed by ad hoc committees.

Exam Probability: **Low**

11. *Answer choices:*

(see index for correct answer)

- a. Unified structured inventive thinking
- b. Task force
- c. Curiosity
- d. Encyclopedia of World Problems and Human Potential

Guidance: level 1

:: Evaluation methods ::

In social psychology, _____ is the process of looking at oneself in order to assess aspects that are important to one's identity. It is one of the motives that drive self-evaluation, along with self-verification and self-enhancement. Sedikides suggests that the _____ motive will prompt people to seek information to confirm their uncertain self-concept rather than their certain self-concept and at the same time people use _____ to enhance their certainty of their own self-knowledge. However, the _____ motive could be seen as quite different from the other two self-evaluation motives. Unlike the other two motives through _____ people are interested in the accuracy of their current self view, rather than improving their self-view. This makes _____ the only self-evaluative motive that may cause a person's self-esteem to be damaged.

Exam Probability: **Medium**

12. *Answer choices:*

(see index for correct answer)

- a. Gender evaluation methodology
- b. Question-focused dataset
- c. Self-assessment
- d. Reality TV confessional

Guidance: level 1

:: Social networks ::

_____ broadly refers to those factors of effectively functioning social groups that include such things as interpersonal relationships, a shared sense of identity, a shared understanding, shared norms, shared values, trust, cooperation, and reciprocity. However, the many views of this complex subject make a single definition difficult.

Exam Probability: **Medium**

13. *Answer choices:*

(see index for correct answer)

- a. Social capital
- b. Crowd computing
- c. Game of Golf Institute
- d. Social networking pedagogy

Guidance: level 1

:: Project management ::

A _____ is a professional in the field of project management. _____s have the responsibility of the planning, procurement and execution of a project, in any undertaking that has a defined scope, defined start and a defined finish; regardless of industry. _____s are first point of contact for any issues or discrepancies arising from within the heads of various departments in an organization before the problem escalates to higher authorities. Project management is the responsibility of a _____. This individual seldom participates directly in the activities that produce the end result, but rather strives to maintain the progress, mutual interaction and tasks of various parties in such a way that reduces the risk of overall failure, maximizes benefits, and minimizes costs.

Exam Probability: **High**

14. *Answer choices:*

(see index for correct answer)

- a. Trenegy Incorporated
- b. Project manager
- c. Gold plating
- d. Flexible product development

Guidance: level 1

:: Leadership ::

_____ /Management is a part of a style of leadership that focuses on supervision, organization, and performance; it is an integral part of the Full Range Leadership Model. _____ is a style of leadership in which leaders promote compliance by followers through both rewards and punishments. Through a rewards and punishments system, transactional leaders are able to keep followers motivated for the short-term. Unlike transformational leaders, those using the transactional approach are not looking to change the future, they look to keep things the same. Leaders using _____ as a model pay attention to followers' work in order to find faults and deviations.

Exam Probability: **Medium**

15. *Answer choices:*

(see index for correct answer)

- a. Leadership analysis
- b. European Center for Leadership Development
- c. Moral example
- d. Transactional leadership

Guidance: level 1

:: Logistics ::

_____ is generally the detailed organization and implementation of a complex operation. In a general business sense, _____ is the management of the flow of things between the point of origin and the point of consumption in order to meet requirements of customers or corporations. The resources managed in _____ may include tangible goods such as materials, equipment, and supplies, as well as food and other consumable items. The _____ of physical items usually involves the integration of information flow, materials handling, production, packaging, inventory, transportation, warehousing, and often security.

Exam Probability: **Medium**

16. *Answer choices:*

(see index for correct answer)

- a. Hubs and Nodes
- b. Logistics center
- c. Phase jitter modulation
- d. Logistics

Guidance: level 1

:: Lean manufacturing ::

_____ is the Sino-Japanese word for "improvement". In business, _____ refers to activities that continuously improve all functions and involve all employees from the CEO to the assembly line workers. It also applies to processes, such as purchasing and logistics, that cross organizational boundaries into the supply chain. It has been applied in healthcare, psychotherapy, life-coaching, government, and banking.

Exam Probability: **Medium**

17. *Answer choices:*

(see index for correct answer)

- a. Kaizen
- b. Production leveling
- c. Muri
- d. takt

Guidance: level 1

:: Generally Accepted Accounting Principles ::

In accounting, _____ is the income that a business have from its normal business activities, usually from the sale of goods and services to customers. _____ is also referred to as sales or turnover. Some companies receive _____ from interest, royalties, or other fees. _____ may refer to business income in general, or it may refer to the amount, in a monetary unit, earned during a period of time, as in "Last year, Company X had _____ of $42 million". Profits or net income generally imply total _____ minus total expenses in a given period. In accounting, in the balance statement it is a subsection of the Equity section and _____ increases equity, it is often referred to as the "top line" due to its position on the income statement at the very top. This is to be contrasted with the "bottom line" which denotes net income.

Exam Probability: **Low**

18. *Answer choices:*

(see index for correct answer)

- a. Chinese accounting standards
- b. Cost principle
- c. Insurance asset management
- d. net realisable value

Guidance: level 1

:: Project management ::

_____ and Theory Y are theories of human work motivation and management. They were created by Douglas McGregor while he was working at the MIT Sloan School of Management in the 1950s, and developed further in the 1960s. McGregor's work was rooted in motivation theory alongside the works of Abraham Maslow, who created the hierarchy of needs. The two theories proposed by McGregor describe contrasting models of workforce motivation applied by managers in human resource management, organizational behavior, organizational communication and organizational development. _____ explains the importance of heightened supervision, external rewards, and penalties, while Theory Y highlights the motivating role of job satisfaction and encourages workers to approach tasks without direct supervision. Management use of _____ and Theory Y can affect employee motivation and productivity in different ways, and managers may choose to implement strategies from both theories into their practices.

Exam Probability: **Medium**

19. *Answer choices:*

(see index for correct answer)

- a. Project initiation document
- b. Feature-driven development
- c. Student syndrome
- d. Theory X

Guidance: level 1

:: Organizational theory ::

_____ is the process of creating, retaining, and transferring knowledge within an organization. An organization improves over time as it gains experience. From this experience, it is able to create knowledge. This knowledge is broad, covering any topic that could better an organization. Examples may include ways to increase production efficiency or to develop beneficial investor relations. Knowledge is created at four different units: individual, group, organizational, and inter organizational.

Exam Probability: **Medium**

20. *Answer choices:*

(see index for correct answer)

- a. Organizational learning
- b. Red tape
- c. Organisational semiotics
- d. Formal consensus

Guidance: level 1

:: ::

In organizational behavior and industrial/organizational psychology, proactivity or _____ behavior by individuals refers to anticipatory, change-oriented and self-initiated behavior in situations. _____ behavior involves acting in advance of a future situation, rather than just reacting. It means taking control and making things happen rather than just adjusting to a situation or waiting for something to happen. _____ employees generally do not need to be asked to act, nor do they require detailed instructions.

Exam Probability: **High**

21. *Answer choices:*

(see index for correct answer)

- a. empathy
- b. Proactive
- c. hierarchical
- d. similarity-attraction theory

Guidance: level 1

:: ::

An _____ is a contingent motivator. Traditional _____ s are extrinsic motivators which reward actions to yield a desired outcome. The effectiveness of traditional _____ s has changed as the needs of Western society have evolved. While the traditional _____ model is effective when there is a defined procedure and goal for a task, Western society started to require a higher volume of critical thinkers, so the traditional model became less effective. Institutions are now following a trend in implementing strategies that rely on intrinsic motivations rather than the extrinsic motivations that the traditional _____ s foster.

Exam Probability: **Low**

22. *Answer choices:*

(see index for correct answer)

- a. Incentive
- b. functional perspective
- c. surface-level diversity
- d. imperative

Guidance: level 1

:: Corporate governance ::

An _____ is generally a person responsible for running an organization, although the exact nature of the role varies depending on the organization. In many militaries, an _____, or "XO," is the second-in-command, reporting to the commanding officer. The XO is typically responsible for the management of day-to-day activities, freeing the commander to concentrate on strategy and planning the unit's next move.

Exam Probability: **Low**

23. *Answer choices:*

(see index for correct answer)

- a. Development director
- b. Dual board
- c. Executive officer
- d. Corporate security

Guidance: level 1

:: Strategic management ::

_____ is a strategic planning technique used to help a person or organization identify strengths, weaknesses, opportunities, and threats related to business competition or project planning. It is intended to specify the objectives of the business venture or project and identify the internal and external factors that are favorable and unfavorable to achieving those objectives. Users of a _____ often ask and answer questions to generate meaningful information for each category to make the tool useful and identify their competitive advantage. SWOT has been described as the tried-and-true tool of strategic analysis.

Exam Probability: **High**

24. *Answer choices:*

(see index for correct answer)

- a. Strategic fit
- b. customer lock-in
- c. SWOT analysis
- d. Management consulting

Guidance: level 1

:: ::

An _____ in international trade is a good or service produced in one country that is bought by someone in another country. The seller of such goods and services is an _____ er; the foreign buyer is an importer.

Exam Probability: **Low**

25. *Answer choices:*

(see index for correct answer)

- a. surface-level diversity
- b. empathy
- c. Export
- d. open system

Guidance: level 1

:: Industrial Revolution ::

The _____, now also known as the First _____, was the transition to new manufacturing processes in Europe and the US, in the period from about 1760 to sometime between 1820 and 1840. This transition included going from hand production methods to machines, new chemical manufacturing and iron production processes, the increasing use of steam power and water power, the development of machine tools and the rise of the mechanized factory system. The _____ also led to an unprecedented rise in the rate of population growth.

Exam Probability: **Low**

26. *Answer choices:*

(see index for correct answer)

- a. Ironworks
- b. Runcorn to Latchford Canal
- c. Spinning frame
- d. American Woolen Company

Guidance: level 1

:: ::

The _____ is a political and economic union of 28 member states that are located primarily in Europe. It has an area of 4,475,757 km2 and an estimated population of about 513 million. The EU has developed an internal single market through a standardised system of laws that apply in all member states in those matters, and only those matters, where members have agreed to act as one. EU policies aim to ensure the free movement of people, goods, services and capital within the internal market, enact legislation in justice and home affairs and maintain common policies on trade, agriculture, fisheries and regional development. For travel within the Schengen Area, passport controls have been abolished. A monetary union was established in 1999 and came into full force in 2002 and is composed of 19 EU member states which use the euro currency.

Exam Probability: **Medium**

27. *Answer choices:*

(see index for correct answer)

- a. European Union
- b. deep-level diversity
- c. imperative
- d. Character

Guidance: level 1

:: Industry ::

_____ describes various measures of the efficiency of production. Often , a _____ measure is expressed as the ratio of an aggregate output to a single input or an aggregate input used in a production process, i.e. output per unit of input. Most common example is the labour _____ measure, e.g., such as GDP per worker. There are many different definitions of _____ and the choice among them depends on the purpose of the _____ measurement and/or data availability. The key source of difference between various _____ measures is also usually related to how the outputs and the inputs are aggregated into scalars to obtain such a ratio-type measure of _____ .

Exam Probability: **Medium**

28. *Answer choices:*

(see index for correct answer)

- a. Productivity
- b. Consciousness Industry
- c. Sensory design
- d. Industrial society

Guidance: level 1

:: ::

A _____ is a problem offering two possibilities, neither of which is unambiguously acceptable or preferable. The possibilities are termed the horns of the _____ , a clichéd usage, but distinguishing the _____ from other kinds of predicament as a matter of usage.

Exam Probability: **Low**

29. *Answer choices:*

(see index for correct answer)

- a. co-culture
- b. Dilemma
- c. hierarchical perspective
- d. open system

Guidance: level 1

:: Management ::

_____ is the identification, evaluation, and prioritization of risks followed by coordinated and economical application of resources to minimize, monitor, and control the probability or impact of unfortunate events or to maximize the realization of opportunities.

Exam Probability: **High**

30. *Answer choices:*

(see index for correct answer)

- a. Total Worker Health
- b. Mobile sales enablement
- c. Managing stage boundaries
- d. Performance indicator

Guidance: level 1

:: Project management ::

A _____ is a team whose members usually belong to different groups, functions and are assigned to activities for the same project. A team can be divided into sub-teams according to need. Usually _____ s are only used for a defined period of time. They are disbanded after the project is deemed complete. Due to the nature of the specific formation and disbandment, _____ s are usually in organizations.

Exam Probability: **High**

31. *Answer choices:*

(see index for correct answer)

- a. Project team
- b. ISO 21500
- c. Bill of quantities
- d. Deployment Plan

Guidance: level 1

:: Organizational theory ::

Decentralisation is the process by which the activities of an organization, particularly those regarding planning and decision making, are distributed or delegated away from a central, authoritative location or group. Concepts of _____ have been applied to group dynamics and management science in private businesses and organizations, political science, law and public administration, economics, money and technology.

Exam Probability: **High**

32. *Answer choices:*

(see index for correct answer)

- a. Resource dependence theory
- b. Organigraph
- c. Decentralization
- d. Organization development

Guidance: level 1

:: Information science ::

_____ is the resolution of uncertainty; it is that which answers the question of "what an entity is" and thus defines both its essence and nature of its characteristics. _____ relates to both data and knowledge, as data is meaningful _____ representing values attributed to parameters, and knowledge signifies understanding of a concept. _____ is uncoupled from an observer, which is an entity that can access _____ and thus discern what it specifies; _____ exists beyond an event horizon for example. In the case of knowledge, the _____ itself requires a cognitive observer to be obtained.

Exam Probability: **Medium**

33. *Answer choices:*

(see index for correct answer)

- a. Information
- b. Evolutionary informatics
- c. ArchiMate
- d. Actionable information logistics

Guidance: level 1

:: ::

_____ is the exchange of capital, goods, and services across international borders or territories.

Exam Probability: **Low**

34. *Answer choices:*

(see index for correct answer)

- a. International trade
- b. Character
- c. process perspective
- d. information systems assessment

Guidance: level 1

:: Organizational theory ::

A _____ is an organizational theory that claims that there is no best way to organize a corporation, to lead a company, or to make decisions. Instead, the optimal course of action is contingent upon the internal and external situation. A contingent leader effectively applies their own style of leadership to the right situation.

Exam Probability: **Medium**

35. *Answer choices:*

(see index for correct answer)

- a. Exit-Voice-Loyalty-Neglect Model
- b. Contingency theory
- c. Organizational engineering
- d. Organizational ecology

Guidance: level 1

:: Statistical terminology ::

_____ es can be learned implicitly within cultural contexts. People may develop _____ es toward or against an individual, an ethnic group, a sexual or gender identity, a nation, a religion, a social class, a political party, theoretical paradigms and ideologies within academic domains, or a species. _____ ed means one-sided, lacking a neutral viewpoint, or not having an open mind. _____ can come in many forms and is related to prejudice and intuition.

Exam Probability: **Low**

36. *Answer choices:*
(see index for correct answer)

- a. Efficiency
- b. Noncentrality parameter
- c. Bias
- d. Iterated conditional modes

Guidance: level 1

:: Supply chain management ::

_____ is the process of finding and agreeing to terms, and acquiring goods, services, or works from an external source, often via a tendering or competitive bidding process. _____ is used to ensure the buyer receives goods, services, or works at the best possible price when aspects such as quality, quantity, time, and location are compared. Corporations and public bodies often define processes intended to promote fair and open competition for their business while minimizing risks such as exposure to fraud and collusion.

Exam Probability: **Medium**

37. *Answer choices:*
(see index for correct answer)

- a. Procurement
- b. Supply chain cyber security
- c. Reverse auction
- d. Calculating demand forecast accuracy

Guidance: level 1

:: ::

A _____ or sample _____ is a single measure of some attribute of a sample. It is calculated by applying a function to the values of the items of the sample, which are known together as a set of data.

Exam Probability: **High**

38. *Answer choices:*

(see index for correct answer)

- a. open system
- b. imperative
- c. Statistic
- d. corporate values

Guidance: level 1

:: Systems thinking ::

In business management, a _____ is a company that facilitates the learning of its members and continuously transforms itself. The concept was coined through the work and research of Peter Senge and his colleagues.

Exam Probability: **Medium**

39. *Answer choices:*

(see index for correct answer)

- a. Ray Hammond
- b. Futuribles International
- c. Learning organization
- d. Interdependence

Guidance: level 1

:: ::

> The business environment is a marketing term and refers to factors and forces that affect a firm's ability to build and maintain successful customer relationships. The business environment has been defined as "the totality of physical and social factors that are taken directly into consideration in the decision-making behaviour of individuals in the organisation."

Exam Probability: **Low**

40. *Answer choices:*

(see index for correct answer)

- a. similarity-attraction theory
- b. levels of analysis
- c. cultural
- d. Environmental scanning

Guidance: level 1

:: Quality management ::

A _____ or quality control circle is a group of workers who do the same or similar work, who meet regularly to identify, analyze and solve work-related problems. Normally small in size, the group is usually led by a supervisor or manager and presents its solutions to management; where possible, workers implement the solutions themselves in order to improve the performance of the organization and motivate employees. _____ s were at their most popular during the 1980s, but continue to exist in the form of Kaizen groups and similar worker participation schemes.

Exam Probability: **Low**

41. *Answer choices:*
(see index for correct answer)

- a. Quality policy
- b. Det Norske Veritas
- c. TL 9000
- d. Quality circle

Guidance: level 1

:: ::

_____ comprises all of the processes of governing – whether undertaken by the government of a state, by a market or by a network – over a social system and whether through the laws, norms, power or language of an organized society. It relates to "the processes of interaction and decision-making among the actors involved in a collective problem that lead to the creation, reinforcement, or reproduction of social norms and institutions". In lay terms, it could be described as the political processes that exist in and between formal institutions.

Exam Probability: **High**

42. *Answer choices:*

(see index for correct answer)

- a. hierarchical perspective
- b. Governance
- c. levels of analysis
- d. information systems assessment

Guidance: level 1

:: Evaluation ::

_____ is a way of preventing mistakes and defects in manufactured products and avoiding problems when delivering products or services to customers; which ISO 9000 defines as "part of quality management focused on providing confidence that quality requirements will be fulfilled". This defect prevention in _____ differs subtly from defect detection and rejection in quality control and has been referred to as a shift left since it focuses on quality earlier in the process.

Exam Probability: **Low**

43. *Answer choices:*

(see index for correct answer)

- a. Summative assessment
- b. Quality assurance
- c. Server Efficiency Rating Tool
- d. Program evaluation

Guidance: level 1

:: Workplace ::

A _____, also referred to as a performance review, performance evaluation, development discussion, or employee appraisal is a method by which the job performance of an employee is documented and evaluated. _____ s are a part of career development and consist of regular reviews of employee performance within organizations.

Exam Probability: **Low**

44. *Answer choices:*

(see index for correct answer)

- a. Workplace deviance
- b. Performance appraisal
- c. Feminisation of the workplace
- d. Work etiquette

Guidance: level 1

:: Management ::

A _____ is a formal written document containing business goals, the methods on how these goals can be attained, and the time frame within which these goals need to be achieved. It also describes the nature of the business, background information on the organization, the organization's financial projections, and the strategies it intends to implement to achieve the stated targets. In its entirety, this document serves as a road map that provides direction to the business.

Exam Probability: **Low**

45. *Answer choices:*

(see index for correct answer)

- a. Total security management

- b. Demand chain management
- c. Business plan
- d. Middle management

Guidance: level 1

:: Strategic alliances ::

A _____ is an agreement between two or more parties to pursue a set of agreed upon objectives needed while remaining independent organizations. A _____ will usually fall short of a legal partnership entity, agency, or corporate affiliate relationship. Typically, two companies form a _____ when each possesses one or more business assets or have expertise that will help the other by enhancing their businesses. _____ s can develop in outsourcing relationships where the parties desire to achieve long-term win-win benefits and innovation based on mutually desired outcomes.

Exam Probability: **Medium**

46. *Answer choices:*

(see index for correct answer)

- a. Defensive termination
- b. Strategic alliance
- c. International joint venture
- d. Cross-licensing

Guidance: level 1

In sales, commerce and economics, a _____ is the recipient of a good, service, product or an idea - obtained from a seller, vendor, or supplier via a financial transaction or exchange for money or some other valuable consideration.

Exam Probability: **Low**

47. *Answer choices:*

(see index for correct answer)

- a. Customer
- b. deep-level diversity
- c. hierarchical
- d. empathy

Guidance: level 1

:: Management occupations ::

_____ is the process of designing, launching and running a new business, which is often initially a small business. The people who create these businesses are called entrepreneurs.

Exam Probability: **High**

48. *Answer choices:*

(see index for correct answer)

- a. entrepreneurial
- b. Vorstandsassistent
- c. Entrepreneurship
- d. Exempt secretary

Guidance: level 1

:: Business models ::

_____ es are privately owned corporations, partnerships, or sole proprietorships that have fewer employees and/or less annual revenue than a regular-sized business or corporation. Businesses are defined as "small" in terms of being able to apply for government support and qualify for preferential tax policy varies depending on the country and industry. _____ es range from fifteen employees under the Australian Fair Work Act 2009, fifty employees according to the definition used by the European Union, and fewer than five hundred employees to qualify for many U.S. _____ Administration programs. While _____ es can also be classified according to other methods, such as annual revenues, shipments, sales, assets, or by annual gross or net revenue or net profits, the number of employees is one of the most widely used measures.

Exam Probability: **Medium**

49. *Answer choices:*

(see index for correct answer)

- a. Product-service system
- b. Lawyers on Demand
- c. Microfranchising
- d. Small business

Guidance: level 1

:: Business process ::

A _____ or business method is a collection of related, structured activities or tasks by people or equipment which in a specific sequence produce a service or product for a particular customer or customers. _____ es occur at all organizational levels and may or may not be visible to the customers. A _____ may often be visualized as a flowchart of a sequence of activities with interleaving decision points or as a process matrix of a sequence of activities with relevance rules based on data in the process. The benefits of using _____ es include improved customer satisfaction and improved agility for reacting to rapid market change. Process-oriented organizations break down the barriers of structural departments and try to avoid functional silos.

Exam Probability: **High**

50. *Answer choices:*

(see index for correct answer)

- a. Closure by stealth
- b. Joget Workflow
- c. Business process
- d. Business process validation

Guidance: level 1

:: Production economics ::

_____ is the creation of a whole that is greater than the simple sum of its parts. The term _____ comes from the Attic Greek word sea synergia from synergos, , meaning "working together".

Exam Probability: **Low**

51. *Answer choices:*

(see index for correct answer)

- a. Division of work
- b. Production theory
- c. Synergy
- d. Capitalist mode of production

Guidance: level 1

:: Management ::

In organizational studies, _____ is the efficient and effective development of an organization's resources when they are needed. Such resources may include financial resources, inventory, human skills, production resources, or information technology and natural resources.

Exam Probability: **Low**

52. *Answer choices:*

(see index for correct answer)

- a. Commercial management
- b. Action item
- c. Resource management
- d. Wireless informatics

Guidance: level 1

:: Management ::

A _____ describes the rationale of how an organization creates, delivers, and captures value, in economic, social, cultural or other contexts. The process of _____ construction and modification is also called _____ innovation and forms a part of business strategy.

Exam Probability: **High**

53. *Answer choices:*

(see index for correct answer)

- a. Overtime rate
- b. Operations research
- c. Power structure
- d. Business model

Guidance: level 1

:: Management ::

In the field of management, _____ involves the formulation and implementation of the major goals and initiatives taken by an organization's top management on behalf of owners, based on consideration of resources and an assessment of the internal and external environments in which the organization operates.

Exam Probability: **High**

54. *Answer choices:*

(see index for correct answer)

- a. Productive efficiency
- b. Strategic management
- c. Six phases of a big project
- d. Supplier relationship management

Guidance: level 1

:: Business ethics ::

_____ is a type of harassment technique that relates to a sexual nature and the unwelcome or inappropriate promise of rewards in exchange for sexual favors. _____ includes a range of actions from mild transgressions to sexual abuse or assault. Harassment can occur in many different social settings such as the workplace, the home, school, churches, etc. Harassers or victims may be of any gender.

Exam Probability: **Medium**

55. *Answer choices:*

(see index for correct answer)

- a. Smart casual
- b. Society for Business Ethics
- c. Employee raiding
- d. Corporate crime

Guidance: level 1

:: ::

A _____ is a fund into which a sum of money is added during an employee's employment years, and from which payments are drawn to support the person's retirement from work in the form of periodic payments. A _____ may be a "defined benefit plan" where a fixed sum is paid regularly to a person, or a "defined contribution plan" under which a fixed sum is invested and then becomes available at retirement age. _____ s should not be confused with severance pay; the former is usually paid in regular installments for life after retirement, while the latter is typically paid as a fixed amount after involuntary termination of employment prior to retirement.

Exam Probability: **High**

56. *Answer choices:*

(see index for correct answer)

- a. information systems assessment
- b. Pension
- c. hierarchical perspective
- d. open system

Guidance: level 1

:: Project management ::

Contemporary business and science treat as a _____ any undertaking, carried out individually or collaboratively and possibly involving research or design, that is carefully planned to achieve a particular aim.

Exam Probability: **Low**

57. *Answer choices:*

(see index for correct answer)

- a. Costab
- b. Rapid Results
- c. Problem domain analysis
- d. Project

Guidance: level 1

:: Employment compensation ::

_____ refers to various incentive plans introduced by businesses that provide direct or indirect payments to employees that depend on company's profitability in addition to employees' regular salary and bonuses. In publicly traded companies these plans typically amount to allocation of shares to employees. One of the earliest pioneers of _____ was Englishman Theodore Cooke Taylor, who is known to have introduced the practice in his woollen mills during the late 1800s.

Exam Probability: **Medium**

58. *Answer choices:*

(see index for correct answer)

- a. salary sacrifice

- b. Salary cap
- c. Stock appreciation right
- d. Profit sharing

Guidance: level 1

:: Grounds for termination of employment ::

_____ is a habitual pattern of absence from a duty or obligation without good reason. Generally, _____ is unplanned absences. _____ has been viewed as an indicator of poor individual performance, as well as a breach of an implicit contract between employee and employer. It is seen as a management problem, and framed in economic or quasi-economic terms. More recent scholarship seeks to understand _____ as an indicator of psychological, medical, or social adjustment to work.

Exam Probability: **Low**

59. *Answer choices:*

(see index for correct answer)

- a. Department of Defense Whistleblower Program
- b. Presidential Policy Directive 19
- c. Sleeping while on duty
- d. Huffman v. Office of Personnel Management

Guidance: level 1

Business law

Corporate law (also known as business law) is the body of law governing the rights, relations, and conduct of persons, companies, organizations and businesses. It refers to the legal practice relating to, or the theory of corporations. Corporate law often describes the law relating to matters which derive directly from the life-cycle of a corporation. It thus encompasses the formation, funding, governance, and death of a corporation.

:: Stock market ::

The _____ of a corporation is all of the shares into which ownership of the corporation is divided. In American English, the shares are commonly known as " _____ s". A single share of the _____ represents fractional ownership of the corporation in proportion to the total number of shares. This typically entitles the _____ holder to that fraction of the company's earnings, proceeds from liquidation of assets , or voting power, often dividing these up in proportion to the amount of money each _____ holder has invested. Not all _____ is necessarily equal, as certain classes of _____ may be issued for example without voting rights, with enhanced voting rights, or with a certain priority to receive profits or liquidation proceeds before or after other classes of shareholders.

Exam Probability: **High**

1. *Answer choices:*

(see index for correct answer)

- a. Earnings call
- b. Underweight
- c. Microcap
- d. Accelerated share repurchase

Guidance: level 1

:: Data management ::

_____ is a form of intellectual property that grants the creator of an original creative work an exclusive legal right to determine whether and under what conditions this original work may be copied and used by others, usually for a limited term of years. The exclusive rights are not absolute but limited by limitations and exceptions to _____ law, including fair use. A major limitation on _____ on ideas is that _____ protects only the original expression of ideas, and not the underlying ideas themselves.

Exam Probability: **High**

2. *Answer choices:*

(see index for correct answer)

- a. Client-side persistent data

- b. Mobile content management system
- c. Copyright
- d. Holistic Data Management

Guidance: level 1

:: Business law ::

A _____ is an offer that will remain open for a certain period or until a certain time or occurrence of a certain event, during which it is incapable of being revoked. As a general rule, all offers are revocable at any time prior to acceptance, even those offers that purport to be irrevocable on their face.

Exam Probability: **High**

3. *Answer choices:*

(see index for correct answer)

- a. TRIPS Agreement
- b. Subordination
- c. Legal tender
- d. Secret rebate

Guidance: level 1

:: ::

_____ Corporation was an American energy, commodities, and services company based in Houston, Texas. It was founded in 1985 as a merger between Houston Natural Gas and InterNorth, both relatively small regional companies. Before its bankruptcy on December 3, 2001, _____ employed approximately 29,000 staff and was a major electricity, natural gas, communications and pulp and paper company, with claimed revenues of nearly $101 billion during 2000. Fortune named _____ "America's Most Innovative Company" for six consecutive years.

Exam Probability: **Low**

4. *Answer choices:*

(see index for correct answer)

- a. empathy
- b. Character
- c. information systems assessment
- d. Enron

Guidance: level 1

:: ::

A federation is a political entity characterized by a union of partially self-governing provinces, states, or other regions under a central _____. In a federation, the self-governing status of the component states, as well as the division of power between them and the central government, is typically constitutionally entrenched and may not be altered by a unilateral decision of either party, the states or the federal political body. Alternatively, federation is a form of government in which sovereign power is formally divided between a central authority and a number of constituent regions so that each region retains some degree of control over its internal affairs. It is often argued that federal states where the central government has the constitutional authority to suspend a constituent state's government by invoking gross mismanagement or civil unrest, or to adopt national legislation that overrides or infringe on the constituent states' powers by invoking the central government's constitutional authority to ensure "peace and good government" or to implement obligations contracted under an international treaty, are not truly federal states.

Exam Probability: **High**

5. *Answer choices:*

(see index for correct answer)

- a. Federal government
- b. Character
- c. surface-level diversity
- d. empathy

Guidance: level 1

:: Contract law ::

An _____, or simply option, is defined as "a promise which meets the requirements for the formation of a contract and limits the promisor's power to revoke an offer."

Exam Probability: **Low**

6. *Answer choices:*

(see index for correct answer)

- a. ConsensusDOCS
- b. Proprietary estoppel
- c. Oral contract
- d. Extinguishment

Guidance: level 1

:: ::

A contract is a legally-binding agreement which recognises and governs the rights and duties of the parties to the agreement. A contract is legally enforceable because it meets the requirements and approval of the law. An agreement typically involves the exchange of goods, services, money, or promises of any of those. In the event of breach of contract, the law awards the injured party access to legal remedies such as damages and cancellation.

Exam Probability: **Low**

7. *Answer choices:*

(see index for correct answer)

- a. hierarchical perspective
- b. Contract law
- c. functional perspective
- d. imperative

Guidance: level 1

:: ::

_____ is the principled guide to action taken by the administrative executive branches of the state with regard to a class of issues, in a manner consistent with law and institutional customs.

Exam Probability: **Low**

8. *Answer choices:*

(see index for correct answer)

- a. levels of analysis
- b. Sarbanes-Oxley act of 2002
- c. information systems assessment
- d. imperative

Guidance: level 1

:: ::

The words "_____" and "testify" both derive from the Latin word testis, referring to the notion of a disinterested third-party witness.

Exam Probability: **Medium**

9. *Answer choices:*

(see index for correct answer)

- a. Testimony
- b. information systems assessment
- c. cultural
- d. imperative

Guidance: level 1

:: Manufactured goods ::

A _____ or final good is any commodity that is produced or consumed by the consumer to satisfy current wants or needs. _____ s are ultimately consumed, rather than used in the production of another good. For example, a microwave oven or a bicycle that is sold to a consumer is a final good or _____ , but the components that are sold to be used in those goods are intermediate goods. For example, textiles or transistors can be used to make some further goods.

Exam Probability: **High**

10. *Answer choices:*

(see index for correct answer)

- a. Household goods
- b. Product ecosystem theory
- c. Bespoke
- d. Final good

Guidance: level 1

:: Competition law ::

In competition law, a _____ is a market in which a particular product or service is sold. It is the intersection of a relevant product market and a relevant geographic market. The European Commission defines a _____ and its product and geographic components as follows.

Exam Probability: **Low**

11. *Answer choices:*

(see index for correct answer)

- a. Small but significant and non-transitory increase in price
- b. Illegal per se
- c. History of competition law

- d. Legal Services Board

Guidance: level 1

:: Business ethics ::

Banking secrecy, alternately known as _____ , banking discretion, or bank safety, is a conditional agreement between a bank and its clients that all foregoing activities remain secure, confidential, and private. While some banking institutions voluntarily impose banking secrecy institutionally, others operate in regions where the practice is legally mandated and protected . Almost all banking secrecy standards prohibit the disclosure of client information to third parties without consent or an accepted criminal complaint. Additional privacy is provided to select clients via numbered bank accounts or underground bank vaults. Most often associated with banking in Switzerland, banking secrecy is prevalent in Luxembourg, Monaco, Hong Kong, Singapore, Ireland, Lebanon and the Cayman Islands, among other off-shore banking institutions.

Exam Probability: **Medium**

12. *Answer choices:*

(see index for correct answer)

- a. Financial privacy
- b. Destructionism
- c. Sherpa
- d. Society for Business Ethics

Guidance: level 1

:: United States corporate law ::

In tort law, a _____ is a legal obligation which is imposed on an individual requiring adherence to a standard of reasonable care while performing any acts that could foreseeably harm others. It is the first element that must be established to proceed with an action in negligence. The claimant must be able to show a _____ imposed by law which the defendant has breached. In turn, breaching a duty may subject an individual to liability. The _____ may be imposed by operation of law between individuals who have no current direct relationship but eventually become related in some manner, as defined by common law.

Exam Probability: **High**

13. *Answer choices:*

(see index for correct answer)

- a. Dunlop Commission on the Future of Worker-Management Relations: Final Report
- b. Duty of care
- c. Corporate law in the United States
- d. New York Business Corporation Law

Guidance: level 1

:: ::

A _____, in law, is a set of facts sufficient to justify a right to sue to obtain money, property, or the enforcement of a right against another party. The term also refers to the legal theory upon which a plaintiff brings suit. The legal document which carries a claim is often called a 'statement of claim' in English law, or a 'complaint' in U.S. federal practice and in many U.S. states. It can be any communication notifying the party to whom it is addressed of an alleged fault which resulted in damages, often expressed in amount of money the receiving party should pay/reimburse.

Exam Probability: **High**

14. *Answer choices:*

(see index for correct answer)

- a. interpersonal communication
- b. Sarbanes-Oxley act of 2002
- c. cultural
- d. Cause of action

Guidance: level 1

:: Project management ::

A _____ is a source or supply from which a benefit is produced and it has some utility. _____ s can broadly be classified upon their availability—they are classified into renewable and non-renewable _____ s. Examples of non renewable _____ s are coal ,crude oil natural gas nuclear energy etc. Examples of renewable _____ s are air,water,wind,solar energy etc. They can also be classified as actual and potential on the basis of level of development and use, on the basis of origin they can be classified as biotic and abiotic, and on the basis of their distribution, as ubiquitous and localized . An item becomes a _____ with time and developing technology. Typically, _____ s are materials, energy, services, staff, knowledge, or other assets that are transformed to produce benefit and in the process may be consumed or made unavailable. Benefits of _____ utilization may include increased wealth, proper functioning of a system, or enhanced well-being. From a human perspective a natural _____ is anything obtained from the environment to satisfy human needs and wants. From a broader biological or ecological perspective a _____ satisfies the needs of a living organism .

Exam Probability: **Low**

15. *Answer choices:*

(see index for correct answer)

- a. Project
- b. Confluence Project Management
- c. Resource
- d. Scope creep

Guidance: level 1

:: Insolvency ::

_____ is a legal process through which people or other entities who cannot repay debts to creditors may seek relief from some or all of their debts. In most jurisdictions, _____ is imposed by a court order, often initiated by the debtor.

Exam Probability: **Low**

16. *Answer choices:*

(see index for correct answer)

- a. Bankruptcy
- b. Preferential creditor
- c. George Samuel Ford
- d. Liquidator

Guidance: level 1

:: Mereology ::

_____ , in the abstract, is what belongs to or with something, whether as an attribute or as a component of said thing. In the context of this article, it is one or more components , whether physical or incorporeal, of a person's estate; or so belonging to, as in being owned by, a person or jointly a group of people or a legal entity like a corporation or even a society. Depending on the nature of the _____ , an owner of _____ has the right to consume, alter, share, redefine, rent, mortgage, pawn, sell, exchange, transfer, give away or destroy it, or to exclude others from doing these things, as well as to perhaps abandon it; whereas regardless of the nature of the _____ , the owner thereof has the right to properly use it , or at the very least exclusively keep it.

Exam Probability: **Medium**

17. *Answer choices:*

(see index for correct answer)

- a. Gunk
- b. Mereotopology
- c. Mereological nihilism
- d. Property

Guidance: level 1

:: ::

_____ is the consumption and saving opportunity gained by an entity within a specified timeframe, which is generally expressed in monetary terms. For households and individuals, "_____ is the sum of all the wages, salaries, profits, interest payments, rents, and other forms of earnings received in a given period of time."

Exam Probability: **High**

18. *Answer choices:*

(see index for correct answer)

- a. Income
- b. interpersonal communication
- c. functional perspective
- d. process perspective

Guidance: level 1

:: Progressive Era in the United States ::

The Clayton Antitrust Act of 1914, was a part of United States antitrust law with the goal of adding further substance to the U.S. antitrust law regime; the _____ sought to prevent anticompetitive practices in their incipiency. That regime started with the Sherman Antitrust Act of 1890, the first Federal law outlawing practices considered harmful to consumers. The _____ specified particular prohibited conduct, the three-level enforcement scheme, the exemptions, and the remedial measures.

Exam Probability: **Medium**

19. *Answer choices:*

(see index for correct answer)

- a. Clayton Antitrust Act
- b. Clayton Act
- c. pragmatism

Guidance: level 1

:: Business law ::

An _____ is a natural person, business, or corporation that provides goods or services to another entity under terms specified in a contract or within a verbal agreement. Unlike an employee, an _____ does not work regularly for an employer but works as and when required, during which time they may be subject to law of agency. _____ s are usually paid on a freelance basis. Contractors often work through a limited company or franchise, which they themselves own, or may work through an umbrella company.

Exam Probability: **High**

20. *Answer choices:*

(see index for correct answer)

- a. Independent contractor
- b. De facto corporation and corporation by estoppel

- c. Lex mercatoria
- d. Bulk transfer

Guidance: level 1

:: ::

A _____ is a formal written enactment of a legislative authority that governs the legal entities of a city, state, or country by way of consent. Typically, _____ s command or prohibit something, or declare policy. _____ s are rules made by legislative bodies; they are distinguished from case law or precedent, which is decided by courts, and regulations issued by government agencies.

Exam Probability: **Medium**

21. *Answer choices:*

(see index for correct answer)

- a. hierarchical
- b. deep-level diversity
- c. open system
- d. Statute

Guidance: level 1

:: Commercial item transport and distribution ::

A _____ in common law countries is a person or company that transports goods or people for any person or company and that is responsible for any possible loss of the goods during transport. A _____ offers its services to the general public under license or authority provided by a regulatory body. The regulatory body has usually been granted "ministerial authority" by the legislation that created it. The regulatory body may create, interpret, and enforce its regulations upon the _____ with independence and finality, as long as it acts within the bounds of the enabling legislation.

Exam Probability: **Medium**

22. *Answer choices:*

(see index for correct answer)

- a. Common carrier
- b. Green logistics
- c. Wholesale
- d. Boat trailer

Guidance: level 1

:: ::

In international relations, _____ is – from the perspective of governments – a voluntary transfer of resources from one country to another.

Exam Probability: **High**

23. Answer choices:

(see index for correct answer)

- a. functional perspective
- b. Aid
- c. hierarchical
- d. Character

Guidance: level 1

:: Business law ::

A _____ is a contractual arrangement calling for the lessee to pay the lessor for use of an asset. Property, buildings and vehicles are common assets that are _____ d. Industrial or business equipment is also _____ d.

Exam Probability: **High**

24. Answer choices:

(see index for correct answer)

- a. Ordinary course of business
- b. Contract A
- c. Statutory liability
- d. Novated lease

Guidance: level 1

:: Majority–minority relations ::

_____ , also known as reservation in India and Nepal, positive discrimination / action in the United Kingdom, and employment equity in Canada and South Africa, is the policy of promoting the education and employment of members of groups that are known to have previously suffered from discrimination. Historically and internationally, support for _____ has sought to achieve goals such as bridging inequalities in employment and pay, increasing access to education, promoting diversity, and redressing apparent past wrongs, harms, or hindrances.

Exam Probability: **High**

25. *Answer choices:*

(see index for correct answer)

- a. cultural Relativism
- b. Affirmative action
- c. cultural dissonance

Guidance: level 1

:: Contract law ::

In jurisprudence, _____ is an equitable doctrine that involves one person taking advantage of a position of power over another person. This inequity in power between the parties can vitiate one party's consent as they are unable to freely exercise their independent will.

Exam Probability: **High**

26. *Answer choices:*

(see index for correct answer)

- a. Doctrine of concurrent delay
- b. Specific performance
- c. Undue influence
- d. Implied warranty

Guidance: level 1

:: ::

Advertising is a marketing communication that employs an openly sponsored, non-personal message to promote or sell a product, service or idea. Sponsors of advertising are typically businesses wishing to promote their products or services. Advertising is differentiated from public relations in that an advertiser pays for and has control over the message. It differs from personal selling in that the message is non-personal, i.e., not directed to a particular individual.Advertising is communicated through various mass media, including traditional media such as newspapers, magazines, television, radio, outdoor advertising or direct mail; and new media such as search results, blogs, social media, websites or text messages. The actual presentation of the message in a medium is referred to as an _____ , or "ad" or advert for short.

Exam Probability: **Low**

27. *Answer choices:*

(see index for correct answer)

- a. similarity-attraction theory
- b. empathy
- c. surface-level diversity
- d. Advertisement

Guidance: level 1

:: Contract law ::

In the law of contracts, the _____ , also referred to as an unequivocal and absolute acceptance requirement, states that an offer must be accepted exactly with no modifications. The offeror is the master of one's own offer. An attempt to accept the offer on different terms instead creates a counter-offer, and this constitutes a rejection of the original offer.

Exam Probability: **Medium**

28. *Answer choices:*

(see index for correct answer)

- a. enforceable
- b. Mandatory rule
- c. Fair Food Program
- d. Unjust enrichment

Guidance: level 1

:: Working time ::

Labour law is the area of law most commonly relating to the relationship between trade unions, employers and the government.

Exam Probability: **Low**

29. *Answer choices:*

(see index for correct answer)

- a. Shift work
- b. Holden v. Hardy
- c. Hot racking
- d. Employment law

Guidance: level 1

:: ::

In financial markets, a share is a unit used as mutual funds, limited partnerships, and real estate investment trusts. The owner of _____ in the corporation/company is a shareholder of the corporation. A share is an indivisible unit of capital, expressing the ownership relationship between the company and the shareholder. The denominated value of a share is its face value, and the total of the face value of issued _____ represent the capital of a company, which may not reflect the market value of those _____.

Exam Probability: **Medium**

30. *Answer choices:*

(see index for correct answer)

- a. deep-level diversity
- b. functional perspective
- c. Shares
- d. imperative

Guidance: level 1

:: Manufacturing ::

A _____ is a building for storing goods. _____s are used by manufacturers, importers, exporters, wholesalers, transport businesses, customs, etc. They are usually large plain buildings in industrial parks on the outskirts of cities, towns or villages.

Exam Probability: **Low**

31. *Answer choices:*

(see index for correct answer)

- a. Part number
- b. Boutique manufacturing
- c. Unhairing
- d. Warehouse

Guidance: level 1

:: ::

According to the philosopher Piyush Mathur, "Tangibility is the property that a phenomenon exhibits if it has and/or transports mass and/or energy and/or momentum".

Exam Probability: **High**

32. *Answer choices:*

(see index for correct answer)

- a. process perspective
- b. cultural
- c. surface-level diversity
- d. similarity-attraction theory

Guidance: level 1

:: Forgery ::

_____ is a white-collar crime that generally refers to the false making or material alteration of a legal instrument with the specific intent to defraud anyone. Tampering with a certain legal instrument may be forbidden by law in some jurisdictions but such an offense is not related to _____ unless the tampered legal instrument was actually used in the course of the crime to defraud another person or entity. Copies, studio replicas, and reproductions are not considered forgeries, though they may later become forgeries through knowing and willful misrepresentations.

Exam Probability: **High**

33. *Answer choices:*

(see index for correct answer)

- a. Forgery
- b. Forgery Act 1870
- c. False evidence
- d. Taggant

Guidance: level 1

:: ::

Employment is a relationship between two parties, usually based on a contract where work is paid for, where one party, which may be a corporation, for profit, not-for-profit organization, co-operative or other entity is the employer and the other is the employee. Employees work in return for payment, which may be in the form of an hourly wage, by piecework or an annual salary, depending on the type of work an employee does or which sector she or he is working in. Employees in some fields or sectors may receive gratuities, bonus payment or stock options. In some types of employment, employees may receive benefits in addition to payment. Benefits can include health insurance, housing, disability insurance or use of a gym. Employment is typically governed by employment laws, regulations or legal contracts.

Exam Probability: **Medium**

34. *Answer choices:*

(see index for correct answer)

- a. Sarbanes-Oxley act of 2002
- b. similarity-attraction theory
- c. Character
- d. co-culture

Guidance: level 1

:: Contract law ::

Offer and acceptance analysis is a traditional approach in contract law. The offer and acceptance formula, developed in the 19th century, identifies a moment of formation when the parties are of one mind. This classical approach to contract formation has been modified by developments in the law of estoppel, misleading conduct, misrepresentation and unjust enrichment.

Exam Probability: **High**

35. *Answer choices:*

(see index for correct answer)

- a. Proprietary estoppel
- b. Seaworthiness
- c. Heads of loss
- d. Offeror

Guidance: level 1

:: Real property law ::

A _____ is any legal instrument in writing which passes, affirms or confirms an interest, right, or property and that is signed, attested, delivered, and in some jurisdictions, sealed. It is commonly associated with transferring title to property. The _____ has a greater presumption of validity and is less rebuttable than an instrument signed by the party to the _____. A _____ can be unilateral or bilateral. _____s include conveyances, commissions, licenses, patents, diplomas, and conditionally powers of attorney if executed as _____s. The _____ is the modern descendant of the medieval charter, and delivery is thought to symbolically replace the ancient ceremony of livery of seisin.

Exam Probability: **High**

36. *Answer choices:*

(see index for correct answer)

- a. Fee farm grant
- b. Exaction
- c. Thomond deeds
- d. Deforce

Guidance: level 1

:: ::

_____ refers to a business or organization attempting to acquire goods or services to accomplish its goals. Although there are several organizations that attempt to set standards in the _____ process, processes can vary greatly between organizations. Typically the word " _____ " is not used interchangeably with the word "procurement", since procurement typically includes expediting, supplier quality, and transportation and logistics in addition to _____ .

Exam Probability: **Medium**

37. *Answer choices:*

(see index for correct answer)

- a. process perspective
- b. Purchasing
- c. Sarbanes-Oxley act of 2002
- d. deep-level diversity

Guidance: level 1

:: Legal terms ::

An _____ is a legal and equitable remedy in the form of a special court order that compels a party to do or refrain from specific acts. "When a court employs the extraordinary remedy of _____ , it directs the conduct of a party, and does so with the backing of its full coercive powers." A party that fails to comply with an _____ faces criminal or civil penalties, including possible monetary sanctions and even imprisonment. They can also be charged with contempt of court. Counter _____ s are _____ s that stop or reverse the enforcement of another _____ .

Exam Probability: **High**

38. *Answer choices:*

(see index for correct answer)

- a. Judicial opinion
- b. Intangible property
- c. Interlocutory injunction
- d. Marital power

Guidance: level 1

:: Contract law ::

_____ is the act of recall or annulment. It is the cancelling of an act, the recalling of a grant or privilege, or the making void of some deed previously existing.

Exam Probability: **High**

39. *Answer choices:*

(see index for correct answer)

- a. Revocation
- b. English clause
- c. End-user license agreement
- d. Penal damages

Guidance: level 1

:: Psychometrics ::

_____ is a dynamic, structured, interactive process where a neutral third party assists disputing parties in resolving conflict through the use of specialized communication and negotiation techniques. All participants in _____ are encouraged to actively participate in the process. _____ is a "party-centered" process in that it is focused primarily upon the needs, rights, and interests of the parties. The mediator uses a wide variety of techniques to guide the process in a constructive direction and to help the parties find their optimal solution. A mediator is facilitative in that she/he manages the interaction between parties and facilitates open communication. _____ is also evaluative in that the mediator analyzes issues and relevant norms, while refraining from providing prescriptive advice to the parties.

Exam Probability: **Low**

40. *Answer choices:*

(see index for correct answer)

- a. Mediation
- b. Equating
- c. Law of comparative judgment
- d. Visual analogue scale

Guidance: level 1

:: Auctioneering ::

An _____ is a process of buying and selling goods or services by offering them up for bid, taking bids, and then selling the item to the highest bidder. The open ascending price _____ is arguably the most common form of _____ in use today. Participants bid openly against one another, with each subsequent bid required to be higher than the previous bid. An _____ eer may announce prices, bidders may call out their bids themselves, or bids may be submitted electronically with the highest current bid publicly displayed. In a Dutch _____, the _____ eer begins with a high asking price for some quantity of like items; the price is lowered until a participant is willing to accept the _____ eer's price for some quantity of the goods in the lot or until the seller's reserve price is met. While _____ s are most associated in the public imagination with the sale of antiques, paintings, rare collectibles and expensive wines, _____ s are also used for commodities, livestock, radio spectrum and used cars. In economic theory, an _____ may refer to any mechanism or set of trading rules for exchange.

Exam Probability: **High**

41. *Answer choices:*

(see index for correct answer)

- a. National Auctioneers Association
- b. Auction chant
- c. Auction
- d. Online trading community

Guidance: level 1

:: Business law ::

The _____ , first published in 1952, is one of a number of Uniform Acts that have been established as law with the goal of harmonizing the laws of sales and other commercial transactions across the United States of America through UCC adoption by all 50 states, the District of Columbia, and the Territories of the United States.

Exam Probability: **Low**

42. *Answer choices:*

(see index for correct answer)

- a. Business courts
- b. Stick licensing
- c. Extraordinary resolution
- d. Uniform Commercial Code

Guidance: level 1

:: Contract law ::

Coercion is the practice of forcing another party to act in an involuntary manner by use of threats or force. It involves a set of various types of forceful actions that violate the free will of an individual to induce a desired response, for example: a bully demanding lunch money from a student or the student gets beaten. These actions may include extortion, blackmail, torture, threats to induce favors, or even sexual assault. In law, coercion is codified as a _____ crime. Such actions are used as leverage, to force the victim to act in a way contrary to their own interests. Coercion may involve the actual infliction of physical pain/injury or psychological harm in order to enhance the credibility of a threat. The threat of further harm may lead to the cooperation or obedience of the person being coerced.

Exam Probability: **Low**

43. *Answer choices:*

(see index for correct answer)

- a. Secured transaction
- b. Duress
- c. Anticipatory repudiation
- d. Garnishment

Guidance: level 1

:: Patent law ::

A _____ is generally any statement intended to specify or delimit the scope of rights and obligations that may be exercised and enforced by parties in a legally recognized relationship. In contrast to other terms for legally operative language, the term _____ usually implies situations that involve some level of uncertainty, waiver, or risk.

Exam Probability: **Medium**

44. *Answer choices:*

(see index for correct answer)

- a. PatentFreedom
- b. Independent inventor
- c. Disclaimer
- d. Sealed crustless sandwich

Guidance: level 1

:: ::

In English law, a _____ or _____ absolute is an estate in land, a form of freehold ownership. It is a way that real estate and land may be owned in common law countries, and is the highest possible ownership interest that can be held in real property. Allodial title is reserved to governments under a civil law structure. The rights of the _____ owner are limited by government powers of taxation, compulsory purchase, police power, and escheat, and it could also be limited further by certain encumbrances or conditions in the deed, such as, for example, a condition that required the land to be used as a public park, with a reversion interest in the grantor if the condition fails; this is a _____ conditional.

Exam Probability: **Low**

45. *Answer choices:*

(see index for correct answer)

- a. Fee simple
- b. cultural
- c. open system
- d. co-culture

Guidance: level 1

:: Business law ::

_____ is where a person's financial liability is limited to a fixed sum, most commonly the value of a person's investment in a company or partnership. If a company with _____ is sued, then the claimants are suing the company, not its owners or investors. A shareholder in a limited company is not personally liable for any of the debts of the company, other than for the amount already invested in the company and for any unpaid amount on the shares in the company, if any. The same is true for the members of a _____ partnership and the limited partners in a limited partnership. By contrast, sole proprietors and partners in general partnerships are each liable for all the debts of the business.

Exam Probability: **Low**

46. *Answer choices:*

(see index for correct answer)

- a. Certificate of incorporation
- b. Independent contractor
- c. Limited liability
- d. Contract A

Guidance: level 1

:: Legal doctrines and principles ::

In the common law of torts, _____ loquitur is a doctrine that infers negligence from the very nature of an accident or injury in the absence of direct evidence on how any defendant behaved. Although modern formulations differ by jurisdiction, common law originally stated that the accident must satisfy the necessary elements of negligence: duty, breach of duty, causation, and injury. In _____ loquitur, the elements of duty of care, breach, and causation are inferred from an injury that does not ordinarily occur without negligence.

Exam Probability: **High**

47. *Answer choices:*

(see index for correct answer)

- a. Attractive nuisance
- b. Abstention doctrine
- c. Res ipsa loquitur
- d. Exclusionary rule

Guidance: level 1

:: ::

A concept of English law, a _____ is an untrue or misleading statement of fact made during negotiations by one party to another, the statement then inducing that other party into the contract. The misled party may normally rescind the contract, and sometimes may be awarded damages as well.

Exam Probability: **High**

48. *Answer choices:*

(see index for correct answer)

- a. co-culture
- b. Misrepresentation
- c. deep-level diversity
- d. open system

Guidance: level 1

:: Marketing ::

_____ or stock is the goods and materials that a business holds for the ultimate goal of resale .

Exam Probability: **High**

49. *Answer choices:*

(see index for correct answer)

- a. Instant rebate
- b. Discounting
- c. City marketing
- d. Inventory

Guidance: level 1

:: ::

_____ is that part of a civil law legal system which is part of the jus commune that involves relationships between individuals, such as the law of contracts or torts , and the law of obligations . It is to be distinguished from public law, which deals with relationships between both natural and artificial persons and the state, including regulatory statutes, penal law and other law that affects the public order. In general terms, _____ involves interactions between private citizens, whereas public law involves interrelations between the state and the general population.

Exam Probability: **High**

50. *Answer choices:*

(see index for correct answer)

- a. hierarchical
- b. Character
- c. information systems assessment
- d. empathy

Guidance: level 1

:: Generally Accepted Accounting Principles ::

In accounting, _____ is the income that a business have from its normal business activities, usually from the sale of goods and services to customers. _____ is also referred to as sales or turnover. Some companies receive _____ from interest, royalties, or other fees. _____ may refer to business income in general, or it may refer to the amount, in a monetary unit, earned during a period of time, as in "Last year, Company X had _____ of $42 million". Profits or net income generally imply total _____ minus total expenses in a given period. In accounting, in the balance statement it is a subsection of the Equity section and _____ increases equity, it is often referred to as the "top line" due to its position on the income statement at the very top. This is to be contrasted with the "bottom line" which denotes net income.

Exam Probability: **High**

51. *Answer choices:*
(see index for correct answer)

- a. Revenue
- b. Gross sales
- c. Closing entries
- d. Fixed investment

Guidance: level 1

_____ is the administration of an organization, whether it is a business, a not-for-profit organization, or government body. _____ includes the activities of setting the strategy of an organization and coordinating the efforts of its employees to accomplish its objectives through the application of available resources, such as financial, natural, technological, and human resources. The term "_____" may also refer to those people who manage an organization.

Exam Probability: **High**

52. *Answer choices:*

(see index for correct answer)

- a. surface-level diversity
- b. Management
- c. co-culture
- d. deep-level diversity

Guidance: level 1

:: ::

The Sherman Antitrust Act of 1890 was a United States antitrust law that regulates competition among enterprises, which was passed by Congress under the presidency of Benjamin Harrison.

Exam Probability: **High**

53. Answer choices:

(see index for correct answer)

- a. personal values
- b. empathy
- c. process perspective
- d. Sherman Act

Guidance: level 1

:: Contract law ::

_____ is a legal process for collecting a monetary judgment on behalf of a plaintiff from a defendant. _____ allows the plaintiff to take the money or property of the debtor from the person or institution that holds that property. A similar legal mechanism called execution allows the seizure of money or property held directly by the debtor.

Exam Probability: **High**

54. Answer choices:

(see index for correct answer)

- a. Shrink wrap contract
- b. Frustration of purpose
- c. Marriage privatization
- d. Pact ink

Guidance: level 1

:: ::

A _____ is an organization, usually a group of people or a company, authorized to act as a single entity and recognized as such in law. Early incorporated entities were established by charter. Most jurisdictions now allow the creation of new _____ s through registration.

Exam Probability: **High**

55. *Answer choices:*

(see index for correct answer)

- a. similarity-attraction theory
- b. information systems assessment
- c. corporate values
- d. Corporation

Guidance: level 1

:: Legal doctrines and principles ::

_____ , land acquisition , compulsory purchase , resumption , resumption/compulsory acquisition , or expropriation is the power of a state, provincial, or national government to take private property for public use. However, this power can be legislatively delegated by the state to municipalities, government subdivisions, or even to private persons or corporations, when they are authorized by the legislature to exercise the functions of public character.

Exam Probability: **High**

56. *Answer choices:*

(see index for correct answer)

- a. Unilateral mistake
- b. Parol evidence
- c. unconscionable contract
- d. compulsory purchase

Guidance: level 1

:: Project management ::

_____ is the right to exercise power, which can be formalized by a state and exercised by way of judges, appointed executives of government, or the ecclesiastical or priestly appointed representatives of a God or other deities.

Exam Probability: **High**

57. Answer choices:

(see index for correct answer)

- a. TELOS
- b. Metra potential method
- c. Drag cost
- d. Task

Guidance: level 1

:: ::

_____ , often abbreviated cert. in the United States, is a process for seeking judicial review and a writ issued by a court that agrees to review. A _____ is issued by a superior court, directing an inferior court, tribunal, or other public authority to send the record of a proceeding for review.

Exam Probability: **Low**

58. Answer choices:

(see index for correct answer)

- a. functional perspective
- b. cultural
- c. imperative
- d. Certiorari

Guidance: level 1

:: Contract law ::

In contract law, a _____ is a promise which is not a condition of the contract or an innominate term: it is a term "not going to the root of the contract", and which only entitles the innocent party to damages if it is breached: i.e. the _____ is not true or the defaulting party does not perform the contract in accordance with the terms of the _____. A _____ is not guarantee. It is a mere promise. It may be enforced if it is breached by an award for the legal remedy of damages.

Exam Probability: **Medium**

59. *Answer choices:*

(see index for correct answer)

- a. Offer and acceptance
- b. Parametric contract
- c. Contract lifecycle management
- d. Warranty

Guidance: level 1

Finance

Finance is a field that is concerned with the allocation (investment) of assets and liabilities over space and time, often under conditions of risk or uncertainty. Finance can also be defined as the science of money management. Participants in the market aim to price assets based on their risk level, fundamental value, and their expected rate of return. Finance can be split into three sub-categories: public finance, corporate finance and personal finance.

:: Debt ::

_____ is the trust which allows one party to provide money or resources to another party wherein the second party does not reimburse the first party immediately, but promises either to repay or return those resources at a later date. In other words, _____ is a method of making reciprocity formal, legally enforceable, and extensible to a large group of unrelated people.

Exam Probability: **Medium**

1. *Answer choices:*

(see index for correct answer)

- a. Default
- b. Peak debt
- c. gearing
- d. Student debt

Guidance: level 1

:: Asset ::

_____ s, also known as tangible assets or property, plant and equipment, is a term used in accounting for assets and property that cannot easily be converted into cash. This can be compared with current assets such as cash or bank accounts, described as liquid assets. In most cases, only tangible assets are referred to as fixed. IAS 16 defines _____ s as assets whose future economic benefit is probable to flow into the entity, whose cost can be measured reliably. _____ s belong to one of 2 types:"Freehold Assets" – assets which are purchased with legal right of ownership and used,and "Leasehold Assets" – assets used by owner without legal right for a particular period of time.

Exam Probability: **High**

2. *Answer choices:*
(see index for correct answer)

- a. Fixed asset
- b. Asset

Guidance: level 1

:: ::

_____ , often abbreviated as B/E in finance, is the point of balance making neither a profit nor a loss. The term originates in finance but the concept has been applied in other fields.

Exam Probability: **Low**

3. Answer choices:

(see index for correct answer)

- a. interpersonal communication
- b. Break-even
- c. open system
- d. Character

Guidance: level 1

:: Management accounting ::

_____ is the process of recording, classifying, analyzing, summarizing, and allocating costs associated with a process, after that developing various courses of action to control the costs. Its goal is to advise the management on how to optimize business practices and processes based on cost efficiency and capability. _____ provides the detailed cost information that management needs to control current operations and plan for the future.

Exam Probability: **Low**

4. Answer choices:

(see index for correct answer)

- a. Owner earnings
- b. Cost accounting
- c. Semi-variable cost
- d. Relevant cost

Guidance: level 1

:: Hazard analysis ::

Broadly speaking, a _____ is the combined effort of 1. identifying and analyzing potential events that may negatively impact individuals, assets, and/or the environment ; and 2. making judgments "on the tolerability of the risk on the basis of a risk analysis" while considering influencing factors . Put in simpler terms, a _____ analyzes what can go wrong, how likely it is to happen, what the potential consequences are, and how tolerable the identified risk is. As part of this process, the resulting determination of risk may be expressed in a quantitative or qualitative fashion. The _____ is an inherent part of an overall risk management strategy, which attempts to, after a _____ , "introduce control measures to eliminate or reduce" any potential risk-related consequences.

Exam Probability: **Low**

5. *Answer choices:*
(see index for correct answer)

- a. Risk assessment
- b. Swiss cheese model
- c. Hazard identification

Guidance: level 1

:: Costs ::

In microeconomic theory, the _____ , or alternative cost, of making a particular choice is the value of the most valuable choice out of those that were not taken. In other words, opportunity that will require sacrifices.

Exam Probability: **Medium**

6. *Answer choices:*

(see index for correct answer)

- a. Implicit cost
- b. Opportunity cost
- c. Further processing cost
- d. Social cost

Guidance: level 1

:: Mathematical finance ::

_____ is the value of an asset at a specific date. It measures the nominal future sum of money that a given sum of money is "worth" at a specified time in the future assuming a certain interest rate, or more generally, rate of return; it is the present value multiplied by the accumulation function. The value does not include corrections for inflation or other factors that affect the true value of money in the future. This is used in time value of money calculations.

Exam Probability: **Medium**

7. Answer choices:

(see index for correct answer)

- a. delta hedging
- b. Alternative beta
- c. Stochastic volatility
- d. Econophysics

Guidance: level 1

:: ::

The _____ of a function of a real variable measures the sensitivity to change of the function value with respect to a change in its argument. _____ s are a fundamental tool of calculus. For example, the _____ of the position of a moving object with respect to time is the object's velocity: this measures how quickly the position of the object changes when time advances.

Exam Probability: **Medium**

8. Answer choices:

(see index for correct answer)

- a. information systems assessment
- b. Derivative
- c. empathy
- d. cultural

Guidance: level 1

:: Portfolio theories ::

In finance, the _____ is a model used to determine a theoretically appropriate required rate of return of an asset, to make decisions about adding assets to a well-diversified portfolio.

Exam Probability: **Low**

9. *Answer choices:*

(see index for correct answer)

- a. Maslowian portfolio theory
- b. Capital asset pricing model
- c. Returns-based style analysis
- d. Intertemporal portfolio choice

Guidance: level 1

:: Loans ::

In corporate finance, a _____ is a medium- to long-term debt instrument used by large companies to borrow money, at a fixed rate of interest. The legal term " _____ " originally referred to a document that either creates a debt or acknowledges it, but in some countries the term is now used interchangeably with bond, loan stock or note. A _____ is thus like a certificate of loan or a loan bond evidencing the fact that the company is liable to pay a specified amount with interest and although the money raised by the _____ s becomes a part of the company's capital structure, it does not become share capital. Senior _____ s get paid before subordinate _____ s, and there are varying rates of risk and payoff for these categories.

Exam Probability: **Medium**

10. *Answer choices:*

(see index for correct answer)

- a. Debenture
- b. Section 502 loans
- c. PIK loan
- d. Small Business Lending Index

Guidance: level 1

:: Accounting terminology ::

Accounts are typically defined by an identifier and a caption or header and are coded by account type. In computerized accounting systems with computable quantity accounting, the accounts can have a quantity measure definition.

Exam Probability: **Low**

11. *Answer choices:*

(see index for correct answer)

- a. Accounts payable
- b. Accrued liabilities
- c. Fair value accounting
- d. Chart of accounts

Guidance: level 1

:: ::

An _____ is an area of the production, distribution, or trade, and consumption of goods and services by different agents. Understood in its broadest sense, 'The _____ is defined as a social domain that emphasize the practices, discourses, and material expressions associated with the production, use, and management of resources`. Economic agents can be individuals, businesses, organizations, or governments. Economic transactions occur when two parties agree to the value or price of the transacted good or service, commonly expressed in a certain currency. However, monetary transactions only account for a small part of the economic domain.

Exam Probability: **Low**

12. *Answer choices:*

(see index for correct answer)

- a. hierarchical
- b. empathy
- c. personal values
- d. Economy

Guidance: level 1

:: Accounting terminology ::

In accounting/accountancy, _____ are journal entries usually made at the end of an accounting period to allocate income and expenditure to the period in which they actually occurred. The revenue recognition principle is the basis of making _____ that pertain to unearned and accrued revenues under accrual-basis accounting. They are sometimes called Balance Day adjustments because they are made on balance day.

Exam Probability: **High**

13. *Answer choices:*

(see index for correct answer)

- a. Basis of accounting
- b. double-entry bookkeeping
- c. Adjusting entries
- d. General ledger

Guidance: level 1

:: Asset ::

In financial accounting, an _____ is any resource owned by the business. Anything tangible or intangible that can be owned or controlled to produce value and that is held by a company to produce positive economic value is an _____. Simply stated, _____ s represent value of ownership that can be converted into cash. The balance sheet of a firm records the monetary value of the _____ s owned by that firm. It covers money and other valuables belonging to an individual or to a business.

Exam Probability: **High**

14. *Answer choices:*

(see index for correct answer)

- a. Asset
- b. Fixed asset

Guidance: level 1

:: ::

A _____ is an individual or institution that legally owns one or more shares of stock in a public or private corporation. _____ s may be referred to as members of a corporation. Legally, a person is not a _____ in a corporation until their name and other details are entered in the corporation's register of _____ s or members.

Exam Probability: **High**

15. *Answer choices:*

(see index for correct answer)

- a. Shareholder
- b. similarity-attraction theory
- c. hierarchical perspective
- d. functional perspective

Guidance: level 1

:: Financial markets ::

_____ s are monetary contracts between parties. They can be created, traded, modified and settled. They can be cash , evidence of an ownership interest in an entity , or a contractual right to receive or deliver cash .

Exam Probability: **Low**

16. *Answer choices:*

(see index for correct answer)

- a. Convertible arbitrage
- b. Financial instrument
- c. Guidance
- d. Convenience yield

Guidance: level 1

:: Global systemically important banks ::

_____ Inc. or Citi is an American multinational investment bank and financial services corporation headquartered in New York City. The company was formed by the merger of banking giant Citicorp and financial conglomerate Travelers Group in 1998; Travelers was subsequently spun off from the company in 2002. _____ owns Citicorp, the holding company for Citibank, as well as several international subsidiaries.

Exam Probability: **Low**

17. *Answer choices:*

(see index for correct answer)

- a. ING Group
- b. Morgan Stanley
- c. Barclays
- d. UniCredit

Guidance: level 1

:: Bonds (finance) ::

An _____ is a legal contract that reflects or covers a debt or purchase obligation. It specifically refers to two types of practices: in historical usage, an _____ d servant status, and in modern usage, it is an instrument used for commercial debt or real estate transaction.

Exam Probability: **High**

18. *Answer choices:*

(see index for correct answer)

- a. Prize Bond
- b. Emerging market debt
- c. Regional Bond Dealers Association
- d. Samurai bond

Guidance: level 1

:: Finance ::

_____ , in finance and accounting, means stated value or face value. From this come the expressions at par , over par and under par .

Exam Probability: **Low**

19. *Answer choices:*

(see index for correct answer)

- a. Personal Composite Instrument
- b. Tick size
- c. CBDC NORTIP
- d. Par value

Guidance: level 1

:: Markets (customer bases) ::

In economics, _____ is the economic price for which a good or service is offered in the marketplace. It is of interest mainly in the study of microeconomics. Market value and _____ are equal only under conditions of market efficiency, equilibrium, and rational expectations.

Exam Probability: **High**

20. *Answer choices:*

(see index for correct answer)

- a. Parity product
- b. Nonmarket forces
- c. Market price
- d. Captive market

Guidance: level 1

:: Inventory ::

Costs are associated with particular goods using one of the several formulas, including specific identification, first-in first-out, or average cost. Costs include all costs of purchase, costs of conversion and other costs that are incurred in bringing the inventories to their present location and condition. Costs of goods made by the businesses include material, labor, and allocated overhead. The costs of those goods which are not yet sold are deferred as costs of inventory until the inventory is sold or written down in value.

Exam Probability: **Medium**

21. *Answer choices:*

(see index for correct answer)

- a. Cost of goods sold
- b. Order fulfillment
- c. Stock control
- d. Periodic inventory

Guidance: level 1

:: Accounting terminology ::

In management accounting or _____, managers use the provisions of accounting information in order to better inform themselves before they decide matters within their organizations, which aids their management and performance of control functions.

Exam Probability: **High**

22. *Answer choices:*

(see index for correct answer)

- a. Accounts payable
- b. profit and loss statement
- c. Record to report
- d. Managerial accounting

Guidance: level 1

:: Pharmaceutical industry ::

A _____ is a document in which data collected for a clinical trial is first recorded. This data is usually later entered in the case report form. The International Conference on Harmonisation of Technical Requirements for Registration of Pharmaceuticals for Human Use guidelines define _____ s as "original documents, data, and records." _____ s contain source data, which is defined as "all information in original records and certified copies of original records of clinical findings, observations, or other activities in a clinical trial necessary for the reconstruction and evaluation of the trial."

Exam Probability: **Low**

23. *Answer choices:*

(see index for correct answer)

- a. Dublin Molecular Medicine Centre
- b. Generic drug
- c. Remote data entry
- d. Standard operating procedure

Guidance: level 1

:: ::

_____ Corporation was an American energy, commodities, and services company based in Houston, Texas. It was founded in 1985 as a merger between Houston Natural Gas and InterNorth, both relatively small regional companies. Before its bankruptcy on December 3, 2001, _____ employed approximately 29,000 staff and was a major electricity, natural gas, communications and pulp and paper company, with claimed revenues of nearly $101 billion during 2000. Fortune named _____ "America's Most Innovative Company" for six consecutive years.

Exam Probability: **Medium**

24. *Answer choices:*
(see index for correct answer)

- a. information systems assessment
- b. empathy
- c. hierarchical perspective
- d. surface-level diversity

Guidance: level 1

:: Debt ::

A _____ is a monetary amount owed to a creditor that is unlikely to be paid and, or which the creditor is not willing to take action to collect for various reasons, often due to the debtor not having the money to pay, for example due to a company going into liquidation or insolvency. There are various technical definitions of what constitutes a _____, depending on accounting conventions, regulatory treatment and the institution provisioning. In the USA, bank loans with more than ninety days' arrears become "problem loans". Accounting sources advise that the full amount of a _____ be written off to the profit and loss account or a provision for _____s as soon as it is foreseen.

Exam Probability: **Medium**

25. *Answer choices:*
(see index for correct answer)

- a. Debit commission
- b. Bad debt
- c. Cohort default rate
- d. Sum certain

Guidance: level 1

:: Monopoly (economics) ::

A _____ is a form of intellectual property that gives its owner the legal right to exclude others from making, using, selling, and importing an invention for a limited period of years, in exchange for publishing an enabling public disclosure of the invention. In most countries _____ rights fall under civil law and the _____ holder needs to sue someone infringing the _____ in order to enforce his or her rights. In some industries _____ s are an essential form of competitive advantage; in others they are irrelevant.

Exam Probability: **Low**

26. *Answer choices:*

(see index for correct answer)

- a. Patent
- b. Monopsony
- c. History of monopoly
- d. Legal monopoly

Guidance: level 1

:: Stock market ::

A share price is the price of a single share of a number of saleable stocks of a company, derivative or other financial asset. In layman's terms, the _____ is the highest amount someone is willing to pay for the stock, or the lowest amount that it can be bought for.

Exam Probability: **Medium**

27. *Answer choices:*

(see index for correct answer)

- a. Free riding
- b. Stock price
- c. Alpha generation platform
- d. Securities offering

Guidance: level 1

:: Fraud ::

In law, _____ is intentional deception to secure unfair or unlawful gain, or to deprive a victim of a legal right. _____ can violate civil law, a criminal law, or it may cause no loss of money, property or legal right but still be an element of another civil or criminal wrong. The purpose of _____ may be monetary gain or other benefits, for example by obtaining a passport, travel document, or driver's license, or mortgage _____, where the perpetrator may attempt to qualify for a mortgage by way of false statements.

Exam Probability: **Medium**

28. *Answer choices:*

(see index for correct answer)

- a. Parcel mule scam
- b. Lip-synching in music
- c. Double billing
- d. Check washing

Guidance: level 1

:: Consumer theory ::

_____ is the quantity of a good that consumers are willing and able to purchase at various prices during a given period of time.

Exam Probability: **Low**

29. *Answer choices:*
(see index for correct answer)

- a. Elasticity of intertemporal substitution
- b. Rational addiction
- c. Demand
- d. Compensated demand

Guidance: level 1

:: ::

In financial markets, a share is a unit used as mutual funds, limited partnerships, and real estate investment trusts. The owner of _____ in the corporation/company is a shareholder of the corporation. A share is an indivisible unit of capital, expressing the ownership relationship between the company and the shareholder. The denominated value of a share is its face value, and the total of the face value of issued _____ represent the capital of a company, which may not reflect the market value of those _____.

Exam Probability: **Medium**

30. *Answer choices:*

(see index for correct answer)

- a. empathy
- b. imperative
- c. Shares
- d. co-culture

Guidance: level 1

An _____ is the production of goods or related services within an economy. The major source of revenue of a group or company is the indicator of its relevant _____. When a large group has multiple sources of revenue generation, it is considered to be working in different industries. Manufacturing _____ became a key sector of production and labour in European and North American countries during the Industrial Revolution, upsetting previous mercantile and feudal economies. This came through many successive rapid advances in technology, such as the production of steel and coal.

Exam Probability: **Low**

31. *Answer choices:*

(see index for correct answer)

- a. imperative
- b. Industry
- c. Character
- d. surface-level diversity

Guidance: level 1

:: Debt ::

_____ is when something, usually money, is owed by one party, the borrower or _____ or, to a second party, the lender or creditor. _____ is a deferred payment, or series of payments, that is owed in the future, which is what differentiates it from an immediate purchase. The _____ may be owed by sovereign state or country, local government, company, or an individual. Commercial _____ is generally subject to contractual terms regarding the amount and timing of repayments of principal and interest. Loans, bonds, notes, and mortgages are all types of _____. The term can also be used metaphorically to cover moral obligations and other interactions not based on economic value. For example, in Western cultures, a person who has been helped by a second person is sometimes said to owe a "_____ of gratitude" to the second person.

Exam Probability: **Medium**

32. *Answer choices:*

(see index for correct answer)

- a. Debt
- b. Compulsive buying disorder
- c. Debt crisis
- d. Financial assistance

Guidance: level 1

:: Generally Accepted Accounting Principles ::

In accounting and finance, earnings before interest and taxes is a measure of a firm's profit that includes all incomes and expenses except interest expenses and income tax expenses.

Exam Probability: **Medium**

33. *Answer choices:*

(see index for correct answer)

- a. Operating Income
- b. Deferral
- c. Cost principle
- d. Generally accepted accounting principles

Guidance: level 1

:: Costs ::

_____ is the sum of costs of all resources consumed in the process of making a product. The _____ is classified into three categories: direct materials cost, direct labor cost and manufacturing overhead.

Exam Probability: **High**

34. *Answer choices:*

(see index for correct answer)

- a. Quality costs
- b. Manufacturing cost
- c. Cost overrun
- d. Sliding scale

Guidance: level 1

:: Accounting terminology ::

A _____ contains all the accounts for recording transactions relating to a company's assets, liabilities, owners' equity, revenue, and expenses. In modern accounting software or ERP, the _____ works as a central repository for accounting data transferred from all subledgers or modules like accounts payable, accounts receivable, cash management, fixed assets, purchasing and projects. The _____ is the backbone of any accounting system which holds financial and non-financial data for an organization. The collection of all accounts is known as the _____ . Each account is known as a ledger account. In a manual or non-computerized system this may be a large book. The statement of financial position and the statement of income and comprehensive income are both derived from the _____ . Each account in the _____ consists of one or more pages. The _____ is where posting to the accounts occurs. Posting is the process of recording amounts as credits , and amounts as debits , in the pages of the _____ . Additional columns to the right hold a running activity total .

Exam Probability: **Low**

35. *Answer choices:*

(see index for correct answer)

- a. Share premium
- b. Accounting equation
- c. General ledger
- d. Basis of accounting

Guidance: level 1

:: Business economics ::

In finance, _____ is the risk of losses caused by interest rate changes. The prices of most financial instruments, such as stocks and bonds move inversely with interest rates, so investors are subject to capital loss when rates rise.

Exam Probability: **Medium**

36. *Answer choices:*

(see index for correct answer)

- a. Lateral expansion
- b. Rate risk
- c. Gross operating surplus
- d. Risk pool

Guidance: level 1

:: Business ::

The seller, or the provider of the goods or services, completes a sale in response to an acquisition, appropriation, requisition or a direct interaction with the buyer at the point of sale. There is a passing of title of the item, and the settlement of a price, in which agreement is reached on a price for which transfer of ownership of the item will occur. The seller, not the purchaser typically executes the sale and it may be completed prior to the obligation of payment. In the case of indirect interaction, a person who sells goods or service on behalf of the owner is known as a _____ man or _____ woman or _____ person, but this often refers to someone selling goods in a store/shop, in which case other terms are also common, including _____ clerk, shop assistant, and retail clerk.

Exam Probability: **High**

37. *Answer choices:*

(see index for correct answer)

- a. Business partnering
- b. American Environmental Assessment and Solutions Inc.
- c. Sales
- d. Shriram Properties

Guidance: level 1

:: Financial markets ::

A _____ is a market in which people trade financial securities and derivatives such as futures and options at low transaction costs. Securities include stocks and bonds, and precious metals.

Exam Probability: **High**

38. *Answer choices:*

(see index for correct answer)

- a. Consolidated Tape System
- b. Head fake
- c. Financial market
- d. Latino Community Foundation

Guidance: level 1

:: Actuarial science ::

The _____ is the greater benefit of receiving money now rather than an identical sum later. It is founded on time preference.

Exam Probability: **Medium**

39. *Answer choices:*

(see index for correct answer)

- a. Time value of money
- b. Statutory reserve
- c. Demography
- d. Esscher transform

Guidance: level 1

:: Money market instruments ::

_____ , in the global financial market, is an unsecured promissory note with a fixed maturity of not more than 270 days.

Exam Probability: **Medium**

40. *Answer choices:*
(see index for correct answer)

- a. Banker's acceptance
- b. Commercial paper

Guidance: level 1

:: Data analysis ::

In statistics, the _____ is a measure that is used to quantify the amount of variation or dispersion of a set of data values. A low _____ indicates that the data points tend to be close to the mean of the set, while a high _____ indicates that the data points are spread out over a wider range of values.

Exam Probability: **Low**

41. *Answer choices:*

(see index for correct answer)

- a. Standard deviation
- b. Training set
- c. Random mapping
- d. Index of dispersion

Guidance: level 1

:: Financial accounting ::

_____ is a financial metric which represents operating liquidity available to a business, organisation or other entity, including governmental entities. Along with fixed assets such as plant and equipment, _____ is considered a part of operating capital. Gross _____ is equal to current assets. _____ is calculated as current assets minus current liabilities. If current assets are less than current liabilities, an entity has a _____ deficiency, also called a _____ deficit.

Exam Probability: **Medium**

42. *Answer choices:*

(see index for correct answer)

- a. Valuation
- b. Working capital
- c. Financial Condition Report
- d. Finance charge

Guidance: level 1

:: Costs ::

> In economics, _____ is the total economic cost of production and is made up of variable cost, which varies according to the quantity of a good produced and includes inputs such as labour and raw materials, plus fixed cost, which is independent of the quantity of a good produced and includes inputs that cannot be varied in the short term: fixed costs such as buildings and machinery, including sunk costs if any. Since cost is measured per unit of time, it is a flow variable.

Exam Probability: **High**

43. *Answer choices:*

(see index for correct answer)

- a. Customer Cost

- b. Cost of products sold
- c. Average variable cost
- d. Total cost

Guidance: level 1

:: ::

An _____ is a contingent motivator. Traditional _____ s are extrinsic motivators which reward actions to yield a desired outcome. The effectiveness of traditional _____ s has changed as the needs of Western society have evolved. While the traditional _____ model is effective when there is a defined procedure and goal for a task, Western society started to require a higher volume of critical thinkers, so the traditional model became less effective. Institutions are now following a trend in implementing strategies that rely on intrinsic motivations rather than the extrinsic motivations that the traditional _____ s foster.

Exam Probability: **Medium**

44. *Answer choices:*

(see index for correct answer)

- a. empathy
- b. Incentive
- c. information systems assessment
- d. interpersonal communication

Guidance: level 1

:: Generally Accepted Accounting Principles ::

_____, also referred to as the bottom line, net income, or net earnings is a measure of the profitability of a venture after accounting for all costs and taxes. It is the actual profit, and includes the operating expenses that are excluded from gross profit.

Exam Probability: **High**

45. *Answer choices:*

(see index for correct answer)

- a. Consolidation
- b. Earnings before interest, taxes and depreciation
- c. Closing entries
- d. Net profit

Guidance: level 1

:: Personal finance ::

_____ is income not spent, or deferred consumption. Methods of _____ include putting money aside in, for example, a deposit account, a pension account, an investment fund, or as cash. _____ also involves reducing expenditures, such as recurring costs. In terms of personal finance, _____ generally specifies low-risk preservation of money, as in a deposit account, versus investment, wherein risk is a lot higher; in economics more broadly, it refers to any income not used for immediate consumption.

Exam Probability: **Medium**

46. *Answer choices:*

(see index for correct answer)

- a. Dissaving
- b. App-o-rama
- c. Saving
- d. Credit history

Guidance: level 1

:: ::

A _____ is the process of presenting a topic to an audience. It is typically a demonstration, introduction, lecture, or speech meant to inform, persuade, inspire, motivate, or to build good will or to present a new idea or product. The term can also be used for a formal or ritualized introduction or offering, as with the _____ of a debutante. _____ s in certain formats are also known as keynote address.

Exam Probability: **High**

47. *Answer choices:*

(see index for correct answer)

- a. surface-level diversity
- b. empathy
- c. interpersonal communication
- d. hierarchical perspective

Guidance: level 1

:: ::

A _____ is any person who contracts to acquire an asset in return for some form of consideration.

Exam Probability: **High**

48. *Answer choices:*

(see index for correct answer)

- a. Buyer
- b. similarity-attraction theory
- c. imperative
- d. personal values

Guidance: level 1

:: Government bonds ::

A _____ or sovereign bond is a bond issued by a national government, generally with a promise to pay periodic interest payments called coupon payments and to repay the face value on the maturity date. The aim of a _____ is to support government spending. _____ s are usually denominated in the country's own currency, in which case the government cannot be forced to default, although it may choose to do so. If a government is close to default on its debt the media often refer to this as a sovereign debt crisis.

Exam Probability: **Low**

49. *Answer choices:*

(see index for correct answer)

- a. Gilt-edged
- b. Gilt-edged securities
- c. Direct operations
- d. GDP-linked bond

Guidance: level 1

:: Marketing ::

A _____ is something that is necessary for an organism to live a healthy life. _____s are distinguished from wants in that, in the case of a _____, a deficiency causes a clear adverse outcome: a dysfunction or death. In other words, a _____ is something required for a safe, stable and healthy life while a want is a desire, wish or aspiration. When _____s or wants are backed by purchasing power, they have the potential to become economic demands.

Exam Probability: **Medium**

50. *Answer choices:*

(see index for correct answer)

- a. Need
- b. Online ethnography
- c. Audience screen
- d. Gatefold

Guidance: level 1

:: Bonds (finance) ::

In finance, a _____ or convertible note or convertible debt is a type of bond that the holder can convert into a specified number of shares of common stock in the issuing company or cash of equal value. It is a hybrid security with debt- and equity-like features. It originated in the mid-19th century, and was used by early speculators such as Jacob Little and Daniel Drew to counter market cornering.

Exam Probability: **Medium**

51. *Answer choices:*

(see index for correct answer)

- a. Emerging market debt
- b. Redemption value
- c. Inflation-indexed bond
- d. Convertible bond

Guidance: level 1

:: Decision theory ::

A _____ is a deliberate system of principles to guide decisions and achieve rational outcomes. A _____ is a statement of intent, and is implemented as a procedure or protocol. Policies are generally adopted by a governance body within an organization. Policies can assist in both subjective and objective decision making. Policies to assist in subjective decision making usually assist senior management with decisions that must be based on the relative merits of a number of factors, and as a result are often hard to test objectively, e.g. work-life balance _____ . In contrast policies to assist in objective decision making are usually operational in nature and can be objectively tested, e.g. password _____ .

Exam Probability: **High**

52. *Answer choices:*

(see index for correct answer)

- a. Decision analysis cycle
- b. Policy
- c. Inference engine
- d. Model-based reasoning

Guidance: level 1

:: Financial economics ::

_____, Inc. is an independent investment research and financial publishing firm based in New York City, New York, United States, founded in 1931 by Arnold Bernhard. _____ is best known for publishing The _____ Investment Survey, a stock analysis newsletter that is among the most highly regarded and widely used independent investment research resources in global investment and trading markets, tracking approximately 1,700 publicly traded stocks in over 99 industries.

Exam Probability: **Medium**

53. *Answer choices:*
(see index for correct answer)

- a. Price discovery
- b. Quasilinear utility
- c. Conditional variance swap
- d. Value Line

Guidance: level 1

:: Management accounting ::

In finance, the _____ or net present worth applies to a series of cash flows occurring at different times. The present value of a cash flow depends on the interval of time between now and the cash flow. It also depends on the discount rate. NPV accounts for the time value of money. It provides a method for evaluating and comparing capital projects or financial products with cash flows spread over time, as in loans, investments, payouts from insurance contracts plus many other applications.

Exam Probability: **Medium**

54. *Answer choices:*
(see index for correct answer)

- a. Direct material price variance
- b. Spend management
- c. Management accounting
- d. Net present value

Guidance: level 1

:: Basic financial concepts ::

_____ is a sustained increase in the general price level of goods and services in an economy over a period of time. When the general price level rises, each unit of currency buys fewer goods and services; consequently, _____ reflects a reduction in the purchasing power per unit of money a loss of real value in the medium of exchange and unit of account within the economy. The measure of _____ is the _____ rate, the annualized percentage change in a general price index, usually the consumer price index, over time. The opposite of _____ is deflation.

Exam Probability: **High**

55. *Answer choices:*

(see index for correct answer)

- a. Short interest
- b. Lodgement
- c. Inflation
- d. Financial transaction

Guidance: level 1

:: Income ::

_____ is a ratio between the net profit and cost of investment resulting from an investment of some resources. A high ROI means the investment's gains favorably to its cost. As a performance measure, ROI is used to evaluate the efficiency of an investment or to compare the efficiencies of several different investments. In purely economic terms, it is one way of relating profits to capital invested. _____ is a performance measure used by businesses to identify the efficiency of an investment or number of different investments.

Exam Probability: **High**

56. *Answer choices:*

(see index for correct answer)

- a. Real estate investing
- b. Salary inversion
- c. Private income
- d. Return on investment

Guidance: level 1

:: Credit cards ::

A _____ is a payment card issued to users to enable the cardholder to pay a merchant for goods and services based on the cardholder's promise to the card issuer to pay them for the amounts plus the other agreed charges. The card issuer creates a revolving account and grants a line of credit to the cardholder, from which the cardholder can borrow money for payment to a merchant or as a cash advance.

Exam Probability: **Low**

57. *Answer choices:*

(see index for correct answer)

- a. SBI Cards
- b. Revolution Money
- c. Credit card
- d. American Express

Guidance: level 1

:: Accounting journals and ledgers ::

The subledger, or _____ , provides details behind entries in the general ledger used in accounting. The subledger shows detail for part of the accounting records such as property and equipment, prepaid expenses, etc. The detail would include such items as date the item was purchased or expense incurred, a description of the item, the original balance, and the net book value. The total of the subledger would match the line item amount on the general ledger. This corresponding line item in the general ledger is referred to as the controlling account. The _____ balance is compared with its controlling account balance as part of the process of preparing a trial balance.

Exam Probability: **High**

58. *Answer choices:*

(see index for correct answer)

- a. Sales journal
- b. Cash receipts journal
- c. Subledger
- d. General journal

Guidance: level 1

:: Accounting terminology ::

_____ are liabilities that reflect expenses that have not yet been paid or logged under accounts payable during an accounting period; in other words, a company's obligation to pay for goods and services that have been provided for which invoices have not yet been received. Examples would include accrued wages payable, accrued sales tax payable, and accrued rent payable.

Exam Probability: **Medium**

59. *Answer choices:*

(see index for correct answer)

- a. Checkoff
- b. Accrued liabilities
- c. Share premium
- d. Capital expenditure

Guidance: level 1

Human resource management

Human resource (HR) management is the strategic approach to the effective management of organization workers so that they help the business gain a competitive advantage. It is designed to maximize employee performance in service of an employer's strategic objectives. HR is primarily concerned with the management of people within organizations, focusing on policies and on systems. HR departments are responsible for overseeing employee-benefits design, employee recruitment, training and development, performance appraisal, and rewarding (e.g., managing pay and benefit systems). HR also concerns itself with organizational change and industrial relations, that is, the balancing of organizational practices with requirements arising from collective bargaining and from governmental laws.

:: Employee relations ::

_____ is a fundamental concept in the effort to understand and describe, both qualitatively and quantitatively, the nature of the relationship between an organization and its employees. An "engaged employee" is defined as one who is fully absorbed by and enthusiastic about their work and so takes positive action to further the organization's reputation and interests. An engaged employee has a positive attitude towards the organization and its values. In contrast, a disengaged employee may range from someone doing the bare minimum at work, up to an employee who is actively damaging the company's work output and reputation.

Exam Probability: **Low**

1. *Answer choices:*

(see index for correct answer)

- a. Employee motivation
- b. Employee engagement
- c. Fringe benefit
- d. employee stock ownership

Guidance: level 1

:: Production and manufacturing ::

_____ consists of organization-wide efforts to "install and make permanent climate where employees continuously improve their ability to provide on demand products and services that customers will find of particular value." "Total" emphasizes that departments in addition to production are obligated to improve their operations; "management" emphasizes that executives are obligated to actively manage quality through funding, training, staffing, and goal setting. While there is no widely agreed-upon approach, TQM efforts typically draw heavily on the previously developed tools and techniques of quality control. TQM enjoyed widespread attention during the late 1980s and early 1990s before being overshadowed by ISO 9000, Lean manufacturing, and Six Sigma.

Exam Probability: **Medium**

2. *Answer choices:*

(see index for correct answer)

- a. Digital materialization
- b. Fiberglass molding
- c. Total Quality Management
- d. Production engineering

Guidance: level 1

:: Trade unions ::

A _____ , in North America, or union branch , in the United Kingdom and other countries, is a local branch of a usually national trade union. The terms used for sub-branches of _____ s vary from country to country and include "shop committee", "shop floor committee", "board of control", "chapel", and others.

Exam Probability: **Medium**

3. *Answer choices:*

(see index for correct answer)

- a. Local union
- b. Agency shop
- c. Unfair list
- d. Directly Affiliated Local Union

Guidance: level 1

:: ::

The _____ or labour force is the labour pool in employment. It is generally used to describe those working for a single company or industry, but can also apply to a geographic region like a city, state, or country. Within a company, its value can be labelled as its " _____ in Place". The _____ of a country includes both the employed and the unemployed. The labour force participation rate, LFPR , is the ratio between the labour force and the overall size of their cohort . The term generally excludes the employers or management, and can imply those involved in manual labour. It may also mean all those who are available for work.

Exam Probability: **Low**

4. *Answer choices:*

(see index for correct answer)

- a. levels of analysis
- b. interpersonal communication
- c. process perspective
- d. Workforce

Guidance: level 1

:: Human resource management ::

The _____ is a free online database that contains hundreds of occupational definitions to help students, job seekers, businesses and workforce development professionals to understand today's world of work in the United States. It was developed under the sponsorship of the US Department of Labor/Employment and Training Administration through a grant to the North Carolina Employment Security Commission during the 1990s. John L. Holland's vocational model, often referred to as the Holland Codes, is used in the "Interests" section of the O*NET.

Exam Probability: **High**

5. *Answer choices:*

(see index for correct answer)

- a. Talascend
- b. Occupational Information Network
- c. Experticity
- d. Organizational chart

Guidance: level 1

:: Human resource management ::

_____, also known as organizational socialization, is management jargon first created in 1988 that refers to the mechanism through which new employees acquire the necessary knowledge, skills, and behaviors in order to become effective organizational members and insiders.

Exam Probability: **High**

6. *Answer choices:*

(see index for correct answer)

- a. Human resource consulting
- b. Employee retention
- c. Skills management
- d. Selection ratio

Guidance: level 1

:: Recruitment ::

_____ is a specialized recruitment service which organizations pay to seek out and recruit highly qualified candidates for senior-level and executive jobs. Headhunters may also seek out and recruit other highly specialized and/or skilled positions in organizations for which there is strong competition in the job market for the top talent, such as senior data analysts or computer programmers. The method usually involves commissioning a third-party organization, typically an _____ firm, but possibly a standalone consultant or consulting firm, to research the availability of suitable qualified candidates working for competitors or related businesses or organizations. Having identified a shortlist of qualified candidates who match the client's requirements, the _____ firm may act as an intermediary to contact the individual and see if they might be interested in moving to a new employer. The _____ firm may also carry out initial screening of the candidate, negotiations on remuneration and benefits, and preparing the employment contract. In some markets there has been a move towards using _____ for lower positions driven by the fact that there are less candidates for some positions even on lower levels than executive.

Exam Probability: **High**

7. *Answer choices:*

(see index for correct answer)

- a. Association of Graduate Recruiters
- b. Referral recruitment
- c. Executive search
- d. Versatilist

Guidance: level 1

:: Unemployment benefits ::

_____ are payments made by back authorized bodies to unemployed people. In the United States, benefits are funded by a compulsory governmental insurance system, not taxes on individual citizens. Depending on the jurisdiction and the status of the person, those sums may be small, covering only basic needs, or may compensate the lost time proportionally to the previous earned salary.

Exam Probability: **High**

8. *Answer choices:*

(see index for correct answer)

- a. Unemployment benefits in Sweden
- b. Unemployment benefits
- c. National Insurance Act 1911
- d. Unemployment benefits in Spain

Guidance: level 1

:: Human resource management ::

_____ is the corporate management term for the act of reorganizing the legal, ownership, operational, or other structures of a company for the purpose of making it more profitable, or better organized for its present needs. Other reasons for _____ include a change of ownership or ownership structure, demerger, or a response to a crisis or major change in the business such as bankruptcy, repositioning, or buyout. _____ may also be described as corporate _____ , debt _____ and financial _____ .

Exam Probability: **Medium**

9. *Answer choices:*

(see index for correct answer)

- a. Restructuring
- b. Labour is not a commodity
- c. Management by observation
- d. Progress, plans, problems

Guidance: level 1

:: Cognitive biases ::

In personality psychology, _____ is the degree to which people believe that they have control over the outcome of events in their lives, as opposed to external forces beyond their control. Understanding of the concept was developed by Julian B. Rotter in 1954, and has since become an aspect of personality studies. A person's "locus" is conceptualized as internal or external .

Exam Probability: **Low**

10. *Answer choices:*

(see index for correct answer)

- a. Certainty effect
- b. Locus of control
- c. Wishful thinking
- d. Pessimism bias

Guidance: level 1

:: Sociological terminology ::

In moral and political philosophy, the _____ is a theory or model that originated during the Age of Enlightenment and usually concerns the legitimacy of the authority of the state over the individual. _____ arguments typically posit that individuals have consented, either explicitly or tacitly, to surrender some of their freedoms and submit to the authority in exchange for protection of their remaining rights or maintenance of the social order. The relation between natural and legal rights is often a topic of _____ theory. The term takes its name from The _____ , a 1762 book by Jean-Jacques Rousseau that discussed this concept. Although the antecedents of _____ theory are found in antiquity, in Greek and Stoic philosophy and Roman and Canon Law, the heyday of the _____ was the mid-17th to early 19th centuries, when it emerged as the leading doctrine of political legitimacy.

Exam Probability: **High**

11. *Answer choices:*

(see index for correct answer)

- a. Social contract
- b. cultural artifact
- c. McDonaldization
- d. Anticipatory socialization

Guidance: level 1

:: Employment compensation ::

Generally PTO hours cover everything from planned vacations to sick days, and are becoming more prevalent in the field of human resource management. Unlike more traditional leave plans, PTO plans don't distinguish employee absences from personal days, vacation days, or sick days. Upon employment, the company determines how many PTO hours will be allotted per year and a "rollover" policy. Some companies let PTO hours accumulate for only a year, and unused hours disappear at year-end. Some PTO plans may also accommodate unexpected or unforeseeable circumstances such as jury duty, military duty, and bereavement leave. PTO bank plans typically do not include short-term or long-term disability leave, workers compensation, family and medical leave, sabbatical, or community service leave.

Exam Probability: **Medium**

12. *Answer choices:*

(see index for correct answer)

- a. Paid time off
- b. Sliding wage scale
- c. Equal pay for equal work
- d. Performance-related pay

Guidance: level 1

:: Types of marketing ::

In microeconomics and management, _____ is an arrangement in which the supply chain of a company is owned by that company. Usually each member of the supply chain produces a different product or service, and the products combine to satisfy a common need. It is contrasted with horizontal integration, wherein a company produces several items which are related to one another. _____ has also described management styles that bring large portions of the supply chain not only under a common ownership, but also into one corporation .

Exam Probability: **Medium**

13. *Answer choices:*
(see index for correct answer)

- a. Consumer Generated Advertising
- b. Close Range Marketing
- c. Customer advocacy
- d. Vertical integration

Guidance: level 1

:: Television terminology ::

Distance education or long- _____ is the education of students who may not always be physically present at a school. Traditionally, this usually involved correspondence courses wherein the student corresponded with the school via post. Today it involves online education. Courses that are conducted are either hybrid, blended or 100% _____ . Massive open online courses , offering large-scale interactive participation and open access through the World Wide Web or other network technologies, are recent developments in distance education. A number of other terms are used roughly synonymously with distance education.

Exam Probability: **Medium**

14. *Answer choices:*

(see index for correct answer)

- a. multiplexing
- b. Distance learning
- c. nonprofit
- d. not-for-profit

Guidance: level 1

:: Offshoring ::

Outsourcing is an agreement in which one company hires another company to be responsible for a planned or existing activity that is or could be done internally, and sometimes involves transferring employees and assets from one firm to another.

Exam Probability: **High**

15. *Answer choices:*

(see index for correct answer)

- a. Nearshoring
- b. Layoff
- c. Offshore custom software development
- d. Antex

Guidance: level 1

:: Employee relations ::

_____ are tools used by organizational leadership to gain feedback on and measure employee engagement, employee morale, and performance. Usually answered anonymously, surveys are also used to gain a holistic picture of employees' feelings on such areas as working conditions, supervisory impact, and motivation that regular channels of communication may not. Surveys are considered effective in this regard provided they are well-designed, effectively administered, have validity, and evoke changes and improvements.

Exam Probability: **Low**

16. *Answer choices:*

(see index for correct answer)

- a. Industry Federation of the State of Rio de Janeiro
- b. Employee motivation
- c. Employee surveys
- d. Employee engagement

Guidance: level 1

:: Recruitment ::

The _____ is an American nonprofit professional association established in 1956 in Bethlehem, Pennsylvania, for college career services, recruiting practitioners, and others who wish to hire the college educated.

Exam Probability: **Low**

17. *Answer choices:*

(see index for correct answer)

- a. National Association of Colleges and Employers
- b. Job fraud
- c. The Select Family of Staffing Companies
- d. Employee referral

Guidance: level 1

:: Unemployment ::

In economics, a _____ is a business cycle contraction when there is a general decline in economic activity. Macroeconomic indicators such as GDP, investment spending, capacity utilization, household income, business profits, and inflation fall, while bankruptcies and the unemployment rate rise. In the United Kingdom, it is defined as a negative economic growth for two consecutive quarters.

Exam Probability: **High**

18. *Answer choices:*

(see index for correct answer)

- a. Hysteresis
- b. Unemployment Convention, 1919
- c. Unemployment Provision Convention, 1934
- d. Functional finance

Guidance: level 1

:: Business models ::

A _____ is a diagram that is used to document the primary strategic goals being pursued by an organization or management team. It is an element of the documentation associated with the Balanced Scorecard, and in particular is characteristic of the second generation of Balanced Scorecard designs that first appeared during the mid-1990s. The first diagrams of this type appeared in the early 1990s, and the idea of using this type of diagram to help document Balanced Scorecard was discussed in a paper by Drs. Robert S. Kaplan and David P. Norton in 1996.

Exam Probability: **Low**

19. *Answer choices:*

(see index for correct answer)

- a. Cooperative
- b. Business model pattern
- c. Business Model Canvas
- d. Strategy map

Guidance: level 1

:: Financial terminology ::

_____ is the cost of maintaining a certain standard of living. Changes in the _____ over time are often operationalized in a cost-of-living index. _____ calculations are also used to compare the cost of maintaining a certain standard of living in different geographic areas. Differences in _____ between locations can also be measured in terms of purchasing power parity rates.

Exam Probability: **Low**

20. *Answer choices:*

(see index for correct answer)

- a. Cost of living
- b. Debtor finance
- c. Financial goal
- d. Nancy Reagan defense

Guidance: level 1

:: Unemployment ::

> _____ is the support service provided by responsible organizations, keen to support individuals who are exiting the business – to help former employees transition to new jobs and help them re-orient themselves in the job market. A consultancy firm usually provides the _____ services which are paid for by the former employer and are achieved usually through practical advice, training materials and workshops. Some companies may offer psychological support.

Exam Probability: **Medium**

21. *Answer choices:*

(see index for correct answer)

- a. JobBridge

- b. Hysteresis
- c. Outplacement
- d. Technological unemployment

Guidance: level 1

:: Income ::

In business and accounting, net income is an entity's income minus cost of goods sold, expenses and taxes for an accounting period. It is computed as the residual of all revenues and gains over all expenses and losses for the period, and has also been defined as the net increase in shareholders' equity that results from a company's operations. In the context of the presentation of financial statements, the IFRS Foundation defines net income as synonymous with profit and loss. The difference between revenue and the cost of making a product or providing a service, before deducting overheads, payroll, taxation, and interest payments. This is different from operating income.

Exam Probability: **High**

22. *Answer choices:*

(see index for correct answer)

- a. Pay grade
- b. Property investment calculator
- c. Return of investment
- d. Bottom line

Guidance: level 1

:: Training ::

_____ refers to practicing newly acquired skills beyond the point of initial mastery. The term is also often used to refer to the pedagogical theory that this form of practice leads to automaticity or other beneficial consequences.

Exam Probability: **Medium**

23. *Answer choices:*
(see index for correct answer)

- a. human resource development
- b. National sports team
- c. Korean Standards Association
- d. Effective safety training

Guidance: level 1

:: Free market ::

Piece work is any type of employment in which a worker is paid a fixed _____ for each unit produced or action performed regardless of time.

Exam Probability: **Medium**

24. *Answer choices:*

(see index for correct answer)

- a. Regulated market
- b. Free market

Guidance: level 1

:: Business ethics ::

> _____ is a type of harassment technique that relates to a sexual nature and the unwelcome or inappropriate promise of rewards in exchange for sexual favors. _____ includes a range of actions from mild transgressions to sexual abuse or assault. Harassment can occur in many different social settings such as the workplace, the home, school, churches, etc. Harassers or victims may be of any gender.

Exam Probability: **Low**

25. *Answer choices:*

(see index for correct answer)

- a. Sexual harassment
- b. Videntifier
- c. Repugnant market
- d. Nishkam Karma

Guidance: level 1

:: Human resource management ::

_____ is an institutional process that maximizes performance levels and competency for an organization. The process includes all the activities needed to maintain a productive workforce, such as field service management, human resource management, performance and training management, data collection, recruiting, budgeting, forecasting, scheduling and analytics.

Exam Probability: **High**

26. *Answer choices:*

(see index for correct answer)

- a. Skill mix
- b. Workforce management
- c. Reward management
- d. Progress, plans, problems

Guidance: level 1

:: Organizational behavior ::

_____ is the state or fact of exclusive rights and control over property, which may be an object, land/real estate or intellectual property. _____ involves multiple rights, collectively referred to as title, which may be separated and held by different parties.

Exam Probability: **High**

27. *Answer choices:*

(see index for correct answer)

- a. Achievement Motivation Inventory
- b. Ownership
- c. Organizational citizenship behavior
- d. Group behaviour

Guidance: level 1

:: ::

_____ is a labor union representing almost 1.9 million workers in over 100 occupations in the United States and Canada. SEIU is focused on organizing workers in three sectors: health care, including hospital, home care and nursing home workers; public services ; and property services .

Exam Probability: **High**

28. *Answer choices:*

(see index for correct answer)

- a. imperative
- b. interpersonal communication
- c. hierarchical perspective

- d. Service Employees International Union

Guidance: level 1

:: Employee relations ::

> _____ ownership, or employee share ownership, is an ownership interest in a company held by the company's workforce. The ownership interest may be facilitated by the company as part of employees' remuneration or incentive compensation for work performed, or the company itself may be employee owned.

Exam Probability: **High**

29. *Answer choices:*

(see index for correct answer)

- a. Employee morale
- b. Employee stock
- c. Employee handbook
- d. Employee motivation

Guidance: level 1

:: Management ::

_____ is the kind of knowledge that is difficult to transfer to another person by means of writing it down or verbalizing it. For example, that London is in the United Kingdom is a piece of explicit knowledge that can be written down, transmitted, and understood by a recipient. However, the ability to speak a language, ride a bicycle, knead dough, play a musical instrument, or design and use complex equipment requires all sorts of knowledge that is not always known explicitly, even by expert practitioners, and which is difficult or impossible to explicitly transfer to other people.

Exam Probability: **Medium**

30. *Answer choices:*

(see index for correct answer)

- a. Submission management
- b. Records manager
- c. Tacit knowledge
- d. Facilitator

Guidance: level 1

:: Management ::

In the field of management, _____ involves the formulation and implementation of the major goals and initiatives taken by an organization's top management on behalf of owners, based on consideration of resources and an assessment of the internal and external environments in which the organization operates.

Exam Probability: **Medium**

31. *Answer choices:*

(see index for correct answer)

- a. Business process mapping
- b. Strategic management
- c. PDCA
- d. Court of Assistants

Guidance: level 1

:: Production and manufacturing ::

_____ is a theory of management that analyzes and synthesizes workflows. Its main objective is improving economic efficiency, especially labor productivity. It was one of the earliest attempts to apply science to the engineering of processes and to management. _____ is sometimes known as Taylorism after its founder, Frederick Winslow Taylor.

Exam Probability: **Low**

32. *Answer choices:*

(see index for correct answer)

- a. Scientific management
- b. Food processing

- c. Miniaturization
- d. Joint product

Guidance: level 1

:: Asset ::

In financial accounting, an _____ is any resource owned by the business. Anything tangible or intangible that can be owned or controlled to produce value and that is held by a company to produce positive economic value is an _____ . Simply stated, _____ s represent value of ownership that can be converted into cash . The balance sheet of a firm records the monetary value of the _____ s owned by that firm. It covers money and other valuables belonging to an individual or to a business.

Exam Probability: **Medium**

33. *Answer choices:*
(see index for correct answer)

- a. Fixed asset
- b. Current asset

Guidance: level 1

:: Offshoring ::

A _____ is the temporary suspension or permanent termination of employment of an employee or, more commonly, a group of employees for business reasons, such as personnel management or downsizing an organization. Originally, _____ referred exclusively to a temporary interruption in work, or employment but this has evolved to a permanent elimination of a position in both British and US English, requiring the addition of "temporary" to specify the original meaning of the word. A _____ is not to be confused with wrongful termination. Laid off workers or displaced workers are workers who have lost or left their jobs because their employer has closed or moved, there was insufficient work for them to do, or their position or shift was abolished. Downsizing in a company is defined to involve the reduction of employees in a workforce. Downsizing in companies became a popular practice in the 1980s and early 1990s as it was seen as a way to deliver better shareholder value as it helps to reduce the costs of employers. Indeed, recent research on downsizing in the U.S., UK, and Japan suggests that downsizing is being regarded by management as one of the preferred routes to help declining organizations, cutting unnecessary costs, and improve organizational performance. Usually a _____ occurs as a cost cutting measure.

Exam Probability: **Low**

34. *Answer choices:*

(see index for correct answer)

- a. Layoff
- b. Programmers Guild
- c. Offshore company
- d. Body shopping

Guidance: level 1

:: Employment discrimination ::

A _____ is a metaphor used to represent an invisible barrier that keeps a given demographic from rising beyond a certain level in a hierarchy.

Exam Probability: **High**

35. *Answer choices:*

(see index for correct answer)

- a. United Kingdom employment equality law
- b. Employment discrimination
- c. Glass ceiling
- d. Employment discrimination law in the European Union

Guidance: level 1

:: Behaviorism ::

In behavioral psychology, _____ is a consequence applied that will strengthen an organism's future behavior whenever that behavior is preceded by a specific antecedent stimulus. This strengthening effect may be measured as a higher frequency of behavior, longer duration, greater magnitude, or shorter latency. There are two types of _____, known as positive _____ and negative _____; positive is where by a reward is offered on expression of the wanted behaviour and negative is taking away an undesirable element in the persons environment whenever the desired behaviour is achieved.

Exam Probability: **Low**

36. *Answer choices:*

(see index for correct answer)

- a. Reinforcement
- b. chaining
- c. Systematic desensitization
- d. social facilitation

Guidance: level 1

:: ::

A _____ is monetary compensation paid by an employer to an employee in exchange for work done. Payment may be calculated as a fixed amount for each task completed , or at an hourly or daily rate , or based on an easily measured quantity of work done.

Exam Probability: **High**

37. *Answer choices:*

(see index for correct answer)

- a. hierarchical perspective
- b. functional perspective
- c. cultural

- d. process perspective

Guidance: level 1

:: Management ::

The term _____ refers to measures designed to increase the degree of autonomy and self-determination in people and in communities in order to enable them to represent their interests in a responsible and self-determined way, acting on their own authority. It is the process of becoming stronger and more confident, especially in controlling one's life and claiming one's rights. _____ as action refers both to the process of self-_____ and to professional support of people, which enables them to overcome their sense of powerlessness and lack of influence, and to recognize and use their resources. To do work with power.

Exam Probability: **Medium**

38. *Answer choices:*

(see index for correct answer)

- a. Supplier relationship management
- b. Empowerment
- c. Extended enterprise
- d. Oriental management

Guidance: level 1

:: Recruitment ::

_____ is a tool companies and organizations use as a way to communicate the good and the bad characteristics of the job during the hiring process of new employees, or as a tool to reestablish job specificity for existing employees. _____ s should provide the individuals with a well-rounded description that details what obligations the individual can expect to perform while working for that specific company. Descriptions may include, but are not limited to, work environment, expectations, and Company policies.

Exam Probability: **Medium**

39. *Answer choices:*

(see index for correct answer)

- a. Silicon Milkroundabout
- b. Staff Selection Commission
- c. Realistic job preview
- d. Labour brokering

Guidance: level 1

:: Validity (statistics) ::

_____ is "the degree to which a test measures what it claims, or purports, to be measuring." In the classical model of test validity, _____ is one of three main types of validity evidence, alongside content validity and criterion validity. Modern validity theory defines _____ as the overarching concern of validity research, subsuming all other types of validity evidence.

Exam Probability: **Low**

40. *Answer choices:*

(see index for correct answer)

- a. Statistical conclusion validity
- b. Test validity
- c. External validity
- d. Ecological validity

Guidance: level 1

:: United States employment discrimination case law ::

_____ , 411 U.S. 792 , is a US employment law case by the United States Supreme Court regarding the burdens and nature of proof in proving a Title VII case and the order in which plaintiffs and defendants present proof. It was the seminal case in the McDonnell Douglas burden-shifting framework.

Exam Probability: **Medium**

41. *Answer choices:*

(see index for correct answer)

- a. Gross v. FBL Financial Services, Inc.
- b. Kloeckner v. Solis
- c. Price Waterhouse v. Hopkins
- d. McDonnell Douglas Corp. v. Green

Guidance: level 1

:: ::

A _____ is an occupation founded upon specialized educational training, the purpose of which is to supply disinterested objective counsel and service to others, for a direct and definite compensation, wholly apart from expectation of other business gain. The term is a truncation of the term "liberal _____", which is, in turn, an Anglicization of the French term " _____ libérale". Originally borrowed by English users in the 19th century, it has been re-borrowed by international users from the late 20th, though the class overtones of the term do not seem to survive retranslation: "liberal _____ s" are, according to the European Union's Directive on Recognition of _____ al Qualifications "those practiced on the basis of relevant _____ al qualifications in a personal, responsible and _____ ally independent capacity by those providing intellectual and conceptual services in the interest of the client and the public".

Exam Probability: **Medium**

42. *Answer choices:*

(see index for correct answer)

- a. Sarbanes-Oxley act of 2002
- b. Profession
- c. similarity-attraction theory
- d. co-culture

Guidance: level 1

:: Employment compensation ::

Compensation and benefits is a sub-discipline of human resources, focused on employee compensation and benefits policy-making. While compensation and benefits are tangible, there are intangible rewards such as recognition, work-life and development. Combined, these are referred to as _____ s. The term "compensation and benefits" refers to the discipline as well as the rewards themselves.

Exam Probability: **Medium**

43. *Answer choices:*
(see index for correct answer)

- a. Total Reward
- b. Lilly Ledbetter Fair Pay Act of 2009
- c. Federal Wage System
- d. Golden handshake

Guidance: level 1

:: Labour law ::

In law, _____ is to give an immediately secured right of present or future deployment. One has a vested right to an asset that cannot be taken away by any third party, even though one may not yet possess the asset. When the right, interest, or title to the present or future possession of a legal estate can be transferred to any other party, it is termed a vested interest.

Exam Probability: **Low**

44. *Answer choices:*

(see index for correct answer)

- a. Vesting
- b. Worker director
- c. Work permit
- d. Negligent retention

Guidance: level 1

:: Trade union legislation ::

The _____ is the name for several legislative bills on US labor law which have been proposed and sometimes introduced into one or both chambers of the U.S. Congress.

Exam Probability: **Low**

45. *Answer choices:*

(see index for correct answer)

- a. Padlock Law
- b. Employee Free Choice Act
- c. Trade Union Act 1984
- d. Trade Disputes and Trade Unions Act 1927

Guidance: level 1

:: Management ::

A _____ is when two or more people come together to discuss one or more topics, often in a formal or business setting, but _____ s also occur in a variety of other environments. Many various types of _____ s exist.

Exam Probability: **High**

46. *Answer choices:*

(see index for correct answer)

- a. Capability management
- b. Personal offshoring
- c. Meeting
- d. manager's right to manage

Guidance: level 1

:: ::

> Domestic violence is violence or other abuse by one person against another in a domestic setting, such as in marriage or cohabitation. It may be termed intimate partner violence when committed by a spouse or partner in an intimate relationship against the other spouse or partner, and can take place in heterosexual or same-sex relationships, or between former spouses or partners. Domestic violence can also involve violence against children, parents, or the elderly. It takes a number of forms, including physical, verbal, emotional, economic, religious, reproductive, and sexual abuse, which can range from subtle, coercive forms to marital rape and to violent physical abuse such as choking, beating, female genital mutilation, and acid throwing that results in disfigurement or death. Domestic murders include stoning, bride burning, honor killings, and dowry deaths.

Exam Probability: **Low**

47. *Answer choices:*

(see index for correct answer)

- a. Family violence
- b. functional perspective
- c. open system
- d. surface-level diversity

Guidance: level 1

:: Trade union legislation ::

The _____ of 1935 is a foundational statute of United States labor law which guarantees the right of private sector employees to organize into trade unions, engage in collective bargaining, and take collective action such as strikes. The act was written by Senator Robert F. Wagner, passed by the 74th United States Congress, and signed into law by President Franklin D. Roosevelt.

Exam Probability: **High**

48. *Answer choices:*

(see index for correct answer)

- a. Trade Disputes and Trade Unions Act 1927
- b. Padlock Law
- c. Employee Free Choice Act
- d. Labor Management Relations Act

Guidance: level 1

:: Learning methods ::

_____ is an approach to problem solving. It involves taking action and reflecting upon the results. This helps improve the problem-solving process as well as simplify the solutions developed by the team.

Exam Probability: **High**

49. *Answer choices:*

(see index for correct answer)

- a. Action learning
- b. Collaborative learning
- c. Audience response system
- d. Double-loop learning

Guidance: level 1

:: Training ::

A _____ is commonly known as an individual taking part in a _____ program or a graduate program within a company after having graduated from university or college.

Exam Probability: **Low**

50. *Answer choices:*
(see index for correct answer)

- a. Trainee
- b. Simulation game
- c. Jeff Phillips
- d. Training camp

Guidance: level 1

:: Employment compensation ::

The _____ has been successfully used by a variety of public and private companies for many decades. These plans combine leadership, total workforce education, and widespread employee participation with a reward system linked to organization performance. The _____ is a gainsharing program in which employees share in pre-established cost savings, based upon employee effort. Formal employee participation is necessary with the _____ , as well as periodic progress reporting and an incentive formula.

Exam Probability: **Low**

51. *Answer choices:*

(see index for correct answer)

- a. Pay scale
- b. Scanlon plan
- c. Employees%27 Compensation Appeals Board
- d. Take-home vehicle

Guidance: level 1

:: Foreign workers ::

A _____ or guest worker is a human who works in a country other than the one of which he or she is a citizen. Some _____s are using a guest worker program in a country with more preferred job prospects than their home country. Guest workers are often either sent or invited to work outside their home country, or have acquired a job before they left their home country, whereas migrant workers often leave their home country without having a specific job at hand.

Exam Probability: **High**

52. *Answer choices:*

(see index for correct answer)

- a. European Voluntary Workers
- b. Foreign worker
- c. Filipinos in Israel
- d. Migrant domestic workers

Guidance: level 1

A _____ is a technical analysis of a biological specimen, for example urine, hair, blood, breath, sweat, and/or oral fluid/saliva—to determine the presence or absence of specified parent drugs or their metabolites. Major applications of _____ ing include detection of the presence of performance enhancing steroids in sport, employers and parole/probation officers screening for drugs prohibited by law and police officers testing for the presence and concentration of alcohol in the blood commonly referred to as BAC . BAC tests are typically administered via a breathalyzer while urinalysis is used for the vast majority of _____ ing in sports and the workplace. Numerous other methods with varying degrees of accuracy, sensitivity , and detection periods exist.

Exam Probability: **High**

53. *Answer choices:*

(see index for correct answer)

- a. personal values
- b. Drug test
- c. process perspective
- d. open system

Guidance: level 1

:: Organizational structure ::

An _____ defines how activities such as task allocation, coordination, and supervision are directed toward the achievement of organizational aims.

Exam Probability: **Medium**

54. *Answer choices:*

(see index for correct answer)

- a. The Starfish and the Spider
- b. Organizational structure
- c. Organization of the New York City Police Department
- d. Unorganisation

Guidance: level 1

:: Human resource management ::

_____ is the application of information technology for both networking and supporting at least two individual or collective actors in their shared performing of HR activities.

Exam Probability: **Low**

55. *Answer choices:*

(see index for correct answer)

- a. Disciplinary probation
- b. E-HRM
- c. Continuing professional development
- d. Virtual management

Guidance: level 1

:: Business terms ::

Centralisation or _____ is the process by which the activities of an organization, particularly those regarding planning and decision-making, framing strategy and policies become concentrated within a particular geographical location group. This moves the important decision-making and planning powers within the center of the organisation.

Exam Probability: **Low**

56. *Answer choices:*

(see index for correct answer)

- a. Mission statement
- b. back office
- c. operating cost
- d. Centralization

Guidance: level 1

:: Employment compensation ::

A _____ is the minimum income necessary for a worker to meet their basic needs. Needs are defined to include food, housing, and other essential needs such as clothing. The goal of a _____ is to allow a worker to afford a basic but decent standard of living. Due to the flexible nature of the term "needs", there is not one universally accepted measure of what a _____ is and as such it varies by location and household type.

Exam Probability: **Medium**

57. *Answer choices:*

(see index for correct answer)

- a. Living wage
- b. Annual enrollment
- c. Long service leave
- d. Gender pay gap in Australia

Guidance: level 1

Refresher/ _____ is the process of learning a new or the same old skill or trade for the same group of personnel. Refresher/ _____ is required to be provided on regular basis to avoid personnel obsolescence due to technological changes & the individuals memory capacity. This short term instruction course shall serve to re-acquaint personnel with skills previously learnt or to bring one's knowledge or skills up-to-date so that skills stay sharp. This kind of training could be provided annually or more frequently as maybe required, based on the importance of consistency of the task of which the skill is involved. Examples of refreshers are cGMP, GDP, HSE trainings. _____ shall also be conducted for an employee, when the employee is rated as 'not qualified' for a skill or knowledge, as determined based on the assessment of answers in the training questionnaire of the employee.

Exam Probability: **Medium**

58. *Answer choices:*

(see index for correct answer)

- a. surface-level diversity
- b. deep-level diversity
- c. information systems assessment
- d. levels of analysis

Guidance: level 1

:: Trade unions ::

An _____ is a form of union security agreement where the employer may hire union or non-union workers, and employees need not join the union in order to remain employed. However, the non-union worker must pay a fee to cover collective bargaining costs. The fee paid by non-union members under the _____ is known as the "agency fee".

Exam Probability: **High**

59. *Answer choices:*

(see index for correct answer)

- a. Agency shop
- b. Directly Affiliated Local Union
- c. Opposition to trade unions
- d. Vigilance committee

Guidance: level 1

Information systems

Information systems (IS) are formal, sociotechnical, organizational systems designed to collect, process, store, and distribute information. In a sociotechnical perspective Information Systems are composed by four components: technology, process, people and organizational structure.

:: Data management ::

Data aggregation is the compiling of information from databases with intent to prepare combined datasets for data processing.

Exam Probability: **High**

1. *Answer choices:*

(see index for correct answer)

- a. National Data Repository
- b. Data aggregator
- c. Content management
- d. Navigational database

Guidance: level 1

:: Service-oriented (business computing) ::

_____ is a software licensing and delivery model in which software is licensed on a subscription basis and is centrally hosted. It is sometimes referred to as "on-demand software", and was formerly referred to as "software plus services" by Microsoft. SaaS is typically accessed by users using a thin client, e.g. via a web browser. SaaS has become a common delivery model for many business applications, including office software, messaging software, payroll processing software, DBMS software, management software, CAD software, development software, gamification, virtualization, accounting, collaboration, customer relationship management, Management Information Systems, enterprise resource planning, invoicing, human resource management, talent acquisition, learning management systems, content management, Geographic Information Systems, and service desk management. SaaS has been incorporated into the strategy of nearly all leading enterprise software companies.

Exam Probability: **High**

2. *Answer choices:*

(see index for correct answer)

- a. Digital nervous system
- b. Barracuda Networks
- c. SOALIB
- d. Software as a service

Guidance: level 1

:: User interfaces ::

The _____, in the industrial design field of human–computer interaction, is the space where interactions between humans and machines occur. The goal of this interaction is to allow effective operation and control of the machine from the human end, whilst the machine simultaneously feeds back information that aids the operators' decision-making process. Examples of this broad concept of _____ s include the interactive aspects of computer operating systems, hand tools, heavy machinery operator controls, and process controls. The design considerations applicable when creating _____ s are related to or involve such disciplines as ergonomics and psychology.

Exam Probability: **High**

3. *Answer choices:*

(see index for correct answer)

- a. Monome
- b. Ludic interface
- c. Direct mode
- d. WYSIWYM

Guidance: level 1

:: Data quality ::

_____ is the maintenance of, and the assurance of the accuracy and consistency of, data over its entire life-cycle, and is a critical aspect to the design, implementation and usage of any system which stores, processes, or retrieves data. The term is broad in scope and may have widely different meanings depending on the specific context even under the same general umbrella of computing. It is at times used as a proxy term for data quality, while data validation is a pre-requisite for _____ . _____ is the opposite of data corruption. The overall intent of any _____ technique is the same: ensure data is recorded exactly as intended and upon later retrieval, ensure the data is the same as it was when it was originally recorded. In short, _____ aims to prevent unintentional changes to information. _____ is not to be confused with data security, the discipline of protecting data from unauthorized parties.

Exam Probability: **High**

4. *Answer choices:*

(see index for correct answer)

- a. Information quality
- b. Dirty data
- c. Data integrity
- d. Data degradation

Guidance: level 1

:: Marketing ::

_____ is a business model in which consumers create value and businesses consume that value. For example, when a consumer writes reviews or when a consumer gives a useful idea for new product development then that consumer is creating value for the business if the business adopts the input.
In the C2B model, a reverse auction or demand collection model, enables buyers to name or demand their own price, which is often binding, for a specific good or service. Inside of a consumer to business market the roles involved in the transaction must be established and the consumer must offer something of value to the business.

Exam Probability: **Medium**

5. *Answer choices:*

(see index for correct answer)

- a. Category management
- b. Consumer-to-business
- c. Immersion marketing
- d. Cross merchandising

Guidance: level 1

:: Online companies ::

_____ is a business directory service and crowd-sourced review forum, and a public company of the same name that is headquartered in San Francisco, California. The company develops, hosts and markets the _____.com website and the _____ mobile app, which publish crowd-sourced reviews about businesses. It also operates an online reservation service called _____ Reservations.

Exam Probability: **Medium**

6. *Answer choices:*

(see index for correct answer)

- a. Aeron chair
- b. Teledesic
- c. Qualir
- d. Indieflix

Guidance: level 1

:: Marketing ::

_____, in marketing, manufacturing, call centres and management, is the use of flexible computer-aided manufacturing systems to produce custom output. Such systems combine the low unit costs of mass production processes with the flexibility of individual customization.

Exam Probability: **Low**

7. *Answer choices:*

(see index for correct answer)

- a. Breakthrough Moments
- b. Mass customization
- c. Fifth screen
- d. Customer franchise

Guidance: level 1

:: Information systems ::

In artificial intelligence, an _____ is a computer system that emulates the decision-making ability of a human expert. _____ s are designed to solve complex problems by reasoning through bodies of knowledge, represented mainly as if–then rules rather than through conventional procedural code. The first _____ s were created in the 1970s and then proliferated in the 1980s. _____ s were among the first truly successful forms of artificial intelligence software. However, some experts point out that _____ s were not part of true artificial intelligence since they lack the ability to learn autonomously from external data. An _____ is divided into two subsystems: the inference engine and the knowledge base. The knowledge base represents facts and rules. The inference engine applies the rules to the known facts to deduce new facts. Inference engines can also include explanation and debugging abilities.

Exam Probability: **High**

8. *Answer choices:*

(see index for correct answer)

- a. European Research Center for Information Systems
- b. MES Hybrid Document Systems
- c. EuResist
- d. Expert system

Guidance: level 1

:: Computer networking ::

A backbone is a part of computer network that interconnects various pieces of network, providing a path for the exchange of information between different LANs or subnetworks. A backbone can tie together diverse networks in the same building, in different buildings in a campus environment, or over wide areas. Normally, the backbone's capacity is greater than the networks connected to it.

Exam Probability: **Medium**

9. *Answer choices:*

(see index for correct answer)

- a. Location information server
- b. DNOS
- c. Slashdot effect
- d. Backbone network

Guidance: level 1

:: Information technology organisations ::

The Internet Corporation for Assigned Names and Numbers is a nonprofit organization responsible for coordinating the maintenance and procedures of several databases related to the namespaces and numerical spaces of the Internet, ensuring the network's stable and secure operation. _____ performs the actual technical maintenance work of the Central Internet Address pools and DNS root zone registries pursuant to the Internet Assigned Numbers Authority function contract. The contract regarding the IANA stewardship functions between _____ and the National Telecommunications and Information Administration of the United States Department of Commerce ended on October 1, 2016, formally transitioning the functions to the global multistakeholder community.

Exam Probability: **Medium**

10. *Answer choices:*
(see index for correct answer)

- a. StrawberryNet
- b. BCSWomen
- c. UK Computer Measurement Group
- d. ICANN

Guidance: level 1

:: Internet advertising ::

_____ , according to the United States federal law known as the Anti _____ Consumer Protection Act, is registering, trafficking in, or using an Internet domain name with bad faith intent to profit from the goodwill of a trademark belonging to someone else. The cybersquatter then offers to sell the domain to the person or company who owns a trademark contained within the name at an inflated price.

Exam Probability: **Low**

11. *Answer choices:*

(see index for correct answer)

- a. Cybersquatting
- b. SiteScreen
- c. Microsoft Corp. v. Shah
- d. Fake blog

Guidance: level 1

:: Payment systems ::

A _____ is any system used to settle financial transactions through the transfer of monetary value. This includes the institutions, instruments, people, rules, procedures, standards, and technologies that make it exchange possible. A common type of _____ is called an operational network that links bank accounts and provides for monetary exchange using bank deposits. Some _____ s also include credit mechanisms, which are essentially a different aspect of payment.

Exam Probability: **Low**

12. *Answer choices:*

(see index for correct answer)

- a. Payment system
- b. Adyen
- c. CHAPS
- d. Letters of credit

Guidance: level 1

:: Virtual economies ::

_____ Inc. is an American social game developer running social video game services founded in April 2007 and headquartered in San Francisco, California, United States. The company primarily focuses on mobile and social networking platforms. _____ states its mission as "connecting the world through games."

Exam Probability: **Medium**

13. *Answer choices:*

(see index for correct answer)

- a. There
- b. Shattered World

- c. Frontier: Elite II
- d. Virtual crime

Guidance: level 1

:: ::

A _____ or data centre is a building, dedicated space within a building, or a group of buildings used to house computer systems and associated components, such as telecommunications and storage systems.

Exam Probability: **Low**

14. *Answer choices:*

(see index for correct answer)

- a. Sarbanes-Oxley act of 2002
- b. information systems assessment
- c. personal values
- d. interpersonal communication

Guidance: level 1

:: Information systems ::

A _____ manages the creation and modification of digital content. It typically supports multiple users in a collaborative environment.

Exam Probability: **Medium**

15. *Answer choices:*

(see index for correct answer)

- a. Field service management
- b. Diablo Data Systems
- c. Content management system
- d. Enhanced publication

Guidance: level 1

:: Service-oriented (business computing) ::

_____ is a style of software design where services are provided to the other components by application components, through a communication protocol over a network. The basic principles of _____ are independent of vendors, products and technologies. A service is a discrete unit of functionality that can be accessed remotely and acted upon and updated independently, such as retrieving a credit card statement online.

Exam Probability: **Low**

16. *Answer choices:*

(see index for correct answer)

- a. JackBe
- b. Web-oriented architecture
- c. Service-oriented architecture
- d. SAP Enterprise Architecture Framework

Guidance: level 1

:: Payment systems ::

An _____ is an electronic telecommunications device that enables customers of financial institutions to perform financial transactions, such as cash withdrawals, deposits, transfer funds, or obtaining account information, at any time and without the need for direct interaction with bank staff.

Exam Probability: **Low**

17. *Answer choices:*

(see index for correct answer)

- a. Automated teller machine
- b. Interac e-Transfer
- c. Saudi Payments Network
- d. Voluntary Collective Licensing

Guidance: level 1

:: Behavioral and social facets of systemic risk ::

_____ is the difficulty in understanding an issue and effectively making decisions when one has too much information about that issue. Generally, the term is associated with the excessive quantity of daily information. _____ most likely originated from information theory, which are studies in the storage, preservation, communication, compression, and extraction of information. The term, _____, was first used in Bertram Gross' 1964 book, The Managing of Organizations, and it was further popularized by Alvin Toffler in his bestselling 1970 book Future Shock. Speier et al. stated.

Exam Probability: **Medium**

18. *Answer choices:*

(see index for correct answer)

- a. Information overload
- b. Moral panic
- c. recommender
- d. Human reliability

Guidance: level 1

:: Multi-agent systems ::

A _____ is a number of Internet-connected devices, each of which is running one or more bots. _____s can be used to perform distributed denial-of-service attack , steal data, send spam, and allows the attacker to access the device and its connection. The owner can control the _____ using command and control software. The word "_____" is a combination of the words "robot" and "network". The term is usually used with a negative or malicious connotation.

Exam Probability: **Low**

19. *Answer choices:*

(see index for correct answer)

- a. Botnet
- b. Cutwail botnet
- c. Bagle
- d. Kelihos botnet

Guidance: level 1

A _____ is a research instrument consisting of a series of questions for the purpose of gathering information from respondents. The _____ was invented by the Statistical Society of London in 1838.

Exam Probability: **Low**

20. Answer choices:

(see index for correct answer)

- a. Questionnaire
- b. cultural
- c. process perspective
- d. Character

Guidance: level 1

:: ::

In linguistics, a _____ is the smallest element that can be uttered in isolation with objective or practical meaning.

Exam Probability: **Low**

21. Answer choices:

(see index for correct answer)

- a. Word
- b. hierarchical
- c. deep-level diversity
- d. surface-level diversity

Guidance: level 1

:: Marketing ::

_____ is the percentage of a market accounted for by a specific entity. In a survey of nearly 200 senior marketing managers, 67% responded that they found the revenue- "dollar _____ " metric very useful, while 61% found "unit _____ " very useful.

Exam Probability: **Low**

22. *Answer choices:*
(see index for correct answer)

- a. Demand generation
- b. Profit chart
- c. Grand cru
- d. Market share

Guidance: level 1

:: Marketing by medium ::

_____ or viral advertising is a business strategy that uses existing social networks to promote a product. Its name refers to how consumers spread information about a product with other people in their social networks, much in the same way that a virus spreads from one person to another. It can be delivered by word of mouth or enhanced by the network effects of the Internet and mobile networks.

Exam Probability: **Medium**

23. *Answer choices:*

(see index for correct answer)

- a. Brand infiltration
- b. New media marketing
- c. Direct Text Marketing
- d. Digital marketing

Guidance: level 1

:: Metadata ::

_____ s usage can be discovered by inspection of software applications or application data files through a process of manual or automated Application Discovery and Understanding. Once _____ s are discovered they can be registered in a metadata registry.

Exam Probability: **Medium**

24. *Answer choices:*

(see index for correct answer)

- a. Data element
- b. Comment
- c. Binary object
- d. Climate and Forecast Metadata Conventions

Guidance: level 1

:: Commerce ::

_____ , Inc. is an American media-services provider headquartered in Los Gatos, California, founded in 1997 by Reed Hastings and Marc Randolph in Scotts Valley, California. The company's primary business is its subscription-based streaming OTT service which offers online streaming of a library of films and television programs, including those produced in-house. As of April 2019, _____ had over 148 million paid subscriptions worldwide, including 60 million in the United States, and over 154 million subscriptions total including free trials. It is available almost worldwide except in mainland China as well as Syria, North Korea, and Crimea . The company also has offices in the Netherlands, Brazil, India, Japan, and South Korea. _____ is a member of the Motion Picture Association of America .

Exam Probability: **Low**

25. *Answer choices:*

(see index for correct answer)

- a. Emerging Markets Index
- b. Netflix
- c. RFM
- d. Drawback

Guidance: level 1

:: ::

A _____ is server software, or hardware dedicated to running said software, that can satisfy World Wide Web client requests. A _____ can, in general, contain one or more websites. A _____ processes incoming network requests over HTTP and several other related protocols.

Exam Probability: **Medium**

26. *Answer choices:*
(see index for correct answer)

- a. Sarbanes-Oxley act of 2002
- b. Web server
- c. hierarchical
- d. functional perspective

Guidance: level 1

:: E-commerce ::

Electronic governance or e-governance is the application of information and communication technology for delivering government services, exchange of information, communication transactions, integration of various stand-alone systems and services between government-to-citizen, government-to-business, _____, government-to-employees as well as back-office processes and interactions within the entire government framework. Through e-governance, government services are made available to citizens in a convenient, efficient, and transparent manner. The three main target groups that can be distinguished in governance concepts are government, citizens, and businesses/interest groups. In e-governance, there are no distinct boundaries.

Exam Probability: **Medium**

27. *Answer choices:*

(see index for correct answer)

- a. Online Revolution
- b. Government-to-government
- c. Transactional Link
- d. BuildDirect

Guidance: level 1

:: Information technology management ::

_____ concerns a cycle of organizational activity: the acquisition of information from one or more sources, the custodianship and the distribution of that information to those who need it, and its ultimate disposition through archiving or deletion.

Exam Probability: **Low**

28. *Answer choices:*

(see index for correct answer)

- a. Business performance management
- b. Change management
- c. Infoblox
- d. Records life-cycle

Guidance: level 1

:: Network performance ::

_____ is a distributed computing paradigm which brings computer data storage closer to the location where it is needed. Computation is largely or completely performed on distributed device nodes. _____ pushes applications, data and computing power away from centralized points to locations closer to the user. The target of _____ is any application or general functionality needing to be closer to the source of the action where distributed systems technology interacts with the physical world. _____ does not need contact with any centralized cloud, although it may interact with one. In contrast to cloud computing, _____ refers to decentralized data processing at the edge of the network.

Exam Probability: **High**

29. *Answer choices:*

(see index for correct answer)

- a. Bandwidth management
- b. Edge computing
- c. WAN optimization
- d. Performance tuning

Guidance: level 1

:: Production economics ::

_____ is a way of producing goods and services that relies on self-organizing communities of individuals. In such communities, the labor of a large number of people is coordinated towards a shared outcome.

Exam Probability: **Low**

30. *Answer choices:*

(see index for correct answer)

- a. Economic batch quantity
- b. Capacity utilization
- c. Peer production
- d. Productive capacity

Guidance: level 1

:: Data interchange standards ::

_____ is the concept of businesses electronically communicating information that was traditionally communicated on paper, such as purchase orders and invoices. Technical standards for EDI exist to facilitate parties transacting such instruments without having to make special arrangements.

Exam Probability: **Low**

31. *Answer choices:*

(see index for correct answer)

- a. Common Alerting Protocol
- b. Domain Application Protocol
- c. Electronic data interchange
- d. Interaction protocol

Guidance: level 1

:: ::

_____ rate is the ratio of users who click on a specific link to the number of total users who view a page, email, or advertisement. It is commonly used to measure the success of an online advertising campaign for a particular website as well as the effectiveness of email campaigns.

Exam Probability: **Low**

32. *Answer choices:*

(see index for correct answer)

- a. co-culture
- b. corporate values
- c. similarity-attraction theory
- d. Click-through

Guidance: level 1

:: Data security ::

_____ are safeguards or countermeasures to avoid, detect, counteract, or minimize security risks to physical property, information, computer systems, or other assets.

Exam Probability: **Medium**

33. *Answer choices:*

(see index for correct answer)

- a. Certified Information Systems Security Professional
- b. Airbackup
- c. Cracking of wireless networks
- d. Information security management system

Guidance: level 1

:: E-commerce ::

_____ is a type of fraud that occurs on the Internet in pay-per-click online advertising. In this type of advertising, the owners of websites that post the ads are paid an amount of money determined by how many visitors to the sites click on the ads. Fraud occurs when a person, automated script or computer program imitates a legitimate user of a web browser, clicking on such an ad without having an actual interest in the target of the ad's link.
_____ is the subject of some controversy and increasing litigation due to the advertising networks being a key beneficiary of the fraud.

Exam Probability: **Medium**

34. *Answer choices:*

(see index for correct answer)

- a. DVD-by-mail
- b. Sears Israel
- c. ESewa
- d. Click fraud

Guidance: level 1

:: ::

In communications and information processing, _____ is a system of rules to convert information—such as a letter, word, sound, image, or gesture—into another form or representation, sometimes shortened or secret, for communication through a communication channel or storage in a storage medium. An early example is the invention of language, which enabled a person, through speech, to communicate what they saw, heard, felt, or thought to others. But speech limits the range of communication to the distance a voice can carry, and limits the audience to those present when the speech is uttered. The invention of writing, which converted spoken language into visual symbols, extended the range of communication across space and time.

Exam Probability: **High**

35. *Answer choices:*

(see index for correct answer)

- a. functional perspective
- b. open system
- c. Code
- d. Sarbanes-Oxley act of 2002

Guidance: level 1

:: Strategic management ::

_____ is a management term for an element that is necessary for an organization or project to achieve its mission. Alternative terms are key result area and key success factor.

Exam Probability: **High**

36. *Answer choices:*

(see index for correct answer)

- a. Critical success factor
- b. BSC SWOT
- c. Core product
- d. The New Age of Innovation

Guidance: level 1

:: ::

_____ is a free email service developed by Google. Users can access _____ on the web and using third-party programs that synchronize email content through POP or IMAP protocols. _____ started as a limited beta release on April 1, 2004 and ended its testing phase on July 7, 2009.

Exam Probability: **Low**

37. *Answer choices:*

(see index for correct answer)

- a. functional perspective
- b. Gmail
- c. similarity-attraction theory
- d. empathy

Guidance: level 1

:: ::

A _____ is a computer file which stores data to be used by a computer application or system, including input and output data. A _____ usually does not contain instructions or code to be executed.

Exam Probability: **High**

38. *Answer choices:*

(see index for correct answer)

- a. cultural
- b. Character
- c. corporate values
- d. Data file

Guidance: level 1

:: Geographic information systems ::

_____ is the computational process of transforming a physical address description to a location on the Earth's surface. Reverse _____, on the other hand, converts geographic coordinates to a description of a location, usually the name of a place or an addressable location. _____ relies on a computer representation of address points, the street / road network, together with postal and administrative boundaries.

Exam Probability: **Medium**

39. *Answer choices:*

(see index for correct answer)

- a. NavTool
- b. Geocoding
- c. Location-allocation
- d. David Mark

Guidance: level 1

:: Computer access control ::

_____ is the act of confirming the truth of an attribute of a single piece of data claimed true by an entity. In contrast with identification, which refers to the act of stating or otherwise indicating a claim purportedly attesting to a person or thing's identity, _____ is the process of actually confirming that identity. It might involve confirming the identity of a person by validating their identity documents, verifying the authenticity of a website with a digital certificate, determining the age of an artifact by carbon dating, or ensuring that a product is what its packaging and labeling claim to be. In other words, _____ often involves verifying the validity of at least one form of identification.

Exam Probability: **Medium**

40. *Answer choices:*
(see index for correct answer)

- a. Access Control Matrix
- b. Security token service
- c. Authentication
- d. VOMS

Guidance: level 1

:: Infographics ::

A _____ is a graphical representation of data, in which "the data is represented by symbols, such as bars in a bar _____, lines in a line _____, or slices in a pie _____". A _____ can represent tabular numeric data, functions or some kinds of qualitative structure and provides different info.

Exam Probability: **High**

41. *Answer choices:*

(see index for correct answer)

- a. Statistical graphics
- b. Chart
- c. Engineering drawing
- d. Cutaway drawing

Guidance: level 1

:: Ergonomics ::

_____ is the design of products, devices, services, or environments for people with disabilities. The concept of accessible design and practice of accessible development ensures both "direct access" and "indirect access" meaning compatibility with a person's assistive technology.

Exam Probability: **High**

42. *Answer choices:*

(see index for correct answer)

- a. Armrest
- b. Accessibility
- c. International Ergonomics Association
- d. Poor posture

Guidance: level 1

:: Network theory ::

A _____ is a social structure made up of a set of social actors, sets of dyadic ties, and other social interactions between actors. The _____ perspective provides a set of methods for analyzing the structure of whole social entities as well as a variety of theories explaining the patterns observed in these structures. The study of these structures uses _____ analysis to identify local and global patterns, locate influential entities, and examine network dynamics.

Exam Probability: **High**

43. *Answer choices:*

(see index for correct answer)

- a. Modularity
- b. Cut-insertion theorem
- c. Social objects

- d. Social network

Guidance: level 1

:: E-commerce ::

_____ , cybersecurity or information technology security is the protection of computer systems from theft or damage to their hardware, software or electronic data, as well as from disruption or misdirection of the services they provide.

Exam Probability: **Medium**

44. *Answer choices:*
(see index for correct answer)

- a. GS1 Sweden
- b. UN/CEFACT
- c. Segundamano
- d. Computer security

Guidance: level 1

:: E-commerce ::

_____, and its now-deprecated predecessor, Secure Sockets Layer, are cryptographic protocols designed to provide communications security over a computer network. Several versions of the protocols find widespread use in applications such as web browsing, email, instant messaging, and voice over IP. Websites can use TLS to secure all communications between their servers and web browsers.

Exam Probability: **Medium**

45. *Answer choices:*

(see index for correct answer)

- a. Webcam Social Shopper
- b. Global Product Classification
- c. Webjet
- d. Transport Layer Security

Guidance: level 1

:: ::

A database is an organized collection of data, generally stored and accessed electronically from a computer system. Where databases are more complex they are often developed using formal design and modeling techniques.

Exam Probability: **High**

46. *Answer choices:*

(see index for correct answer)

- a. co-culture
- b. hierarchical perspective
- c. Sarbanes-Oxley act of 2002
- d. Database management system

Guidance: level 1

:: E-commerce ::

_____ is a method of e-commerce where shoppers' friends become involved in the shopping experience. _____ attempts to use technology to mimic the social interactions found in physical malls and stores. With the rise of mobile devices, _____ is now extending beyond the online world and into the offline world of shopping.

Exam Probability: **Medium**

47. *Answer choices:*

(see index for correct answer)

- a. Social shopping
- b. Quisk
- c. Ecash
- d. Product finder

Guidance: level 1

:: Economic globalization ::

_____ is an agreement in which one company hires another company to be responsible for a planned or existing activity that is or could be done internally, and sometimes involves transferring employees and assets from one firm to another.

Exam Probability: **High**

48. *Answer choices:*

(see index for correct answer)

- a. global financial
- b. Outsourcing

Guidance: level 1

:: Global Positioning System ::

The _____ , originally Navstar GPS, is a satellite-based radionavigation system owned by the United States government and operated by the United States Air Force. It is a global navigation satellite system that provides geolocation and time information to a GPS receiver anywhere on or near the Earth where there is an unobstructed line of sight to four or more GPS satellites. Obstacles such as mountains and buildings block the relatively weak GPS signals.

Exam Probability: **Medium**

49. *Answer choices:*

(see index for correct answer)

- a. Gpsd
- b. SK-42 reference system
- c. Wayfinder
- d. Global Positioning System

Guidance: level 1

:: Information retrieval ::

_____ is the practice of making content from multiple enterprise-type sources, such as databases and intranets, searchable to a defined audience .

Exam Probability: **Low**

50. *Answer choices:*

(see index for correct answer)

- a. Enterprise search
- b. Policy framework
- c. Audio mining
- d. Literature-based discovery

Guidance: level 1

:: Consumer behaviour ::

_____ is the ratio of users who click on a specific link to the number of total users who view a page, email, or advertisement. It is commonly used to measure the success of an online advertising campaign for a particular website as well as the effectiveness of email campaigns.

Exam Probability: **Medium**

51. *Answer choices:*

(see index for correct answer)

- a. Gruppi di Acquisto Solidale
- b. Click-through rate
- c. Shopping Neutral
- d. Ernest Dichter

Guidance: level 1

:: Information technology management ::

_____ s or pop-ups are forms of online advertising on the World Wide Web. A pop-up is a graphical user interface display area, usually a small window, that suddenly appears in the foreground of the visual interface. The pop-up window containing an advertisement is usually generated by JavaScript that uses cross-site scripting, sometimes with a secondary payload that uses Adobe Flash. They can also be generated by other vulnerabilities/security holes in browser security.

Exam Probability: **Low**

52. *Answer choices:*

(see index for correct answer)

- a. OpenACS
- b. Capability Maturity Model
- c. Pop-up ad
- d. Run Book Automation

Guidance: level 1

:: ::

_____, Inc. was a company that provided human resource management systems, Financial Management Solutions, supply chain management, customer relationship management, and enterprise performance management software, as well as software for manufacturing, and student administration to large corporations, governments, and organizations. It existed as an independent corporation until its acquisition by Oracle Corporation in 2005. The _____ name and product line are now marketed by Oracle.

Exam Probability: **High**

53. *Answer choices:*

(see index for correct answer)

- a. imperative
- b. levels of analysis
- c. deep-level diversity
- d. similarity-attraction theory

Guidance: level 1

:: Data management ::

_____, or IG, is the management of information at an organization. _____ balances the use and security of information. _____ helps with legal compliance, operational transparency, and reducing expenditures associated with legal discovery. An organization can establish a consistent and logical framework for employees to handle data through their _____ policies and procedures. These policies guide proper behavior regarding how organizations and their employees handle electronically stored information.

Exam Probability: **Low**

54. *Answer choices:*

(see index for correct answer)

- a. Information governance
- b. Master data management
- c. Sales intelligence
- d. SciDB

Guidance: level 1

:: Data management ::

An _____ is any kind of information system which improves the functions of enterprise business processes by integration. This means typically offering high quality of service, dealing with large volumes of data and capable of supporting some large and possibly complex organization or enterprise. An EIS must be able to be used by all parts and all levels of an enterprise.

Exam Probability: **High**

55. *Answer choices:*

(see index for correct answer)

- a. CA Gen
- b. Linear medium

- c. Enterprise information system
- d. Information integration

Guidance: level 1

:: Information technology ::

_____ is the use of computers to store, retrieve, transmit, and manipulate data, or information, often in the context of a business or other enterprise. IT is considered to be a subset of information and communications technology. An _____ system is generally an information system, a communications system or, more specifically speaking, a computer system – including all hardware, software and peripheral equipment – operated by a limited group of users.

Exam Probability: **High**

56. *Answer choices:*

(see index for correct answer)

- a. Local Government ICT Network
- b. Mobile file management
- c. Information technology
- d. Hard copy

Guidance: level 1

:: E-commerce ::

A _____ is a plastic payment card that can be used instead of cash when making purchases. It is similar to a credit card, but unlike a credit card, the money is immediately transferred directly from the cardholder's bank account when performing a transaction.

Exam Probability: **Medium**

57. *Answer choices:*

(see index for correct answer)

- a. Gazaro
- b. Debit card
- c. Pay at the pump
- d. Mobile payment

Guidance: level 1

:: Management ::

Porter's Five Forces Framework is a tool for analyzing competition of a business. It draws from industrial organization economics to derive five forces that determine the competitive intensity and, therefore, the attractiveness of an industry in terms of its profitability. An "unattractive" industry is one in which the effect of these five forces reduces overall profitability. The most unattractive industry would be one approaching "pure competition", in which available profits for all firms are driven to normal profit levels. The five-forces perspective is associated with its originator, Michael E. Porter of Harvard University. This framework was first published in Harvard Business Review in 1979.

Exam Probability: **Low**

58. *Answer choices:*

(see index for correct answer)

- a. Economic production quantity
- b. Enterprise planning system
- c. Strategic group
- d. Porter five forces analysis

Guidance: level 1

:: Information science ::

In discourse-based grammatical theory, _____ is any tracking of referential information by speakers. Information may be new, just introduced into the conversation; given, already active in the speakers' consciousness; or old, no longer active. The various types of activation, and how these are defined, are model-dependent.

Exam Probability: **Medium**

59. *Answer choices:*
(see index for correct answer)

- a. International Coalition for GeoInformatics
- b. Sound and music computing
- c. Subject indexing
- d. Information flow

Guidance: level 1

Marketing

Marketing is the study and management of exchange relationships. Marketing is the business process of creating relationships with and satisfying customers. With its focus on the customer, marketing is one of the premier components of business management.

Marketing is defined by the American Marketing Association as "the activity, set of institutions, and processes for creating, communicating, delivering, and exchanging offerings that have value for customers, clients, partners, and society at large."

:: Management ::

A _____ is a promise of value to be delivered, communicated, and acknowledged. It is also a belief from the customer about how value will be delivered, experienced and acquired.

Exam Probability: **Low**

1. *Answer choices:*

(see index for correct answer)

- a. Business process mapping
- b. Cynefin
- c. Middle management
- d. Concept of operations

Guidance: level 1

:: Supply chain management ::

_____ is the removal of intermediaries in economics from a supply chain, or cutting out the middlemen in connection with a transaction or a series of transactions. Instead of going through traditional distribution channels, which had some type of intermediary , companies may now deal with customers directly, for example via the Internet. Hence, the use of factory direct and direct from the factory to mean the same thing.

Exam Probability: **Low**

2. *Answer choices:*

(see index for correct answer)

- a. Disintermediation
- b. Delivery Performance
- c. Supply chain surplus
- d. Spend analysis

Guidance: level 1

:: Network theory ::

A _____ is a social structure made up of a set of social actors , sets of dyadic ties, and other social interactions between actors. The _____ perspective provides a set of methods for analyzing the structure of whole social entities as well as a variety of theories explaining the patterns observed in these structures. The study of these structures uses _____ analysis to identify local and global patterns, locate influential entities, and examine network dynamics.

Exam Probability: **Medium**

3. *Answer choices:*

(see index for correct answer)

- a. Agent network topology
- b. Similarity
- c. Complex network

- d. Social network

Guidance: level 1

:: Contract law ::

In contract law, a _____ is a promise which is not a condition of the contract or an innominate term: it is a term "not going to the root of the contract", and which only entitles the innocent party to damages if it is breached: i.e. the _____ is not true or the defaulting party does not perform the contract in accordance with the terms of the _____ . A _____ is not guarantee. It is a mere promise. It may be enforced if it is breached by an award for the legal remedy of damages.

Exam Probability: **Medium**

4. *Answer choices:*
(see index for correct answer)

- a. Offeree
- b. Non-repudiation
- c. Unenforceable contract
- d. Handshake deal

Guidance: level 1

:: ::

In _____ relations and communication science, _____ s are groups of individual people, and the _____ is the totality of such groupings. This is a different concept to the sociological concept of the Öffentlichkeit or _____ sphere. The concept of a _____ has also been defined in political science, psychology, marketing, and advertising. In _____ relations and communication science, it is one of the more ambiguous concepts in the field. Although it has definitions in the theory of the field that have been formulated from the early 20th century onwards, it has suffered in more recent years from being blurred, as a result of conflation of the idea of a _____ with the notions of audience, market segment, community, constituency, and stakeholder.

Exam Probability: **Low**

5. *Answer choices:*

(see index for correct answer)

- a. Public
- b. hierarchical
- c. similarity-attraction theory
- d. surface-level diversity

Guidance: level 1

:: ::

A _____ is a person who trades in commodities produced by other people. Historically, a _____ is anyone who is involved in business or trade. _____ s have operated for as long as industry, commerce, and trade have existed. During the 16th-century, in Europe, two different terms for _____ s emerged: One term, meerseniers, described local traders such as bakers, grocers, etc.; while a new term, koopman (Dutch: koopman, described _____ s who operated on a global stage, importing and exporting goods over vast distances, and offering added-value services such as credit and finance.

Exam Probability: **Low**

6. *Answer choices:*

(see index for correct answer)

- a. open system
- b. levels of analysis
- c. Merchant
- d. hierarchical

Guidance: level 1

:: Pricing ::

_____ is a pricing strategy in which the selling price is determined by adding a specific amount markup to a product's unit cost. An alternative pricing method is value-based pricing.

Exam Probability: **Low**

7. *Answer choices:*

(see index for correct answer)

- a. The price of milk
- b. Cost-plus pricing
- c. Reference price
- d. Peak-load pricing

Guidance: level 1

:: Brokered programming ::

An _____ is a form of television commercial, which generally includes a toll-free telephone number or website. Most often used as a form of direct response television, long-form _____ s are typically 28:30 or 58:30 minutes in length. _____ s are also known as paid programming. This phenomenon started in the United States, where _____ s were typically shown overnight, outside peak prime time hours for commercial broadcasters. Some television stations chose to air _____ s as an alternative to the former practice of signing off. Some channels air _____ s 24 hours. Some stations also choose to air _____ s during the daytime hours mostly on weekends to fill in for unscheduled network or syndicated programming. By 2009, most _____ spending in the U.S. occurred during the early morning, daytime and evening hours, or in the afternoon. Stations in most countries around the world have instituted similar media structures. The _____ industry is worth over $200 billion.

Exam Probability: **Low**

8. *Answer choices:*

(see index for correct answer)

- a. Toonzai
- b. Infomercial
- c. One Magnificent Morning
- d. Brokered programming

Guidance: level 1

:: Types of marketing ::

_____ is "marketing on a worldwide scale reconciling or taking commercial advantage of global operational differences, similarities and opportunities in order to meet global objectives".

Exam Probability: **Medium**

9. *Answer choices:*
(see index for correct answer)

- a. Direct response
- b. Menu engineering
- c. Global marketing
- d. Vertical integration

Guidance: level 1

:: Meetings ::

A _____ is a body of one or more persons that is subordinate to a deliberative assembly. Usually, the assembly sends matters into a _____ as a way to explore them more fully than would be possible if the assembly itself were considering them. _____ s may have different functions and their type of work differ depending on the type of the organization and its needs.

Exam Probability: **Medium**

10. *Answer choices:*
(see index for correct answer)

- a. Moment of silence
- b. Stand-up meeting
- c. Unconference
- d. Moderator

Guidance: level 1

:: ::

_____ characterises the behaviour of a system or model whose components interact in multiple ways and follow local rules, meaning there is no reasonable higher instruction to define the various possible interactions.

Exam Probability: **Medium**

11. *Answer choices:*

(see index for correct answer)

- a. interpersonal communication
- b. cultural
- c. functional perspective
- d. Complexity

Guidance: level 1

:: Direct selling ::

_____ consists of two main business models: single-level marketing, in which a direct seller makes money by buying products from a parent organization and selling them directly to customers, and multi-level marketing , in which the direct seller may earn money from both direct sales to customers and by sponsoring new direct sellers and potentially earning a commission from their efforts.

Exam Probability: **Medium**

12. *Answer choices:*

(see index for correct answer)

- a. Direct Selling Association
- b. Direct selling

- c. CVSL
- d. The Longaberger Company

Guidance: level 1

:: Problem solving ::

In other words, _____ is a situation where a group of people meet to generate new ideas and solutions around a specific domain of interest by removing inhibitions. People are able to think more freely and they suggest as many spontaneous new ideas as possible. All the ideas are noted down and those ideas are not criticized and after _____ session the ideas are evaluated. The term was popularized by Alex Faickney Osborn in the 1953 book Applied Imagination.

Exam Probability: **Medium**

13. *Answer choices:*

(see index for correct answer)

- a. Working memory training
- b. Calculation
- c. Cognitive acceleration
- d. Creative Education Foundation

Guidance: level 1

:: Electronic feedback ::

_____ occurs when outputs of a system are routed back as inputs as part of a chain of cause-and-effect that forms a circuit or loop. The system can then be said to feed back into itself. The notion of cause-and-effect has to be handled carefully when applied to _____ systems.

Exam Probability: **High**

14. *Answer choices:*

(see index for correct answer)

- a. Feedback
- b. Positive feedback

Guidance: level 1

:: ::

In regulatory jurisdictions that provide for it, _____ is a group of laws and organizations designed to ensure the rights of consumers as well as fair trade, competition and accurate information in the marketplace. The laws are designed to prevent the businesses that engage in fraud or specified unfair practices from gaining an advantage over competitors. They may also provides additional protection for those most vulnerable in society. _____ laws are a form of government regulation that aim to protect the rights of consumers. For example, a government may require businesses to disclose detailed information about products—particularly in areas where safety or public health is an issue, such as food.

Exam Probability: **High**

15. *Answer choices:*

(see index for correct answer)

- a. process perspective
- b. Sarbanes-Oxley act of 2002
- c. personal values
- d. Consumer Protection

Guidance: level 1

:: ::

_____ is both a research area and a practical skill encompassing the ability of an individual or organization to "lead" or guide other individuals, teams, or entire organizations. Specialist literature debates various viewpoints, contrasting Eastern and Western approaches to _____ , and also United States versus European approaches. U.S. academic environments define _____ as "a process of social influence in which a person can enlist the aid and support of others in the accomplishment of a common task".

Exam Probability: **Low**

16. *Answer choices:*

(see index for correct answer)

- a. Leadership

- b. information systems assessment
- c. hierarchical
- d. hierarchical perspective

Guidance: level 1

:: Project management ::

A _____ is a source or supply from which a benefit is produced and it has some utility. _____ s can broadly be classified upon their availability—they are classified into renewable and non-renewable _____ s. Examples of non renewable _____ s are coal ,crude oil natural gas nuclear energy etc. Examples of renewable _____ s are air, water, wind, solar energy etc. They can also be classified as actual and potential on the basis of level of development and use, on the basis of origin they can be classified as biotic and abiotic, and on the basis of their distribution, as ubiquitous and localized . An item becomes a _____ with time and developing technology. Typically, _____ s are materials, energy, services, staff, knowledge, or other assets that are transformed to produce benefit and in the process may be consumed or made unavailable. Benefits of _____ utilization may include increased wealth, proper functioning of a system, or enhanced well-being. From a human perspective a natural _____ is anything obtained from the environment to satisfy human needs and wants. From a broader biological or ecological perspective a _____ satisfies the needs of a living organism .

Exam Probability: **Low**

17. *Answer choices:*

(see index for correct answer)

- a. Logical framework approach

- b. P3M3
- c. Product description
- d. Financial plan

Guidance: level 1

:: Marketing ::

> _____ is the process of using surveys to evaluate consumer acceptance of a new product idea prior to the introduction of a product to the market. It is important not to confuse _____ with advertising testing, brand testing and packaging testing; as is sometimes done. _____ focuses on the basic product idea, without the embellishments and puffery inherent in advertising.

Exam Probability: **High**

18. *Answer choices:*

(see index for correct answer)

- a. Lead management
- b. Concept testing
- c. Nutraceutical
- d. Bayesian inference in marketing

Guidance: level 1

:: Direct marketing ::

_____ is a method of direct marketing in which a salesperson solicits prospective customers to buy products or services, either over the phone or through a subsequent face to face or Web conferencing appointment scheduled during the call. _____ can also include recorded sales pitches programmed to be played over the phone via automatic dialing.

Exam Probability: **Medium**

19. *Answer choices:*

(see index for correct answer)

- a. Telemarketing
- b. Colony Brands
- c. Arthur Schiff
- d. Large-group awareness training

Guidance: level 1

:: Reputation management ::

A _____ is an astronomical object consisting of a luminous spheroid of plasma held together by its own gravity. The nearest _____ to Earth is the Sun. Many other _____ s are visible to the naked eye from Earth during the night, appearing as a multitude of fixed luminous points in the sky due to their immense distance from Earth. Historically, the most prominent _____ s were grouped into constellations and asterisms, the brightest of which gained proper names. Astronomers have assembled _____ catalogues that identify the known _____ s and provide standardized stellar designations. However, most of the estimated 300 sextillion _____ s in the Universe are invisible to the naked eye from Earth, including all _____ s outside our galaxy, the Milky Way.

Exam Probability: **Medium**

20. *Answer choices:*

(see index for correct answer)

- a. Star
- b. Raph Levien
- c. Moderation system
- d. Hilltop algorithm

Guidance: level 1

:: Market research ::

_____ is the action of defining, gathering, analyzing, and distributing intelligence about products, customers, competitors, and any aspect of the environment needed to support executives and managers in strategic decision making for an organization.

Exam Probability: **Low**

21. *Answer choices:*

(see index for correct answer)

- a. Early adopter
- b. Marketing research mix
- c. Competitive intelligence
- d. Confidence interval

Guidance: level 1

:: Retailing ::

A _____ is a retail establishment offering a wide range of consumer goods in different product categories known as "departments". In modern major cities, the _____ made a dramatic appearance in the middle of the 19th century, and permanently reshaped shopping habits, and the definition of service and luxury. Similar developments were under way in London, in Paris and in New York.

Exam Probability: **High**

22. *Answer choices:*

(see index for correct answer)

- a. Stock rotation
- b. Non-store retailing
- c. Department store
- d. Endcap

Guidance: level 1

:: Monopoly (economics) ::

A _____ exists when a specific person or enterprise is the only supplier of a particular commodity. This contrasts with a monopsony which relates to a single entity's control of a market to purchase a good or service, and with oligopoly which consists of a few sellers dominating a market. Monopolies are thus characterized by a lack of economic competition to produce the good or service, a lack of viable substitute goods, and the possibility of a high _____ price well above the seller's marginal cost that leads to a high _____ profit. The verb monopolise or monopolize refers to the process by which a company gains the ability to raise prices or exclude competitors. In economics, a _____ is a single seller. In law, a _____ is a business entity that has significant market power, that is, the power to charge overly high prices. Although monopolies may be big businesses, size is not a characteristic of a _____ . A small business may still have the power to raise prices in a small industry .

Exam Probability: **Medium**

23. *Answer choices:*

(see index for correct answer)

- a. Wartime Law on Industrial Property
- b. Price-cap regulation
- c. Monopoly
- d. Tesco Town

Guidance: level 1

:: ::

> Employment is a relationship between two parties, usually based on a contract where work is paid for, where one party, which may be a corporation, for profit, not-for-profit organization, co-operative or other entity is the employer and the other is the employee. Employees work in return for payment, which may be in the form of an hourly wage, by piecework or an annual salary, depending on the type of work an employee does or which sector she or he is working in. Employees in some fields or sectors may receive gratuities, bonus payment or stock options. In some types of employment, employees may receive benefits in addition to payment. Benefits can include health insurance, housing, disability insurance or use of a gym. Employment is typically governed by employment laws, regulations or legal contracts.

Exam Probability: **Low**

24. *Answer choices:*

(see index for correct answer)

- a. co-culture

- b. hierarchical perspective
- c. Personnel
- d. deep-level diversity

Guidance: level 1

:: Planning ::

_____ is a high level plan to achieve one or more goals under conditions of uncertainty. In the sense of the "art of the general," which included several subsets of skills including tactics, siegecraft, logistics etc., the term came into use in the 6th century C.E. in East Roman terminology, and was translated into Western vernacular languages only in the 18th century. From then until the 20th century, the word "_____" came to denote "a comprehensive way to try to pursue political ends, including the threat or actual use of force, in a dialectic of wills" in a military conflict, in which both adversaries interact.

Exam Probability: **High**

25. *Answer choices:*

(see index for correct answer)

- a. Territorialist School
- b. Strategy
- c. Plano Trienal
- d. BLUF

Guidance: level 1

:: Product management ::

A _____, trade mark, or trade-mark is a recognizable sign, design, or expression which identifies products or services of a particular source from those of others, although _____ s used to identify services are usually called service marks. The _____ owner can be an individual, business organization, or any legal entity. A _____ may be located on a package, a label, a voucher, or on the product itself. For the sake of corporate identity, _____ s are often displayed on company buildings. It is legally recognized as a type of intellectual property.

Exam Probability: **High**

26. *Answer choices:*

(see index for correct answer)

- a. Trademark
- b. Tipping point
- c. Requirement prioritization
- d. Technology acceptance model

Guidance: level 1

:: ::

In financial markets, a share is a unit used as mutual funds, limited partnerships, and real estate investment trusts. The owner of _____ in the corporation/company is a shareholder of the corporation. A share is an indivisible unit of capital, expressing the ownership relationship between the company and the shareholder. The denominated value of a share is its face value, and the total of the face value of issued _____ represent the capital of a company, which may not reflect the market value of those _____.

Exam Probability: **High**

27. *Answer choices:*

(see index for correct answer)

- a. cultural
- b. Shares
- c. deep-level diversity
- d. open system

Guidance: level 1

:: Management ::

A _____ is an idea of the future or desired result that a person or a group of people envisions, plans and commits to achieve. People endeavor to reach _____ s within a finite time by setting deadlines.

Exam Probability: **Medium**

28. *Answer choices:*

(see index for correct answer)

- a. Goal
- b. Best current practice
- c. Bed management
- d. Libertarian management

Guidance: level 1

:: ::

> _____ are interactive computer-mediated technologies that facilitate the creation and sharing of information, ideas, career interests and other forms of expression via virtual communities and networks. The variety of stand-alone and built-in _____ services currently available introduces challenges of definition; however, there are some common features.

Exam Probability: **Medium**

29. *Answer choices:*

(see index for correct answer)

- a. Social media
- b. Sarbanes-Oxley act of 2002
- c. surface-level diversity
- d. hierarchical perspective

Guidance: level 1

:: Marketing ::

A _____ is an overall experience of a customer that distinguishes an organization or product from its rivals in the eyes of the customer. _____ s are used in business, marketing, and advertising. Name _____ s are sometimes distinguished from generic or store _____ s.

Exam Probability: **Low**

30. *Answer choices:*

(see index for correct answer)

- a. Health marketing
- b. Licensing International Expo
- c. Brand
- d. One Town One Product

Guidance: level 1

:: Packaging ::

In work place, _____ or job _____ means good ranking with the hypothesized conception of requirements of a role. There are two types of job _____ s: contextual and task. Task _____ is related to cognitive ability while contextual _____ is dependent upon personality. Task _____ are behavioral roles that are recognized in job descriptions and by remuneration systems, they are directly related to organizational _____, whereas, contextual _____ are value based and additional behavioral roles that are not recognized in job descriptions and covered by compensation; they are extra roles that are indirectly related to organizational _____.
Citizenship _____ like contextual _____ means a set of individual activity/contribution that supports the organizational culture.

Exam Probability: **High**

31. *Answer choices:*

(see index for correct answer)

- a. Modified atmosphere
- b. Self-heating food packaging
- c. Active packaging
- d. Performance

Guidance: level 1

:: Debt ::

_____ is the trust which allows one party to provide money or resources to another party wherein the second party does not reimburse the first party immediately, but promises either to repay or return those resources at a later date. In other words, _____ is a method of making reciprocity formal, legally enforceable, and extensible to a large group of unrelated people.

Exam Probability: **Medium**

32. *Answer choices:*

(see index for correct answer)

- a. Legal liability
- b. Interest
- c. Extendible bond
- d. Credit

Guidance: level 1

:: Management ::

In business, a _____ is the attribute that allows an organization to outperform its competitors. A _____ may include access to natural resources, such as high-grade ores or a low-cost power source, highly skilled labor, geographic location, high entry barriers, and access to new technology.

Exam Probability: **Low**

33. *Answer choices:*

(see index for correct answer)

- a. Fleet management
- b. Management buyout
- c. Overtime rate
- d. Competitive advantage

Guidance: level 1

:: Management ::

A _____ is a comprehensive document or blueprint that outlines the advertising and marketing efforts for the coming year. It describes business activities involved in accomplishing specific marketing objectives within a set time frame. A _____ also includes a description of the current marketing position of a business, a discussion of the target market and a description of the marketing mix that a business will use to achieve their marketing goals. A _____ has a formal structure, but can be used as a formal or informal document which makes it very flexible. It contains some historical data, future predictions, and methods or strategies to achieve the marketing objectives. _____ s start with the identification of customer needs through a market research and how the business can satisfy these needs while generating an acceptable return. This includes processes such as market situation analysis, action programs, budgets, sales forecasts, strategies and projected financial statements. A _____ can also be described as a technique that helps a business to decide on the best use of its resources to achieve corporate objectives. It can also contain a full analysis of the strengths and weaknesses of a company, its organization and its products.

Exam Probability: **High**

34. Answer choices:

(see index for correct answer)

- a. Event to knowledge
- b. Project team builder
- c. Marketing plan
- d. Quick response manufacturing

Guidance: level 1

:: Behaviorism ::

In behavioral psychology, _____ is a consequence applied that will strengthen an organism's future behavior whenever that behavior is preceded by a specific antecedent stimulus. This strengthening effect may be measured as a higher frequency of behavior, longer duration, greater magnitude, or shorter latency. There are two types of _____, known as positive _____ and negative _____; positive is where by a reward is offered on expression of the wanted behaviour and negative is taking away an undesirable element in the persons environment whenever the desired behaviour is achieved.

Exam Probability: **High**

35. Answer choices:

(see index for correct answer)

- a. social facilitation
- b. Systematic desensitization

- c. Reinforcement
- d. Matching Law

Guidance: level 1

:: Marketing ::

A _____ is something that is necessary for an organism to live a healthy life. _____ s are distinguished from wants in that, in the case of a _____ , a deficiency causes a clear adverse outcome: a dysfunction or death. In other words, a _____ is something required for a safe, stable and healthy life while a want is a desire, wish or aspiration. When _____ s or wants are backed by purchasing power, they have the potential to become economic demands.

Exam Probability: **High**

36. *Answer choices:*

(see index for correct answer)

- a. BEC
- b. Movie packaging
- c. Need
- d. Marketing warfare strategies

Guidance: level 1

:: ::

_____ is the practice of deliberately managing the spread of information between an individual or an organization and the public. _____ may include an organization or individual gaining exposure to their audiences using topics of public interest and news items that do not require direct payment. This differentiates it from advertising as a form of marketing communications. _____ is the idea of creating coverage for clients for free, rather than marketing or advertising. But now, advertising is also a part of greater PR Activities. An example of good _____ would be generating an article featuring a client, rather than paying for the client to be advertised next to the article. The aim of _____ is to inform the public, prospective customers, investors, partners, employees, and other stakeholders and ultimately persuade them to maintain a positive or favorable view about the organization, its leadership, products, or political decisions. _____ professionals typically work for PR and marketing firms, businesses and companies, government, and public officials as PIOs and nongovernmental organizations, and nonprofit organizations. Jobs central to _____ include account coordinator, account executive, account supervisor, and media relations manager.

Exam Probability: **Medium**

37. *Answer choices:*

(see index for correct answer)

- a. process perspective
- b. corporate values
- c. Public relations
- d. co-culture

Guidance: level 1

:: Consumer theory ::

A _____ is a technical term in psychology, economics and philosophy usually used in relation to choosing between alternatives. For example, someone prefers A over B if they would rather choose A than B.

Exam Probability: **High**

38. *Answer choices:*

(see index for correct answer)

- a. Expenditure function
- b. Slutsky equation
- c. Consumer service
- d. Preference

Guidance: level 1

:: Promotion and marketing communications ::

Advertising mail, also known as _____ , junk mail , mailshot or admail, is the delivery of advertising material to recipients of postal mail. The delivery of advertising mail forms a large and growing service for many postal services, and direct-mail marketing forms a significant portion of the direct marketing industry. Some organizations attempt to help people opt out of receiving advertising mail, in many cases motivated by a concern over its negative environmental impact.

Exam Probability: **High**

39. *Answer choices:*

(see index for correct answer)

- a. Direct mail
- b. Sales force automation
- c. Air Miles
- d. Slogan

Guidance: level 1

:: ::

In logic and philosophy, an _____ is a series of statements , called the premises or premisses , intended to determine the degree of truth of another statement, the conclusion. The logical form of an _____ in a natural language can be represented in a symbolic formal language, and independently of natural language formally defined " _____ s" can be made in math and computer science.

Exam Probability: **Low**

40. *Answer choices:*

(see index for correct answer)

- a. Argument
- b. open system
- c. Character
- d. similarity-attraction theory

Guidance: level 1

:: ::

In the broadest sense, _____ is any practice which contributes to the sale of products to a retail consumer. At a retail in-store level, _____ refers to the variety of products available for sale and the display of those products in such a way that it stimulates interest and entices customers to make a purchase.

Exam Probability: **Medium**

41. *Answer choices:*

(see index for correct answer)

- a. Merchandising
- b. open system

- c. hierarchical
- d. similarity-attraction theory

Guidance: level 1

:: Market research ::

An _____ or lighthouse customer is an early customer of a given company, product, or technology. The term originates from Everett M. Rogers' Diffusion of Innovations.

Exam Probability: **High**

42. *Answer choices:*

(see index for correct answer)

- a. Vehicle Dependability Study
- b. LRMR
- c. Portable People Meter
- d. Early adopter

Guidance: level 1

:: ::

A _____ is the process of presenting a topic to an audience. It is typically a demonstration, introduction, lecture, or speech meant to inform, persuade, inspire, motivate, or to build good will or to present a new idea or product. The term can also be used for a formal or ritualized introduction or offering, as with the _____ of a debutante. _____ s in certain formats are also known as keynote address.

Exam Probability: **High**

43. *Answer choices:*

(see index for correct answer)

- a. Sarbanes-Oxley act of 2002
- b. co-culture
- c. interpersonal communication
- d. empathy

Guidance: level 1

:: Marketing ::

_____ is a growth strategy that identifies and develops new market segments for current products. A _____ strategy targets non-buying customers in currently targeted segments. It also targets new customers in new segments.

Exam Probability: **Low**

44. Answer choices:

(see index for correct answer)

- a. Packshot
- b. Double bottom line
- c. Concept testing
- d. LIDA

Guidance: level 1

:: Marketing ::

A _____ is the quantity of payment or compensation given by one party to another in return for one unit of goods or services.. A _____ is influenced by both production costs and demand for the product. A _____ may be determined by a monopolist or may be imposed on the firm by market conditions.

Exam Probability: **High**

45. Answer choices:

(see index for correct answer)

- a. Demand signal repository
- b. Discoverability
- c. Generic brand
- d. Market development

Guidance: level 1

:: Marketing ::

A _____ is the people, organizations, and activities necessary to transfer the ownership of goods from the point of production to the point of consumption. It is the way products get to the end-user, the consumer; and is also known as a distribution channel. A _____ is a useful tool for management, and is crucial to creating an effective and well-planned marketing strategy.

Exam Probability: **Medium**

46. *Answer choices:*

(see index for correct answer)

- a. Performance-based advertising
- b. Marketing channel
- c. Democratized transactional giving
- d. Decoy effect

Guidance: level 1

:: ::

_____ is an abstract concept of management of complex systems according to a set of rules and trends. In systems theory, these types of rules exist in various fields of biology and society, but the term has slightly different meanings according to context. For example.

Exam Probability: **High**

47. *Answer choices:*

(see index for correct answer)

- a. empathy
- b. deep-level diversity
- c. levels of analysis
- d. Regulation

Guidance: level 1

Advertising is a marketing communication that employs an openly sponsored, non-personal message to promote or sell a product, service or idea. Sponsors of advertising are typically businesses wishing to promote their products or services. Advertising is differentiated from public relations in that an advertiser pays for and has control over the message. It differs from personal selling in that the message is non-personal, i.e., not directed to a particular individual.Advertising is communicated through various mass media, including traditional media such as newspapers, magazines, television, radio, outdoor advertising or direct mail; and new media such as search results, blogs, social media, websites or text messages. The actual presentation of the message in a medium is referred to as an _____ , or "ad" or advert for short.

Exam Probability: **Medium**

48. *Answer choices:*

(see index for correct answer)

- a. deep-level diversity
- b. Sarbanes-Oxley act of 2002
- c. co-culture
- d. Advertisement

Guidance: level 1

:: ::

In international relations, _____ is – from the perspective of governments – a voluntary transfer of resources from one country to another.

Exam Probability: **High**

49. *Answer choices:*

(see index for correct answer)

- a. Sarbanes-Oxley act of 2002
- b. information systems assessment
- c. Aid
- d. personal values

Guidance: level 1

:: Marketing ::

_____ is a pricing strategy where the price of a product is initially set low to rapidly reach a wide fraction of the market and initiate word of mouth. The strategy works on the expectation that customers will switch to the new brand because of the lower price. _____ is most commonly associated with marketing objectives of enlarging market share and exploiting economies of scale or experience.

Exam Probability: **High**

50. *Answer choices:*

(see index for correct answer)

- a. Leverage
- b. Branded asset management

- c. Penetration pricing
- d. Product bundling

Guidance: level 1

:: Marketing ::

_____ is the marketing of products that are presumed to be environmentally safe. It incorporates a broad range of activities, including product modification, changes to the production process, sustainable packaging, as well as modifying advertising. Yet defining _____ is not a simple task where several meanings intersect and contradict each other; an example of this will be the existence of varying social, environmental and retail definitions attached to this term. Other similar terms used are environmental marketing and ecological marketing.

Exam Probability: **Medium**

51. *Answer choices:*
(see index for correct answer)

- a. Primary research
- b. Kidification
- c. Green marketing
- d. Mass marketing

Guidance: level 1

:: bad_topic ::

Sponsoring something is the act of supporting an event, activity, person, or organization financially or through the provision of products or services. The individual or group that provides the support, similar to a benefactor, is known as sponsor.

Exam Probability: **Low**

52. *Answer choices:*

(see index for correct answer)

- a. conative
- b. Sponsorship
- c. Vision statement
- d. Veritas Software

Guidance: level 1

:: ::

_____ is change in the heritable characteristics of biological populations over successive generations. These characteristics are the expressions of genes that are passed on from parent to offspring during reproduction. Different characteristics tend to exist within any given population as a result of mutation, genetic recombination and other sources of genetic variation. _____ occurs when _____ ary processes such as natural selection and genetic drift act on this variation, resulting in certain characteristics becoming more common or rare within a population. It is this process of _____ that has given rise to biodiversity at every level of biological organisation, including the levels of species, individual organisms and molecules.

Exam Probability: **High**

53. *Answer choices:*

(see index for correct answer)

- a. co-culture
- b. Character
- c. levels of analysis
- d. Evolution

Guidance: level 1

:: Cognitive dissonance ::

In the field of psychology, _____ is the mental discomfort experienced by a person who holds two or more contradictory beliefs, ideas, or values. This discomfort is triggered by a situation in which a person's belief clashes with new evidence perceived by the person. When confronted with facts that contradict beliefs, ideals, and values, people will try to find a way to resolve the contradiction to reduce their discomfort.

Exam Probability: **High**

54. *Answer choices:*

(see index for correct answer)

- a. Hypocrisy
- b. Cognitive dissonance
- c. Double standard
- d. Self-refuting idea

Guidance: level 1

:: ::

_____ is a process whereby a person assumes the parenting of another, usually a child, from that person's biological or legal parent or parents. Legal _____ s permanently transfers all rights and responsibilities, along with filiation, from the biological parent or parents.

Exam Probability: **High**

55. Answer choices:

(see index for correct answer)

- a. Sarbanes-Oxley act of 2002
- b. hierarchical
- c. Adoption
- d. hierarchical perspective

Guidance: level 1

:: Stochastic processes ::

_____ in its modern meaning is a "new idea, creative thoughts, new imaginations in form of device or method". _____ is often also viewed as the application of better solutions that meet new requirements, unarticulated needs, or existing market needs. Such _____ takes place through the provision of more-effective products, processes, services, technologies, or business models that are made available to markets, governments and society. An _____ is something original and more effective and, as a consequence, new, that "breaks into" the market or society. _____ is related to, but not the same as, invention, as _____ is more apt to involve the practical implementation of an invention to make a meaningful impact in the market or society, and not all _____ s require an invention. _____ often manifests itself via the engineering process, when the problem being solved is of a technical or scientific nature. The opposite of _____ is exnovation.

Exam Probability: **Low**

56. Answer choices:

(see index for correct answer)

- a. Gaussian noise
- b. Traffic equations
- c. Law of the iterated logarithm
- d. Innovation

Guidance: level 1

:: Materials ::

A _____ , also known as a feedstock, unprocessed material, or primary commodity, is a basic material that is used to produce goods, finished products, energy, or intermediate materials which are feedstock for future finished products. As feedstock, the term connotes these materials are bottleneck assets and are highly important with regard to producing other products. An example of this is crude oil, which is a _____ and a feedstock used in the production of industrial chemicals, fuels, plastics, and pharmaceutical goods; lumber is a _____ used to produce a variety of products including all types of furniture. The term "_____" denotes materials in minimally processed or unprocessed in states; e.g., raw latex, crude oil, cotton, coal, raw biomass, iron ore, air, logs, or water i.e. "...any product of agriculture, forestry, fishing and any other mineral that is in its natural form or which has undergone the transformation required to prepare it for internationally marketing in substantial volumes."

Exam Probability: **High**

57. *Answer choices:*

(see index for correct answer)

- a. Solid surface

- b. Ebonite
- c. Raw material
- d. Nanophase material

Guidance: level 1

:: Services management and marketing ::

> _____ is a specialised branch of marketing. _____ emerged as a separate field of study in the early 1980s, following the recognition that the unique characteristics of services required different strategies compared with the marketing of physical goods.

Exam Probability: **Low**

58. *Answer choices:*

(see index for correct answer)

- a. Service provider
- b. Integrated customer management
- c. Service delivery framework
- d. Night service

Guidance: level 1

:: ::

_____ is a marketing communication that employs an openly sponsored, non-personal message to promote or sell a product, service or idea. Sponsors of _____ are typically businesses wishing to promote their products or services. _____ is differentiated from public relations in that an advertiser pays for and has control over the message. It differs from personal selling in that the message is non-personal, i.e., not directed to a particular individual. _____ is communicated through various mass media, including traditional media such as newspapers, magazines, television, radio, outdoor _____ or direct mail; and new media such as search results, blogs, social media, websites or text messages. The actual presentation of the message in a medium is referred to as an advertisement, or "ad" or advert for short.

Exam Probability: **Low**

59. *Answer choices:*

(see index for correct answer)

- a. personal values
- b. information systems assessment
- c. Advertising
- d. surface-level diversity

Guidance: level 1

Manufacturing

Manufacturing is the production of merchandise for use or sale using labor and machines, tools, chemical and biological processing, or formulation. The term may refer to a range of human activity, from handicraft to high tech, but is most commonly applied to industrial design , in which raw materials are transformed into finished goods on a large scale. Such finished goods may be sold to other manufacturers for the production of other, more complex products, such as aircraft, household appliances, furniture, sports equipment or automobiles, or sold to wholesalers, who in turn sell them to retailers, who then sell them to end users and consumers.

:: Costs ::

In microeconomic theory, the _____, or alternative cost, of making a particular choice is the value of the most valuable choice out of those that were not taken. In other words, opportunity that will require sacrifices.

Exam Probability: **High**

1. *Answer choices:*

(see index for correct answer)

- a. Flyaway cost
- b. Total cost
- c. Opportunity cost
- d. Cost competitiveness of fuel sources

Guidance: level 1

:: Data interchange standards ::

_____ is the concept of businesses electronically communicating information that was traditionally communicated on paper, such as purchase orders and invoices. Technical standards for EDI exist to facilitate parties transacting such instruments without having to make special arrangements.

Exam Probability: **High**

2. *Answer choices:*

(see index for correct answer)

- a. Domain Application Protocol
- b. Electronic data interchange
- c. Uniform Communication Standard
- d. Data Interchange Standards Association

Guidance: level 1

:: Auditing ::

_____ is the process of systematic examination of a quality system carried out by an internal or external _____ or or an audit team. It is an important part of an organization's quality management system and is a key element in the ISO quality system standard, ISO 9001.

Exam Probability: **Medium**

3. *Answer choices:*
(see index for correct answer)

- a. Verified Audit Circulation
- b. Legal auditing
- c. Risk based internal audit
- d. Quality audit

Guidance: level 1

:: Management ::

_____ is the process of thinking about the activities required to achieve a desired goal. It is the first and foremost activity to achieve desired results. It involves the creation and maintenance of a plan, such as psychological aspects that require conceptual skills. There are even a couple of tests to measure someone's capability of _____ well. As such, _____ is a fundamental property of intelligent behavior. An important further meaning, often just called "_____" is the legal context of permitted building developments.

Exam Probability: **High**

4. *Answer choices:*

(see index for correct answer)

- a. Planning
- b. Continuous-flow manufacturing
- c. Design management
- d. Continuous monitoring

Guidance: level 1

:: Product development ::

In business and engineering, _____ covers the complete process of bringing a new product to market. A central aspect of NPD is product design, along with various business considerations. _____ is described broadly as the transformation of a market opportunity into a product available for sale. The product can be tangible or intangible, though sometimes services and other processes are distinguished from "products." NPD requires an understanding of customer needs and wants, the competitive environment, and the nature of the market. Cost, time and quality are the main variables that drive customer needs. Aiming at these three variables, innovative companies develop continuous practices and strategies to better satisfy customer requirements and to increase their own market share by a regular development of new products. There are many uncertainties and challenges which companies must face throughout the process. The use of best practices and the elimination of barriers to communication are the main concerns for the management of the NPD.

Exam Probability: **Medium**

5. *Answer choices:*

(see index for correct answer)

- a. New product development
- b. Minimum viable product
- c. Design brief
- d. Virtual product development

Guidance: level 1

:: Computer memory companies ::

_____ Corporation is a Japanese multinational conglomerate headquartered in Tokyo, Japan. Its diversified products and services include information technology and communications equipment and systems, electronic components and materials, power systems, industrial and social infrastructure systems, consumer electronics, household appliances, medical equipment, office equipment, as well as lighting and logistics.

Exam Probability: **Medium**

6. *Answer choices:*

(see index for correct answer)

- a. Virage Logic
- b. Toshiba
- c. Grandis
- d. OCZ Storage Solutions

Guidance: level 1

:: Building materials ::

_____ is an alloy of iron and carbon, and sometimes other elements. Because of its high tensile strength and low cost, it is a major component used in buildings, infrastructure, tools, ships, automobiles, machines, appliances, and weapons.

Exam Probability: **Medium**

7. Answer choices:

(see index for correct answer)

- a. Bungaroosh
- b. Building-integrated photovoltaics
- c. Wychert
- d. Steel

Guidance: level 1

:: Supply chain management ::

_____ is the process of finding and agreeing to terms, and acquiring goods, services, or works from an external source, often via a tendering or competitive bidding process. _____ is used to ensure the buyer receives goods, services, or works at the best possible price when aspects such as quality, quantity, time, and location are compared. Corporations and public bodies often define processes intended to promote fair and open competition for their business while minimizing risks such as exposure to fraud and collusion.

Exam Probability: **Low**

8. Answer choices:

(see index for correct answer)

- a. Delayed differentiation
- b. Irancode
- c. Disintermediation

- d. ISO/PAS 28000

Guidance: level 1

:: Data management ::

_____ refers to a data-driven improvement cycle used for improving, optimizing and stabilizing business processes and designs. The _____ improvement cycle is the core tool used to drive Six Sigma projects. However, _____ is not exclusive to Six Sigma and can be used as the framework for other improvement applications.

Exam Probability: **Low**

9. *Answer choices:*

(see index for correct answer)

- a. Commit
- b. Data auditing
- c. DMAIC
- d. Data bank

Guidance: level 1

:: Teams ::

A _____ usually refers to a group of individuals who work together from different geographic locations and rely on communication technology such as email, FAX, and video or voice conferencing services in order to collaborate. The term can also refer to groups or teams that work together asynchronously or across organizational levels. Powell, Piccoli and Ives define _____ s as "groups of geographically, organizationally and/or time dispersed workers brought together by information and telecommunication technologies to accomplish one or more organizational tasks." According to Ale Ebrahim et. al. , _____ s can also be defined as "small temporary groups of geographically, organizationally and/or time dispersed knowledge workers who coordinate their work predominantly with electronic information and communication technologies in order to accomplish one or more organization tasks."

Exam Probability: **Low**

10. *Answer choices:*

(see index for correct answer)

- a. Virtual team
- b. team composition

Guidance: level 1

:: Project management ::

A _____ is a professional in the field of project management. _____ s have the responsibility of the planning, procurement and execution of a project, in any undertaking that has a defined scope, defined start and a defined finish; regardless of industry. _____ s are first point of contact for any issues or discrepancies arising from within the heads of various departments in an organization before the problem escalates to higher authorities. Project management is the responsibility of a _____. This individual seldom participates directly in the activities that produce the end result, but rather strives to maintain the progress, mutual interaction and tasks of various parties in such a way that reduces the risk of overall failure, maximizes benefits, and minimizes costs.

Exam Probability: **Medium**

11. *Answer choices:*

(see index for correct answer)

- a. Risk management plan
- b. Project manager
- c. Iteration
- d. Bottleneck

Guidance: level 1

:: Quality assurance ::

Organizations that issue credentials or certify third parties against official standards are themselves formally accredited by _____ bodies ; hence they are sometimes known as "accredited certification bodies". The _____ process ensures that their certification practices are acceptable, typically meaning that they are competent to test and certify third parties, behave ethically and employ suitable quality assurance.

Exam Probability: **Low**

12. *Answer choices:*

<small>(see index for correct answer)</small>

- a. Healthcare Facilities Accreditation Program
- b. Quality Assurance Agency for Higher Education
- c. Joint Commission
- d. Swiss quality label for further education institutions

Guidance: level 1

:: Unit operations ::

_____ is a discipline of thermal engineering that concerns the generation, use, conversion, and exchange of thermal energy between physical systems. _____ is classified into various mechanisms, such as thermal conduction, thermal convection, thermal radiation, and transfer of energy by phase changes. Engineers also consider the transfer of mass of differing chemical species, either cold or hot, to achieve _____ . While these mechanisms have distinct characteristics, they often occur simultaneously in the same system.

Exam Probability: **Medium**

13. *Answer choices:*

(see index for correct answer)

- a. Unit Operations of Chemical Engineering
- b. Heat transfer
- c. Sedimentation coefficient
- d. Theoretical plate

Guidance: level 1

:: Accounting source documents ::

A _____ is a commercial document and first official offer issued by a buyer to a seller indicating types, quantities, and agreed prices for products or services. It is used to control the purchasing of products and services from external suppliers. _____ s can be an essential part of enterprise resource planning system orders.

Exam Probability: **Low**

14. *Answer choices:*

(see index for correct answer)

- a. Air waybill
- b. Invoice

- c. Bank statement
- d. Purchase order

Guidance: level 1

:: ::

_____ is the production of products for use or sale using labour and machines, tools, chemical and biological processing, or formulation. The term may refer to a range of human activity, from handicraft to high tech, but is most commonly applied to industrial design, in which raw materials are transformed into finished goods on a large scale. Such finished goods may be sold to other manufacturers for the production of other, more complex products, such as aircraft, household appliances, furniture, sports equipment or automobiles, or sold to wholesalers, who in turn sell them to retailers, who then sell them to end users and consumers.

Exam Probability: **Medium**

15. *Answer choices:*
(see index for correct answer)

- a. hierarchical perspective
- b. Sarbanes-Oxley act of 2002
- c. empathy
- d. similarity-attraction theory

Guidance: level 1

:: Project management ::

_____ is a process of setting goals, planning and/or controlling the organizing and leading the execution of any type of activity, such as.

Exam Probability: **Low**

16. *Answer choices:*
(see index for correct answer)

- a. Management process
- b. Research program
- c. Collaborative planning software
- d. Metra potential method

Guidance: level 1

:: Production economics ::

In economics and related disciplines, a _____ is a cost in making any economic trade when participating in a market.

Exam Probability: **Low**

17. *Answer choices:*

(see index for correct answer)

- a. Value and Capital
- b. Transaction cost
- c. Economic batch quantity
- d. Marginal cost of capital schedule

Guidance: level 1

:: ::

In sales, commerce and economics, a _____ is the recipient of a good, service, product or an idea - obtained from a seller, vendor, or supplier via a financial transaction or exchange for money or some other valuable consideration.

Exam Probability: **Low**

18. *Answer choices:*

(see index for correct answer)

- a. levels of analysis
- b. cultural
- c. Customer
- d. empathy

Guidance: level 1

:: ::

_____ is the process of finding an estimate, or approximation, which is a value that is usable for some purpose even if input data may be incomplete, uncertain, or unstable. The value is nonetheless usable because it is derived from the best information available. Typically, _____ involves "using the value of a statistic derived from a sample to estimate the value of a corresponding population parameter". The sample provides information that can be projected, through various formal or informal processes, to determine a range most likely to describe the missing information. An estimate that turns out to be incorrect will be an overestimate if the estimate exceeded the actual result, and an underestimate if the estimate fell short of the actual result.

Exam Probability: **High**

19. *Answer choices:*

(see index for correct answer)

- a. hierarchical perspective
- b. deep-level diversity
- c. personal values
- d. similarity-attraction theory

Guidance: level 1

:: Occupational safety and health ::

_____ is a chemical element with symbol Pb and atomic number 82. It is a heavy metal that is denser than most common materials. _____ is soft and malleable, and also has a relatively low melting point. When freshly cut, _____ is silvery with a hint of blue; it tarnishes to a dull gray color when exposed to air. _____ has the highest atomic number of any stable element and three of its isotopes are endpoints of major nuclear decay chains of heavier elements.

Exam Probability: **Medium**

20. *Answer choices:*

(see index for correct answer)

- a. Hierarchy of hazard control
- b. Lead
- c. Specific inhalation challenge
- d. Diacetyl

Guidance: level 1

:: Management ::

_____ , also known as natural process limits, are horizontal lines drawn on a statistical process control chart, usually at a distance of ±3 standard deviations of the plotted statistic from the statistic's mean.

Exam Probability: **Medium**

21. *Answer choices:*

(see index for correct answer)

- a. Control limits
- b. Opera management
- c. Social business model
- d. Project cost management

Guidance: level 1

:: Commerce ::

A _____ is an employee within a company, business or other organization who is responsible at some level for buying or approving the acquisition of goods and services needed by the company. Responsible for buying the best quality products, goods and services for their company at the most competitive prices, _____ s work in a wide range of sectors for many different organizations. The position responsibilities may be the same as that of a buyer or purchasing agent, or may include wider supervisory or managerial responsibilities. A _____ may oversee the acquisition of materials needed for production, general supplies for offices and facilities, equipment, or construction contracts. A _____ often supervises purchasing agents and buyers, but in small companies the _____ may also be the purchasing agent or buyer. The _____ position may also carry the title "Procurement Manager" or in the public sector, "Procurement Officer". He or she can come from both an Engineering or Economics background.

Exam Probability: **High**

22. *Answer choices:*

(see index for correct answer)

- a. Trade in services statistics
- b. Bunker adjustment factor
- c. Oniomania
- d. Purchasing manager

Guidance: level 1

:: Management ::

A _____ is an idea of the future or desired result that a person or a group of people envisions, plans and commits to achieve. People endeavor to reach _____ s within a finite time by setting deadlines.

Exam Probability: **Medium**

23. *Answer choices:*

(see index for correct answer)

- a. Goal
- b. Central administration
- c. Six phases of a big project
- d. Logistics management

Guidance: level 1

:: Natural resources ::

_____s are resources that exist without actions of humankind. This includes all valued characteristics such as magnetic, gravitational, electrical properties and forces etc. On Earth it includes sunlight, atmosphere, water, land along with all vegetation, crops and animal life that naturally subsists upon or within the heretofore identified characteristics and substances.

Exam Probability: **High**

24. *Answer choices:*

(see index for correct answer)

- a. Ecosystem Health
- b. Natural Resources Acts
- c. I-Tree
- d. Natural resource

Guidance: level 1

:: Management ::

_____ is a method of quality control which employs statistical methods to monitor and control a process. This helps to ensure that the process operates efficiently, producing more specification-conforming products with less waste . SPC can be applied to any process where the "conforming product" output can be measured. Key tools used in SPC include run charts, control charts, a focus on continuous improvement, and the design of experiments. An example of a process where SPC is applied is manufacturing lines.

Exam Probability: **Medium**

25. *Answer choices:*

(see index for correct answer)

- a. Event chain methodology
- b. Distributed management
- c. Board of governors
- d. Statistical process control

Guidance: level 1

:: Finance ::

_____ is a financial estimate intended to help buyers and owners determine the direct and indirect costs of a product or system. It is a management accounting concept that can be used in full cost accounting or even ecological economics where it includes social costs.

Exam Probability: **Medium**

26. *Answer choices:*

(see index for correct answer)

- a. Reverse greenshoe
- b. Target benefit plan
- c. Separation property
- d. Total return swap

Guidance: level 1

:: Project management ::

In political science, an _____ is a means by which a petition signed by a certain minimum number of registered voters can force a government to choose to either enact a law or hold a public vote in parliament in what is called indirect _____, or under direct _____, the proposition is immediately put to a plebiscite or referendum, in what is called a Popular initiated Referendum or citizen-initiated referendum).

Exam Probability: **Low**

27. *Answer choices:*

(see index for correct answer)

- a. Collaborative project management
- b. Task management
- c. ISO 21500
- d. Initiative

Guidance: level 1

:: Industrial engineering ::

The _____ is the design of any task that aims to describe or explain the variation of information under conditions that are hypothesized to reflect the variation. The term is generally associated with experiments in which the design introduces conditions that directly affect the variation, but may also refer to the design of quasi-experiments, in which natural conditions that influence the variation are selected for observation.

Exam Probability: **Low**

28. *Answer choices:*

(see index for correct answer)

- a. Design of experiments
- b. Work Measurement
- c. Operation chart
- d. Pilot plant

Guidance: level 1

:: Project management ::

_____ is a work methodology emphasizing the parallelisation of tasks, which is sometimes called simultaneous engineering or integrated product development using an integrated product team approach. It refers to an approach used in product development in which functions of design engineering, manufacturing engineering, and other functions are integrated to reduce the time required to bring a new product to market.

Exam Probability: **Medium**

29. *Answer choices:*

(see index for correct answer)

- a. Product-based planning
- b. Student syndrome
- c. Concurrent engineering
- d. Pre-mortem

Guidance: level 1

:: Project management ::

Rolling-wave planning is the process of project planning in waves as the project proceeds and later details become clearer; similar to the techniques used in agile software development approaches like Scrum..

Exam Probability: **High**

30. *Answer choices:*

(see index for correct answer)

- a. Rolling Wave planning
- b. Bill of quantities
- c. Project blog
- d. Design structure matrix

Guidance: level 1

:: Information technology management ::

_____ concerns a cycle of organizational activity: the acquisition of information from one or more sources, the custodianship and the distribution of that information to those who need it, and its ultimate disposition through archiving or deletion.

Exam Probability: **High**

31. *Answer choices:*

(see index for correct answer)

- a. Computer-aided manufacturing
- b. Service desk
- c. Grey problem
- d. Information management

Guidance: level 1

:: E-commerce ::

_____ is the activity of buying or selling of products on online services or over the Internet. Electronic commerce draws on technologies such as mobile commerce, electronic funds transfer, supply chain management, Internet marketing, online transaction processing, electronic data interchange , inventory management systems, and automated data collection systems.

Exam Probability: **Medium**

32. *Answer choices:*

(see index for correct answer)

- a. Government-to-business
- b. Online locator service
- c. Cleaning card
- d. EPAS

Guidance: level 1

:: Supply chain management terms ::

In business and finance, _____ is a system of organizations, people, activities, information, and resources involved in moving a product or service from supplier to customer. _____ activities involve the transformation of natural resources, raw materials, and components into a finished product that is delivered to the end customer. In sophisticated _____ systems, used products may re-enter the _____ at any point where residual value is recyclable. _____ s link value chains.

Exam Probability: **High**

33. *Answer choices:*

(see index for correct answer)

- a. Work in process
- b. Supply chain
- c. Consumables
- d. Cool Chain Quality Indicator

Guidance: level 1

:: Production and manufacturing ::

_____ is the process of determining the production capacity needed by an organization to meet changing demands for its products. In the context of _____ , design capacity is the maximum amount of work that an organization is capable of completing in a given period. Effective capacity is the maximum amount of work that an organization is capable of completing in a given period due to constraints such as quality problems, delays, material handling, etc.

Exam Probability: **High**

34. *Answer choices:*

(see index for correct answer)

- a. EFQM Excellence Model
- b. Six Sigma
- c. Seweasy
- d. Variable rate feeder

Guidance: level 1

:: Sampling (statistics) ::

_____ uses statistical sampling to determine whether to accept or reject a production lot of material. It has been a common quality control technique used in industry. It is usually done as products leaves the factory, or in some cases even within the factory. Most often a producer supplies a consumer a number of items and a decision to accept or reject the items is made by determining the number of defective items in a sample from the lot. The lot is accepted if the number of defects falls below where the acceptance number or otherwise the lot is rejected.

Exam Probability: **Low**

35. *Answer choices:*

(see index for correct answer)

- a. Inclusion probability
- b. Judgment sample
- c. Selection bias
- d. Acceptance sampling

Guidance: level 1

:: Management ::

A process is a unique combination of tools, materials, methods, and people engaged in producing a measurable output; for example a manufacturing line for machine parts. All processes have inherent statistical variability which can be evaluated by statistical methods.

Exam Probability: **High**

36. *Answer choices:*
(see index for correct answer)

- a. Product breakdown structure
- b. Process capability
- c. Inside job
- d. Context analysis

Guidance: level 1

:: Project management ::

A _____ is a team whose members usually belong to different groups, functions and are assigned to activities for the same project. A team can be divided into sub-teams according to need. Usually _____ s are only used for a defined period of time. They are disbanded after the project is deemed complete. Due to the nature of the specific formation and disbandment, _____ s are usually in organizations.

Exam Probability: **Medium**

37. *Answer choices:*
(see index for correct answer)

- a. SQEP
- b. Enterprise project management
- c. Sequence step algorithm
- d. Project team

Guidance: level 1

:: Knowledge representation ::

_____ s are causal diagrams created by Kaoru Ishikawa that show the causes of a specific event.

Exam Probability: **High**

38. *Answer choices:*

(see index for correct answer)

- a. Linguistic value
- b. IDIS
- c. Scripts
- d. Ishikawa diagram

Guidance: level 1

:: Mereology ::

_____ , in the abstract, is what belongs to or with something, whether as an attribute or as a component of said thing. In the context of this article, it is one or more components , whether physical or incorporeal, of a person's estate; or so belonging to, as in being owned by, a person or jointly a group of people or a legal entity like a corporation or even a society. Depending on the nature of the _____ , an owner of _____ has the right to consume, alter, share, redefine, rent, mortgage, pawn, sell, exchange, transfer, give away or destroy it, or to exclude others from doing these things, as well as to perhaps abandon it; whereas regardless of the nature of the _____ , the owner thereof has the right to properly use it , or at the very least exclusively keep it.

Exam Probability: **High**

39. *Answer choices:*

(see index for correct answer)

- a. Mereological nihilism
- b. Gunk
- c. Property
- d. Mereology

Guidance: level 1

:: Quality management ::

_____ ensures that an organization, product or service is consistent. It has four main components: quality planning, quality assurance, quality control and quality improvement. _____ is focused not only on product and service quality, but also on the means to achieve it. _____ , therefore, uses quality assurance and control of processes as well as products to achieve more consistent quality. What a customer wants and is willing to pay for it determines quality. It is written or unwritten commitment to a known or unknown consumer in the market . Thus, quality can be defined as fitness for intended use or, in other words, how well the product performs its intended function

Exam Probability: **Low**

40. *Answer choices:*

(see index for correct answer)

- a. Flemish Quality Management Center
- b. Det Norske Veritas
- c. Quality management
- d. Germanischer Lloyd

Guidance: level 1

:: Evaluation ::

_____ is a way of preventing mistakes and defects in manufactured products and avoiding problems when delivering products or services to customers; which ISO 9000 defines as "part of quality management focused on providing confidence that quality requirements will be fulfilled". This defect prevention in _____ differs subtly from defect detection and rejection in quality control and has been referred to as a shift left since it focuses on quality earlier in the process.

Exam Probability: **Medium**

41. *Answer choices:*
(see index for correct answer)

- a. Health technology assessment
- b. Career portfolio
- c. Appraisal
- d. Quality assurance

Guidance: level 1

:: Quality ::

The _____ , formerly the _____ Control , is a knowledge-based global community of quality professionals, with nearly 80,000 members dedicated to promoting and advancing quality tools, principles, and practices in their workplaces and communities.

Exam Probability: **High**

42. *Answer choices:*

(see index for correct answer)

- a. American Society for Quality
- b. Quality of life
- c. European Practice Assessment
- d. Quality by Design

Guidance: level 1

:: Process management ::

A _____ is a diagram commonly used in chemical and process engineering to indicate the general flow of plant processes and equipment. The PFD displays the relationship between major equipment of a plant facility and does not show minor details such as piping details and designations. Another commonly used term for a PFD is a flowsheet.

Exam Probability: **Medium**

43. *Answer choices:*

(see index for correct answer)

- a. Planning horizon
- b. Turnaround
- c. Process modeling
- d. Process flow diagram

Guidance: level 1

:: Data management ::

_____ is the ability of a physical product to remain functional, without requiring excessive maintenance or repair, when faced with the challenges of normal operation over its design lifetime. There are several measures of _____ in use, including years of life, hours of use, and number of operational cycles. In economics, goods with a long usable life are referred to as durable goods.

Exam Probability: **Low**

44. *Answer choices:*

(see index for correct answer)

- a. Single customer view
- b. Linear medium
- c. Durability
- d. Operational database

Guidance: level 1

:: Management ::

An _____ is a loosely coupled, self-organizing network of firms that combine their economic output to provide products and services offerings to the market. Firms in the _____ may operate independently, for example, through market mechanisms, or cooperatively through agreements and contracts. They provide value added service or product to the OEM .

Exam Probability: **High**

45. *Answer choices:*

(see index for correct answer)

- a. Completed Staff Work
- b. Extended enterprise
- c. Outrage constraint
- d. Energy monitoring and targeting

Guidance: level 1

:: Materials ::

A _____, also known as a feedstock, unprocessed material, or primary commodity, is a basic material that is used to produce goods, finished products, energy, or intermediate materials which are feedstock for future finished products. As feedstock, the term connotes these materials are bottleneck assets and are highly important with regard to producing other products. An example of this is crude oil, which is a _____ and a feedstock used in the production of industrial chemicals, fuels, plastics, and pharmaceutical goods; lumber is a _____ used to produce a variety of products including all types of furniture. The term "_____" denotes materials in minimally processed or unprocessed in states; e.g., raw latex, crude oil, cotton, coal, raw biomass, iron ore, air, logs, or water i.e. "...any product of agriculture, forestry, fishing and any other mineral that is in its natural form or which has undergone the transformation required to prepare it for internationally marketing in substantial volumes."

Exam Probability: **High**

46. *Answer choices:*

(see index for correct answer)

- a. Monocrystalline whisker
- b. Solid surface
- c. Rubblization
- d. Raw material

Guidance: level 1

:: Project management ::

A _____ is a source or supply from which a benefit is produced and it has some utility. _____ s can broadly be classified upon their availability—they are classified into renewable and non-renewable _____ s. Examples of non renewable _____ s are coal, crude oil natural gas nuclear energy etc. Examples of renewable _____ s are air, water, wind, solar energy etc. They can also be classified as actual and potential on the basis of level of development and use, on the basis of origin they can be classified as biotic and abiotic, and on the basis of their distribution, as ubiquitous and localized. An item becomes a _____ with time and developing technology. Typically, _____ s are materials, energy, services, staff, knowledge, or other assets that are transformed to produce benefit and in the process may be consumed or made unavailable. Benefits of _____ utilization may include increased wealth, proper functioning of a system, or enhanced well-being. From a human perspective a natural _____ is anything obtained from the environment to satisfy human needs and wants. From a broader biological or ecological perspective a _____ satisfies the needs of a living organism.

Exam Probability: **High**

47. *Answer choices:*

(see index for correct answer)

- a. Resource
- b. Theory X
- c. Australian Institute of Project Management
- d. Concept note

Guidance: level 1

:: Help desk ::

Data center management is the collection of tasks performed by those responsible for managing ongoing operation of a data center This includes Business service management and planning for the future.

Exam Probability: **High**

48. *Answer choices:*

(see index for correct answer)

- a. AetherPal
- b. Technical support
- c. KnowledgeBase Manager Pro
- d. EHelp Corporation

Guidance: level 1

:: Process management ::

When used in the context of communication networks, such as Ethernet or packet radio, _____ or network _____ is the rate of successful message delivery over a communication channel. The data these messages belong to may be delivered over a physical or logical link, or it can pass through a certain network node. _____ is usually measured in bits per second, and sometimes in data packets per second or data packets per time slot.

Exam Probability: **Low**

49. *Answer choices:*

(see index for correct answer)

- a. Process consultant
- b. Throughput
- c. Stock clearance
- d. Business process orientation

Guidance: level 1

:: Quality management ::

In quality management system, a _____ is a document developed by management to express the directive of the top management with respect to quality. _____ management is a strategic item.

Exam Probability: **Medium**

50. *Answer choices:*

(see index for correct answer)

- a. External quality assessment
- b. Quality policy
- c. E-TQM College
- d. Product quality risk in supply chain

Guidance: level 1

:: Monopoly (economics) ::

_____ are "efficiencies formed by variety, not volume". For example, a gas station that sells gasoline can sell soda, milk, baked goods, etc through their customer service representatives and thus achieve gasoline companies _____.

Exam Probability: **Medium**

51. *Answer choices:*

(see index for correct answer)

- a. Statute of Monopolies
- b. Supracompetitive pricing
- c. Economies of scope
- d. Eisenkammer Pirna

Guidance: level 1

:: Waste ::

_____ are unwanted or unusable materials. _____ is any substance which is discarded after primary use, or is worthless, defective and of no use. A by-product by contrast is a joint product of relatively minor economic value. A _____ product may become a by-product, joint product or resource through an invention that raises a _____ product's value above zero.

Exam Probability: **Medium**

52. *Answer choices:*

(see index for correct answer)

- a. Spent caustic
- b. Toxic waste
- c. Coffee wastewater
- d. Post-consumer waste

Guidance: level 1

:: Procurement ::

> Purchasing is the formal process of buying goods and services. The _____ can vary from one organization to another, but there are some common key elements.

Exam Probability: **Medium**

53. *Answer choices:*

(see index for correct answer)

- a. Request for tender
- b. Swiss challenge
- c. Bid and proposal
- d. Tender board

Guidance: level 1

:: Metal heat treatments ::

_____ is a group of industrial and metalworking processes used to alter the physical, and sometimes chemical, properties of a material. The most common application is metallurgical. Heat treatments are also used in the manufacture of many other materials, such as glass. Heat treatment involves the use of heating or chilling, normally to extreme temperatures, to achieve a desired result such as hardening or softening of a material. Heat treatment techniques include annealing, case hardening, precipitation strengthening, tempering, carburizing, normalizing and quenching. It is noteworthy that while the term heat treatment applies only to processes where the heating and cooling are done for the specific purpose of altering properties intentionally, heating and cooling often occur incidentally during other manufacturing processes such as hot forming or welding.

Exam Probability: **Medium**

54. *Answer choices:*

(see index for correct answer)

- a. Carbonitriding
- b. Boriding
- c. Ferritic nitrocarburizing
- d. Austempering

Guidance: level 1

:: Supply chain management ::

A _____ is a type of auction in which the traditional roles of buyer and seller are reversed. Thus, there is one buyer and many potential sellers. In an ordinary auction, buyers compete to obtain goods or services by offering increasingly higher prices. In contrast, in a _____ , the sellers compete to obtain business from the buyer and prices will typically decrease as the sellers underbid each other.

Exam Probability: **Medium**

55. *Answer choices:*
(see index for correct answer)

- a. Demand sensing
- b. Suppliers and Parts database
- c. Service management
- d. Calculating demand forecast accuracy

Guidance: level 1

:: Process management ::

_____ is a statistics package developed at the Pennsylvania State University by researchers Barbara F. Ryan, Thomas A. Ryan, Jr., and Brian L. Joiner in 1972. It began as a light version of OMNITAB 80, a statistical analysis program by NIST. Statistical analysis software such as _____ automates calculations and the creation of graphs, allowing the user to focus more on the analysis of data and the interpretation of results. It is compatible with other _____, Inc. software.

Exam Probability: **Low**

56. *Answer choices:*

(see index for correct answer)

- a. Stock clearance
- b. YAWL
- c. Artifact-centric business process model
- d. Minitab

Guidance: level 1

:: Production and manufacturing ::

_____ is the production under license of technology developed elsewhere. It is an especially prominent commercial practice in developing nations, which often approach _____ as a starting point for indigenous industrial development.

Exam Probability: **Low**

57. *Answer choices:*

(see index for correct answer)

- a. Production equipment control
- b. Report generator
- c. STEP-NC
- d. Division of labour

Guidance: level 1

:: Decision theory ::

_____ is a method developed in Japan beginning in 1966 to help transform the voice of the customer into engineering characteristics for a product. Yoji Akao, the original developer, described QFD as a "method to transform qualitative user demands into quantitative parameters, to deploy the functions forming quality, and to deploy methods for achieving the design quality into subsystems and component parts, and ultimately to specific elements of the manufacturing process." The author combined his work in quality assurance and quality control points with function deployment used in value engineering.

Exam Probability: **High**

58. *Answer choices:*

(see index for correct answer)

- a. Clarity test
- b. ELECTRE

- c. Consensus-seeking decision-making
- d. Binary decision

Guidance: level 1

:: Product management ::

_____s, also known as Shewhart charts or process-behavior charts, are a statistical process control tool used to determine if a manufacturing or business process is in a state of control.

Exam Probability: **High**

59. *Answer choices:*
(see index for correct answer)

- a. Control chart
- b. Brand extension
- c. Swing tag
- d. Trademark

Guidance: level 1

Commerce

Commerce relates to "the exchange of goods and services, especially on a large scale." It includes legal, economic, political, social, cultural and technological systems that operate in any country or internationally.

:: Management accounting ::

_____ , or dollar contribution per unit, is the selling price per unit minus the variable cost per unit. "Contribution" represents the portion of sales revenue that is not consumed by variable costs and so contributes to the coverage of fixed costs. This concept is one of the key building blocks of break-even analysis.

Exam Probability: **Medium**

1. *Answer choices:*

(see index for correct answer)

- a. Institute of Certified Management Accountants
- b. Contribution margin
- c. Spend management
- d. Bridge life-cycle cost analysis

Guidance: level 1

:: ::

In Western musical notation, the staff or stave is a set of five horizontal lines and four spaces that each represent a different musical pitch or in the case of a percussion staff, different percussion instruments. Appropriate music symbols, depending on the intended effect, are placed on the staff according to their corresponding pitch or function. Musical notes are placed by pitch, percussion notes are placed by instrument, and rests and other symbols are placed by convention.

Exam Probability: **Low**

2. *Answer choices:*

(see index for correct answer)

- a. Character

- b. information systems assessment
- c. imperative
- d. Sarbanes-Oxley act of 2002

Guidance: level 1

:: Commercial item transport and distribution ::

In a contract of carriage, the _____ is the entity who is financially responsible for the receipt of a shipment. Generally, but not always, the _____ is the same as the receiver.

Exam Probability: **Low**

3. *Answer choices:*

(see index for correct answer)

- a. Fulfillment house
- b. Hydrogen pipeline transport
- c. Consignee
- d. Skid unit

Guidance: level 1

:: Dot-com bubble ::

_____ was an online grocery business that filed bankruptcy in 2001 after 3 years of operation and was later folded into Amazon.com. It was headquartered in Foster City, California, United States. It delivered products to customers' homes within a 30-minute window of their choosing. At its peak, it offered service in ten US markets: the San Francisco Bay Area; Dallas; Sacramento; San Diego; Los Angeles; Orange County, California; Chicago; Seattle; Portland, Oregon; and Atlanta, Georgia. The company had hoped to expand to 26 cities by 2001.

Exam Probability: **High**

4. *Answer choices:*

(see index for correct answer)

- a. AllAdvantage
- b. Dot-com company
- c. Think Tools
- d. Webvan

Guidance: level 1

:: Supply chain management ::

_____ is the process of finding and agreeing to terms, and acquiring goods, services, or works from an external source, often via a tendering or competitive bidding process. _____ is used to ensure the buyer receives goods, services, or works at the best possible price when aspects such as quality, quantity, time, and location are compared. Corporations and public bodies often define processes intended to promote fair and open competition for their business while minimizing risks such as exposure to fraud and collusion.

Exam Probability: **Low**

5. *Answer choices:*

(see index for correct answer)

- a. Procurement
- b. ERFx
- c. Netchain analysis
- d. ClearOrbit

Guidance: level 1

:: Project management ::

In political science, an _____ is a means by which a petition signed by a certain minimum number of registered voters can force a government to choose to either enact a law or hold a public vote in parliament in what is called indirect _____ , or under direct _____ , the proposition is immediately put to a plebiscite or referendum, in what is called a Popular initiated Referendum or citizen-initiated referendum).

Exam Probability: **Low**

6. *Answer choices:*

(see index for correct answer)

- a. Social project management
- b. Soft Costs
- c. Initiative
- d. Jeff Sutherland

Guidance: level 1

:: Management accounting ::

_____s are costs that change as the quantity of the good or service that a business produces changes. _____s are the sum of marginal costs over all units produced. They can also be considered normal costs. Fixed costs and _____s make up the two components of total cost. Direct costs are costs that can easily be associated with a particular cost object. However, not all _____s are direct costs. For example, variable manufacturing overhead costs are _____s that are indirect costs, not direct costs. _____s are sometimes called unit-level costs as they vary with the number of units produced.

Exam Probability: **High**

7. *Answer choices:*

(see index for correct answer)

- a. Variable cost
- b. Cash and cash equivalents
- c. Owner earnings
- d. Certified Management Accountants of Canada

Guidance: level 1

:: Market structure and pricing ::

_____ has historically emerged in two separate types of discussions in economics, that of Adam Smith on the one hand, and that of Karl Marx on the other hand. Adam Smith in his writing on economics stressed the importance of laissez-faire principles outlining the operation of the market in the absence of dominant political mechanisms of control, while Karl Marx discussed the working of the market in the presence of a controlled economy sometimes referred to as a command economy in the literature. Both types of _____ have been in historical evidence throughout the twentieth century and twenty-first century.

Exam Probability: **High**

8. *Answer choices:*

(see index for correct answer)

- a. Market structure
- b. industry concentration
- c. Open source
- d. Open-source economics

Guidance: level 1

:: Materials ::

A _____, also known as a feedstock, unprocessed material, or primary commodity, is a basic material that is used to produce goods, finished products, energy, or intermediate materials which are feedstock for future finished products. As feedstock, the term connotes these materials are bottleneck assets and are highly important with regard to producing other products. An example of this is crude oil, which is a _____ and a feedstock used in the production of industrial chemicals, fuels, plastics, and pharmaceutical goods; lumber is a _____ used to produce a variety of products including all types of furniture. The term "_____" denotes materials in minimally processed or unprocessed in states; e.g., raw latex, crude oil, cotton, coal, raw biomass, iron ore, air, logs, or water i.e. "...any product of agriculture, forestry, fishing and any other mineral that is in its natural form or which has undergone the transformation required to prepare it for internationally marketing in substantial volumes."

Exam Probability: **Medium**

9. *Answer choices:*

(see index for correct answer)

- a. Biocompatible material
- b. Orthotropic material
- c. Tortoiseshell
- d. Technora

Guidance: level 1

:: Asset ::

In financial accounting, an _____ is any resource owned by the business. Anything tangible or intangible that can be owned or controlled to produce value and that is held by a company to produce positive economic value is an _____ . Simply stated, _____ s represent value of ownership that can be converted into cash . The balance sheet of a firm records the monetary value of the _____ s owned by that firm. It covers money and other valuables belonging to an individual or to a business.

Exam Probability: **Medium**

10. *Answer choices:*

(see index for correct answer)

- a. Asset
- b. Current asset

Guidance: level 1

:: ::

A _____ is monetary compensation paid by an employer to an employee in exchange for work done. Payment may be calculated as a fixed amount for each task completed , or at an hourly or daily rate , or based on an easily measured quantity of work done.

Exam Probability: **Medium**

11. *Answer choices:*

(see index for correct answer)

- a. Wage
- b. cultural
- c. process perspective
- d. hierarchical perspective

Guidance: level 1

:: Debt ::

_____ is the trust which allows one party to provide money or resources to another party wherein the second party does not reimburse the first party immediately, but promises either to repay or return those resources at a later date. In other words, _____ is a method of making reciprocity formal, legally enforceable, and extensible to a large group of unrelated people.

Exam Probability: **Medium**

12. *Answer choices:*

(see index for correct answer)

- a. Peak debt
- b. Debtors Anonymous

- c. Odious debt
- d. External financing

Guidance: level 1

:: Evaluation ::

_____ is a way of preventing mistakes and defects in manufactured products and avoiding problems when delivering products or services to customers; which ISO 9000 defines as "part of quality management focused on providing confidence that quality requirements will be fulfilled". This defect prevention in _____ differs subtly from defect detection and rejection in quality control and has been referred to as a shift left since it focuses on quality earlier in the process .

Exam Probability: **High**

13. *Answer choices:*
(see index for correct answer)

- a. Australian Drug Evaluation Committee
- b. Goddard College
- c. Quality assurance
- d. Appraisal

Guidance: level 1

:: Meetings ::

A _____ is a body of one or more persons that is subordinate to a deliberative assembly. Usually, the assembly sends matters into a _____ as a way to explore them more fully than would be possible if the assembly itself were considering them. _____s may have different functions and their type of work differ depending on the type of the organization and its needs.

Exam Probability: **Low**

14. *Answer choices:*
(see index for correct answer)

- a. Open town meeting
- b. Committee
- c. Altenberg Workshops in Theoretical Biology
- d. Convention

Guidance: level 1

:: ::

_____ is the provision of service to customers before, during and after a purchase. The perception of success of such interactions is dependent on employees "who can adjust themselves to the personality of the guest". _____ concerns the priority an organization assigns to _____ relative to components such as product innovation and pricing. In this sense, an organization that values good _____ may spend more money in training employees than the average organization or may proactively interview customers for feedback.

Exam Probability: **Medium**

15. *Answer choices:*

(see index for correct answer)

- a. surface-level diversity
- b. Customer service
- c. interpersonal communication
- d. functional perspective

Guidance: level 1

:: Marketing ::

_____ comes from the Latin neg and otsia referring to businessmen who, unlike the patricians, had no leisure time in their industriousness; it held the meaning of business until the 17th century when it took on the diplomatic connotation as a dialogue between two or more people or parties intended to reach a beneficial outcome over one or more issues where a conflict exists with respect to at least one of these issues. Thus, _____ is a process of combining divergent positions into a joint agreement under a decision rule of unanimity.

Exam Probability: **Medium**

16. *Answer choices:*

(see index for correct answer)

- a. Niche market
- b. Negotiation
- c. Immersion marketing
- d. Food marketing

Guidance: level 1

:: Summary statistics ::

_____ is the number of occurrences of a repeating event per unit of time. It is also referred to as temporal _____, which emphasizes the contrast to spatial _____ and angular _____. The period is the duration of time of one cycle in a repeating event, so the period is the reciprocal of the _____. For example: if a newborn baby's heart beats at a _____ of 120 times a minute, its period—the time interval between beats—is half a second. _____ is an important parameter used in science and engineering to specify the rate of oscillatory and vibratory phenomena, such as mechanical vibrations, audio signals, radio waves, and light.

Exam Probability: **High**

17. *Answer choices:*

(see index for correct answer)

- a. Frequency
- b. Multiple of the median
- c. Mean percentage error
- d. Robin Hood index

Guidance: level 1

:: ::

In marketing jargon, product lining is offering several related products for sale individually. Unlike product bundling, where several products are combined into one group, which is then offered for sale as a units, product lining involves offering the products for sale separately. A line can comprise related products of various sizes, types, colors, qualities, or prices. Line depth refers to the number of subcategories a category has. Line consistency refers to how closely related the products that make up the line are. Line vulnerability refers to the percentage of sales or profits that are derived from only a few products in the line.

Exam Probability: **Medium**

18. *Answer choices:*

(see index for correct answer)

- a. co-culture
- b. empathy
- c. process perspective
- d. Product line

Guidance: level 1

:: ::

_____ is a means of protection from financial loss. It is a form of risk management, primarily used to hedge against the risk of a contingent or uncertain loss

Exam Probability: **High**

19. *Answer choices:*

(see index for correct answer)

- a. deep-level diversity
- b. co-culture
- c. Character
- d. Insurance

Guidance: level 1

:: Hospitality industry ::

_____ refers to the relationship between a guest and a host, wherein the host receives the guest with goodwill, including the reception and entertainment of guests, visitors, or strangers. Louis, chevalier de Jaucourt describes _____ in the Encyclopédie as the virtue of a great soul that cares for the whole universe through the ties of humanity.

Exam Probability: **Low**

20. *Answer choices:*

(see index for correct answer)

- a. Travel insurance
- b. Hospitality

- c. Hospitality industry
- d. Hospitality law

Guidance: level 1

:: ::

A federation is a political entity characterized by a union of partially self-governing provinces, states, or other regions under a central _____. In a federation, the self-governing status of the component states, as well as the division of power between them and the central government, is typically constitutionally entrenched and may not be altered by a unilateral decision of either party, the states or the federal political body. Alternatively, federation is a form of government in which sovereign power is formally divided between a central authority and a number of constituent regions so that each region retains some degree of control over its internal affairs. It is often argued that federal states where the central government has the constitutional authority to suspend a constituent state's government by invoking gross mismanagement or civil unrest, or to adopt national legislation that overrides or infringe on the constituent states' powers by invoking the central government's constitutional authority to ensure "peace and good government" or to implement obligations contracted under an international treaty, are not truly federal states.

Exam Probability: **High**

21. *Answer choices:*

(see index for correct answer)

- a. similarity-attraction theory
- b. imperative

- c. functional perspective
- d. Federal government

Guidance: level 1

:: Human resource management ::

_____ are the people who make up the workforce of an organization, business sector, or economy. "Human capital" is sometimes used synonymously with "_____", although human capital typically refers to a narrower effect. Likewise, other terms sometimes used include manpower, talent, labor, personnel, or simply people.

Exam Probability: **High**

22. *Answer choices:*

(see index for correct answer)

- a. Employeeship
- b. Illness rate
- c. Training and development
- d. Human resources

Guidance: level 1

:: Management ::

_____ is the process of thinking about the activities required to achieve a desired goal. It is the first and foremost activity to achieve desired results. It involves the creation and maintenance of a plan, such as psychological aspects that require conceptual skills. There are even a couple of tests to measure someone's capability of _____ well. As such, _____ is a fundamental property of intelligent behavior. An important further meaning, often just called "_____" is the legal context of permitted building developments.

Exam Probability: **Low**

23. *Answer choices:*

(see index for correct answer)

- a. Formula for change
- b. Scenario planning
- c. Extended enterprise
- d. Planning

Guidance: level 1

:: ::

An _____ is a systematic and independent examination of books, accounts, statutory records, documents and vouchers of an organization to ascertain how far the financial statements as well as non-financial disclosures present a true and fair view of the concern. It also attempts to ensure that the books of accounts are properly maintained by the concern as required by law. _____ing has become such a ubiquitous phenomenon in the corporate and the public sector that academics started identifying an "_____ Society". The _____ or perceives and recognises the propositions before them for examination, obtains evidence, evaluates the same and formulates an opinion on the basis of his judgement which is communicated through their _____ing report.

Exam Probability: **High**

24. *Answer choices:*

(see index for correct answer)

- a. Character
- b. deep-level diversity
- c. Sarbanes-Oxley act of 2002
- d. Audit

Guidance: level 1

:: ::

_____ is "property consisting of land and the buildings on it, along with its natural resources such as crops, minerals or water; immovable property of this nature; an interest vested in this an item of real property, buildings or housing in general. Also: the business of _____ ; the profession of buying, selling, or renting land, buildings, or housing." It is a legal term used in jurisdictions whose legal system is derived from English common law, such as India, England, Wales, Northern Ireland, United States, Canada, Pakistan, Australia, and New Zealand.

Exam Probability: **Medium**

25. *Answer choices:*

(see index for correct answer)

- a. similarity-attraction theory
- b. levels of analysis
- c. hierarchical perspective
- d. Real estate

Guidance: level 1

:: Marketing by medium ::

_____ , also called online marketing or Internet advertising or web advertising, is a form of marketing and advertising which uses the Internet to deliver promotional marketing messages to consumers. Many consumers find _____ disruptive and have increasingly turned to ad blocking for a variety of reasons. When software is used to do the purchasing, it is known as programmatic advertising.

Exam Probability: **High**

26. *Answer choices:*

(see index for correct answer)

- a. Viral marketing
- b. Social marketing intelligence
- c. Digital marketing
- d. New media marketing

Guidance: level 1

:: Human resource management ::

An organizational chart is a diagram that shows the structure of an organization and the relationships and relative ranks of its parts and positions/jobs. The term is also used for similar diagrams, for example ones showing the different elements of a field of knowledge or a group of languages.

Exam Probability: **Medium**

27. *Answer choices:*

(see index for correct answer)

- a. Job knowledge
- b. Service record
- c. Organization chart

- d. Turnover

Guidance: level 1

:: ::

_____ is the extraction of valuable minerals or other geological materials from the earth, usually from an ore body, lode, vein, seam, reef or placer deposit. These deposits form a mineralized package that is of economic interest to the miner.

Exam Probability: **High**

28. *Answer choices:*

(see index for correct answer)

- a. open system
- b. Mining
- c. similarity-attraction theory
- d. corporate values

Guidance: level 1

:: Payment systems ::

Amazon Pay is an online payments processing service that is owned by Amazon. Launched in 2007, Amazon Pay uses the consumer base of Amazon.com and focuses on giving users the option to pay with their Amazon accounts on external merchant websites. As of January 2019 the service is available in Austria, Belgium, Cyprus, Germany, Denmark, Spain, France, Hungary, Luxembourg, Republic of Ireland, India, Italy, Japan, Netherlands, Portugal, Sweden, United Kingdom, United States.

Exam Probability: **Medium**

29. *Answer choices:*

(see index for correct answer)

- a. Honesty bar
- b. TIPANET
- c. FreshBooks
- d. Amazon Payments

Guidance: level 1

:: International trade ::

In finance, an _____ is the rate at which one currency will be exchanged for another. It is also regarded as the value of one country's currency in relation to another currency. For example, an interbank _____ of 114 Japanese yen to the United States dollar means that ¥114 will be exchanged for each US$1 or that US$1 will be exchanged for each ¥114. In this case it is said that the price of a dollar in relation to yen is ¥114, or equivalently that the price of a yen in relation to dollars is $1/114.

Exam Probability: **Medium**

30. *Answer choices:*

(see index for correct answer)

- a. Directive on services in the internal market
- b. Commercial invoice
- c. Exchange rate
- d. Home country control

Guidance: level 1

:: Real estate ::

_____ s serve several societal needs – primarily as shelter from weather, security, living space, privacy, to store belongings, and to comfortably live and work. A _____ as a shelter represents a physical division of the human habitat and the outside.

Exam Probability: **Low**

31. *Answer choices:*

(see index for correct answer)

- a. Landed property
- b. Infrastructure Lifecycle Management
- c. Plantation

- d. Land monopoly

Guidance: level 1

:: ::

In law, an _____ is the process in which cases are reviewed, where parties request a formal change to an official decision. _____s function both as a process for error correction as well as a process of clarifying and interpreting law. Although appellate courts have existed for thousands of years, common law countries did not incorporate an affirmative right to _____ into their jurisprudence until the 19th century.

Exam Probability: **Low**

32. *Answer choices:*

(see index for correct answer)

- a. personal values
- b. surface-level diversity
- c. functional perspective
- d. Appeal

Guidance: level 1

:: ::

_____ Corporation is an American multinational technology company with headquarters in Redmond, Washington. It develops, manufactures, licenses, supports and sells computer software, consumer electronics, personal computers, and related services. Its best known software products are the _____ Windows line of operating systems, the _____ Office suite, and the Internet Explorer and Edge Web browsers. Its flagship hardware products are the Xbox video game consoles and the _____ Surface lineup of touchscreen personal computers. As of 2016, it is the world's largest software maker by revenue, and one of the world's most valuable companies. The word "_____" is a portmanteau of "microcomputer" and "software". _____ is ranked No. 30 in the 2018 Fortune 500 rankings of the largest United States corporations by total revenue.

Exam Probability: **High**

33. *Answer choices:*

(see index for correct answer)

- a. levels of analysis
- b. Microsoft
- c. hierarchical
- d. corporate values

Guidance: level 1

_____ are electronic transfer of money from one bank account to another, either within a single financial institution or across multiple institutions, via computer-based systems, without the direct intervention of bank staff.

Exam Probability: **Low**

34. *Answer choices:*

(see index for correct answer)

- a. imperative
- b. personal values
- c. Electronic funds transfer
- d. similarity-attraction theory

Guidance: level 1

:: ::

_____ or standardisation is the process of implementing and developing technical standards based on the consensus of different parties that include firms, users, interest groups, standards organizations and governments. _____ can help maximize compatibility, interoperability, safety, repeatability, or quality. It can also facilitate commoditization of formerly custom processes. In social sciences, including economics, the idea of _____ is close to the solution for a coordination problem, a situation in which all parties can realize mutual gains, but only by making mutually consistent decisions. This view includes the case of "spontaneous _____ processes", to produce de facto standards.

Exam Probability: **Low**

35. *Answer choices:*

(see index for correct answer)

- a. surface-level diversity
- b. co-culture
- c. Standardization
- d. empathy

Guidance: level 1

:: Commerce ::

_____ relates to "the exchange of goods and services, especially on a large scale". It includes legal, economic, political, social, cultural and technological systems that operate in a country or in international trade.

Exam Probability: **Low**

36. *Answer choices:*

(see index for correct answer)

- a. Export restriction
- b. Card association
- c. Haul video
- d. Reseller

Guidance: level 1

:: Business law ::

A _____ is a group of people who jointly supervise the activities of an organization, which can be either a for-profit business, nonprofit organization, or a government agency. Such a board's powers, duties, and responsibilities are determined by government regulations and the organization's own constitution and bylaws. These authorities may specify the number of members of the board, how they are to be chosen, and how often they are to meet.

Exam Probability: **Low**

37. *Answer choices:*

(see index for correct answer)

- a. Registered agent
- b. Novated lease
- c. Board of directors
- d. Ordinary course of business

Guidance: level 1

:: Production economics ::

In economics and related disciplines, a _____ is a cost in making any economic trade when participating in a market.

Exam Probability: **Low**

38. *Answer choices:*

(see index for correct answer)

- a. Partial productivity
- b. Division of work
- c. Productive capacity
- d. Marginal cost

Guidance: level 1

:: Industry ::

_____ describes various measures of the efficiency of production. Often, a _____ measure is expressed as the ratio of an aggregate output to a single input or an aggregate input used in a production process, i.e. output per unit of input. Most common example is the labour _____ measure, e.g., such as GDP per worker. There are many different definitions of _____ and the choice among them depends on the purpose of the _____ measurement and/or data availability. The key source of difference between various _____ measures is also usually related to how the outputs and the inputs are aggregated into scalars to obtain such a ratio-type measure of _____ .

Exam Probability: **High**

39. *Answer choices:*

(see index for correct answer)

- a. Primary sector of the economy
- b. Sunrise industry
- c. Straw plaiting
- d. Mass production

Guidance: level 1

:: ::

_____ is the practical authority granted to a legal body to administer justice within a defined field of responsibility, e.g., Michigan tax law. In federations like the United States, areas of _____ apply to local, state, and federal levels; e.g. the court has _____ to apply federal law.

Exam Probability: **Medium**

40. *Answer choices:*

(see index for correct answer)

- a. levels of analysis
- b. Jurisdiction
- c. co-culture

- d. surface-level diversity

Guidance: level 1

:: ::

A _____ is a fund into which a sum of money is added during an employee's employment years, and from which payments are drawn to support the person's retirement from work in the form of periodic payments. A _____ may be a "defined benefit plan" where a fixed sum is paid regularly to a person, or a "defined contribution plan" under which a fixed sum is invested and then becomes available at retirement age. _____ s should not be confused with severance pay; the former is usually paid in regular installments for life after retirement, while the latter is typically paid as a fixed amount after involuntary termination of employment prior to retirement.

Exam Probability: **Medium**

41. *Answer choices:*

(see index for correct answer)

- a. Character
- b. process perspective
- c. personal values
- d. Pension

Guidance: level 1

:: Commercial item transport and distribution ::

Wholesaling or distributing is the sale of goods or merchandise to retailers; to industrial, commercial, institutional, or other professional business users; or to other _____ rs and related subordinated services. In general, it is the sale of goods to anyone other than a standard consumer.

Exam Probability: **Low**

42. *Answer choices:*

(see index for correct answer)

- a. Wholesale
- b. Private carrier
- c. Shipbroking
- d. SAP EWM

Guidance: level 1

:: ::

_____ is the process of removing or reducing state regulations, typically in the economic sphere. It is the repeal of governmental regulation of the economy. It became common in advanced industrial economies in the 1970s and 1980s, as a result of new trends in economic thinking about the inefficiencies of government regulation, and the risk that regulatory agencies would be controlled by the regulated industry to its benefit, and thereby hurt consumers and the wider economy.

Exam Probability: **Low**

43. *Answer choices:*

(see index for correct answer)

- a. Deregulation
- b. imperative
- c. interpersonal communication
- d. surface-level diversity

Guidance: level 1

:: Dot-com bubble ::

Yahoo! _____ was a web hosting service. It was founded in November 1994 by David Bohnett and John Rezner, and was called Beverly Hills Internet for a very short time before being named _____ .

Exam Probability: **High**

44. *Answer choices:*

(see index for correct answer)

- a. GovWorks
- b. Pay to surf
- c. Fucked Company
- d. GeoCities

Guidance: level 1

:: Export and import control ::

" _____ " means the Government Service which is responsible for the administration of _____ law and the collection of duties and taxes and which also has the responsibility for the application of other laws and regulations relating to the importation, exportation, movement or storage of goods.

Exam Probability: **Medium**

45. *Answer choices:*

(see index for correct answer)

- a. Arms Export Control Act
- b. Customs
- c. Bureau of Industry and Security
- d. Export of cryptography

Guidance: level 1

:: Price fixing convictions ::

_____ is the flag carrier airline of the United Kingdom, headquartered at Waterside, Harmondsworth. It is the second largest airline in the United Kingdom, based on fleet size and passengers carried, behind easyJet. The airline is based in Waterside near its main hub at London Heathrow Airport. In January 2011 BA merged with Iberia, creating the International Airlines Group, a holding company registered in Madrid, Spain. IAG is the world's third-largest airline group in terms of annual revenue and the second-largest in Europe. It is listed on the London Stock Exchange and in the FTSE 100 Index. _____ is the first passenger airline to have generated more than $1 billion on a single air route in a year.

Exam Probability: **Low**

46. *Answer choices:*

(see index for correct answer)

- a. SK Foods
- b. Asahi Glass Co.
- c. ThyssenKrupp
- d. British Airways

Guidance: level 1

In legal terminology, a _____ is any formal legal document that sets out the facts and legal reasons that the filing party or parties believes are sufficient to support a claim against the party or parties against whom the claim is brought that entitles the plaintiff to a remedy. For example, the Federal Rules of Civil Procedure that govern civil litigation in United States courts provide that a civil action is commenced with the filing or service of a pleading called a _____ . Civil court rules in states that have incorporated the Federal Rules of Civil Procedure use the same term for the same pleading.

Exam Probability: **Medium**

47. *Answer choices:*

(see index for correct answer)

- a. open system
- b. hierarchical
- c. co-culture
- d. Complaint

Guidance: level 1

:: Workplace ::

_____ is asystematic determination of a subject's merit, worth and significance, using criteria governed by a set of standards. It can assist an organization, program, design, project or any other intervention or initiative to assess any aim, realisable concept/proposal, or any alternative, to help in decision-making; or to ascertain the degree of achievement or value in regard to the aim and objectives and results of any such action that has been completed. The primary purpose of _____ , in addition to gaining insight into prior or existing initiatives, is to enable reflection and assist in the identification of future change.

Exam Probability: **Medium**

48. *Answer choices:*

(see index for correct answer)

- a. Workplace deviance
- b. Workplace incivility
- c. Feminisation of the workplace
- d. Workplace spirituality

Guidance: level 1

:: Fraud ::

In law, _____ is intentional deception to secure unfair or unlawful gain, or to deprive a victim of a legal right. _____ can violate civil law, a criminal law, or it may cause no loss of money, property or legal right but still be an element of another civil or criminal wrong. The purpose of _____ may be monetary gain or other benefits, for example by obtaining a passport, travel document, or driver's license, or mortgage _____, where the perpetrator may attempt to qualify for a mortgage by way of false statements.

Exam Probability: **Medium**

49. *Answer choices:*
(see index for correct answer)

- a. Fraud
- b. Intrinsic fraud
- c. Pharma fraud
- d. Selling Hitler

Guidance: level 1

:: ::

An _____ is an area of the production, distribution, or trade, and consumption of goods and services by different agents. Understood in its broadest sense, 'The _____ is defined as a social domain that emphasize the practices, discourses, and material expressions associated with the production, use, and management of resources'. Economic agents can be individuals, businesses, organizations, or governments. Economic transactions occur when two parties agree to the value or price of the transacted good or service, commonly expressed in a certain currency. However, monetary transactions only account for a small part of the economic domain.

Exam Probability: **Medium**

50. *Answer choices:*

(see index for correct answer)

- a. open system
- b. Economy
- c. similarity-attraction theory
- d. personal values

Guidance: level 1

:: ::

_____ s and acquisitions are transactions in which the ownership of companies, other business organizations, or their operating units are transferred or consolidated with other entities. As an aspect of strategic management, M&A can allow enterprises to grow or downsize, and change the nature of their business or competitive position.

Exam Probability: **Low**

51. *Answer choices:*

(see index for correct answer)

- a. Character
- b. Merger
- c. open system
- d. corporate values

Guidance: level 1

:: Business law ::

A _____ is a business entity created by two or more parties, generally characterized by shared ownership, shared returns and risks, and shared governance. Companies typically pursue _____ s for one of four reasons: to access a new market, particularly emerging markets; to gain scale efficiencies by combining assets and operations; to share risk for major investments or projects; or to access skills and capabilities.

Exam Probability: **High**

52. *Answer choices:*

(see index for correct answer)

- a. Joint venture
- b. Process agent

- c. Country of origin
- d. Business method patent

Guidance: level 1

:: ::

The _____ or just chief executive, is the most senior corporate, executive, or administrative officer in charge of managing an organization especially an independent legal entity such as a company or nonprofit institution. CEOs lead a range of organizations, including public and private corporations, non-profit organizations and even some government organizations. The CEO of a corporation or company typically reports to the board of directors and is charged with maximizing the value of the entity, which may include maximizing the share price, market share, revenues or another element. In the non-profit and government sector, CEOs typically aim at achieving outcomes related to the organization's mission, such as reducing poverty, increasing literacy, etc.

Exam Probability: **Medium**

53. *Answer choices:*

(see index for correct answer)

- a. functional perspective
- b. process perspective
- c. similarity-attraction theory
- d. Chief executive officer

Guidance: level 1

:: Commerce ::

_____ , also known as duty _____ is defined by the United States Customs and Border Protection as the refund of certain duties, internal and revenue taxes and certain fees collected upon the importation of goods. Such refunds are only allowed upon the exportation or destruction of goods under U.S. Customs and Border Protection supervision. Duty _____ is an export promotions program sanctioned by the World Trade Organization and allows the refund of certain duties taxes and fees paid upon importation which was established in 1789 in order to promote U.S. innovation and manufacturing across the global market.

Exam Probability: **Low**

54. *Answer choices:*

(see index for correct answer)

- a. Factory
- b. Drawback
- c. European Retail Round Table
- d. Agio

Guidance: level 1

:: ::

A _____ is a professional who provides expert advice in a particular area such as security, management, education, accountancy, law, human resources, marketing, finance, engineering, science or any of many other specialized fields.

Exam Probability: **Low**

55. *Answer choices:*

(see index for correct answer)

- a. cultural
- b. Consultant
- c. levels of analysis
- d. open system

Guidance: level 1

:: Commercial item transport and distribution ::

A _____ , forwarder, or forwarding agent, also known as a non-vessel operating common carrier , is a person or company that organizes shipments for individuals or corporations to get goods from the manufacturer or producer to a market, customer or final point of distribution. Forwarders contract with a carrier or often multiple carriers to move the goods. A forwarder does not move the goods but acts as an expert in the logistics network. These carriers can use a variety of shipping modes, including ships, airplanes, trucks, and railroads, and often do utilize multiple modes for a single shipment. For example, the _____ may arrange to have cargo moved from a plant to an airport by truck, flown to the destination city, then moved from the airport to a customer's building by another truck.

Exam Probability: **Low**

56. *Answer choices:*

(see index for correct answer)

- a. Freight forwarder
- b. Steam wagon
- c. Fulfillment house
- d. Refrigerator truck

Guidance: level 1

:: Basic financial concepts ::

_____ is a sustained increase in the general price level of goods and services in an economy over a period of time. When the general price level rises, each unit of currency buys fewer goods and services; consequently, _____ reflects a reduction in the purchasing power per unit of money a loss of real value in the medium of exchange and unit of account within the economy. The measure of _____ is the _____ rate, the annualized percentage change in a general price index, usually the consumer price index, over time. The opposite of _____ is deflation.

Exam Probability: **Low**

57. *Answer choices:*

(see index for correct answer)

- a. Lodgement
- b. Inflation
- c. Short interest
- d. Tax shield

Guidance: level 1

:: Management ::

Logistics is generally the detailed organization and implementation of a complex operation. In a general business sense, logistics is the management of the flow of things between the point of origin and the point of consumption in order to meet requirements of customers or corporations. The resources managed in logistics may include tangible goods such as materials, equipment, and supplies, as well as food and other consumable items. The logistics of physical items usually involves the integration of information flow, materials handling, production, packaging, inventory, transportation, warehousing, and often security.

Exam Probability: **Low**

58. *Answer choices:*

(see index for correct answer)

- a. Security management
- b. Board of governors
- c. Planning
- d. Logistics Management

Guidance: level 1

:: ::

_____ is an emotion involving pleasure, , or anxiety in considering or awaiting an expected event.

Exam Probability: **Medium**

59. *Answer choices:*

(see index for correct answer)

- a. process perspective
- b. co-culture
- c. Anticipation
- d. hierarchical

Guidance: level 1

Business ethics

Business ethics (also known as corporate ethics) is a form of applied ethics or professional ethics, that examines ethical principles and moral or ethical problems that can arise in a business environment. It applies to all aspects of business conduct and is relevant to the conduct of individuals and entire organizations. These ethics originate from individuals, organizational statements or from the legal system. These norms, values, ethical, and unethical practices are what is used to guide business. They help those businesses maintain a better connection with their stakeholders.

:: Competition regulators ::

The _____ is an independent agency of the United States government, established in 1914 by the _____ Act. Its principal mission is the promotion of consumer protection and the elimination and prevention of anticompetitive business practices, such as coercive monopoly. It is headquartered in the _____ Building in Washington, D.C.

Exam Probability: **High**

1. *Answer choices:*

(see index for correct answer)

- a. Federal Trade Commission
- b. Competition Commission of India
- c. Competition Bureau
- d. Fair Trade Commission

Guidance: level 1

:: ::

The _____ of 1906 was the first of a series of significant consumer protection laws which was enacted by Congress in the 20th century and led to the creation of the Food and Drug Administration. Its main purpose was to ban foreign and interstate traffic in adulterated or mislabeled food and drug products, and it directed the U.S. Bureau of Chemistry to inspect products and refer offenders to prosecutors. It required that active ingredients be placed on the label of a drug's packaging and that drugs could not fall below purity levels established by the United States Pharmacopeia or the National Formulary. The Jungle by Upton Sinclair with its graphic and revolting descriptions of unsanitary conditions and unscrupulous practices rampant in the meatpacking industry, was an inspirational piece that kept the public's attention on the important issue of unhygienic meat processing plants that later led to food inspection legislation. Sinclair quipped, "I aimed at the public's heart and by accident I hit it in the stomach," as outraged readers demanded and got the pure food law.

Exam Probability: **Medium**

2. *Answer choices:*

(see index for correct answer)

- a. personal values
- b. interpersonal communication
- c. cultural
- d. open system

Guidance: level 1

:: Social enterprise ::

Corporate social responsibility is a type of international private business self-regulation. While once it was possible to describe CSR as an internal organisational policy or a corporate ethic strategy, that time has passed as various international laws have been developed and various organisations have used their authority to push it beyond individual or even industry-wide initiatives. While it has been considered a form of corporate self-regulation for some time, over the last decade or so it has moved considerably from voluntary decisions at the level of individual organisations, to mandatory schemes at regional, national and even transnational levels.

Exam Probability: **High**

3. *Answer choices:*
(see index for correct answer)

- a. Social venture
- b. Social enterprise

Guidance: level 1

:: Dutch inventions ::

The Fairtrade certification initiative was created to form a new method for economic trade. This method takes an ethical standpoint, and considers the producers first.

Exam Probability: **Low**

4. Answer choices:

(see index for correct answer)

- a. Fairtrade
- b. Dijkstra's algorithm

Guidance: level 1

:: ::

A _____ is the ability to carry out a task with determined results often within a given amount of time, energy, or both. _____ s can often be divided into domain-general and domain-specific _____ s. For example, in the domain of work, some general _____ s would include time management, teamwork and leadership, self-motivation and others, whereas domain-specific _____ s would be used only for a certain job. _____ usually requires certain environmental stimuli and situations to assess the level of _____ being shown and used.

Exam Probability: **Medium**

5. Answer choices:

(see index for correct answer)

- a. Character
- b. personal values
- c. Sarbanes-Oxley act of 2002
- d. imperative

Guidance: level 1

:: ::

_____ is the introduction of contaminants into the natural environment that cause adverse change. _____ can take the form of chemical substances or energy, such as noise, heat or light. Pollutants, the components of _____ , can be either foreign substances/energies or naturally occurring contaminants. _____ is often classed as point source or nonpoint source _____ .In 2015, _____ killed 9 million people in the world.

Exam Probability: **Medium**

6. *Answer choices:*

(see index for correct answer)

- a. Sarbanes-Oxley act of 2002
- b. hierarchical perspective
- c. Pollution
- d. deep-level diversity

Guidance: level 1

:: Agricultural labor ::

The _____ of America, or more commonly just _____, is a labor union for farmworkers in the United States. It originated from the merger of two workers' rights organizations, the Agricultural Workers Organizing Committee led by organizer Larry Itliong, and the National Farm Workers Association led by César Chávez and Dolores Huerta. They became allied and transformed from workers' rights organizations into a union as a result of a series of strikes in 1965, when the mostly Filipino farmworkers of the AWOC in Delano, California initiated a grape strike, and the NFWA went on strike in support. As a result of the commonality in goals and methods, the NFWA and the AWOC formed the _____ Organizing Committee on August 22, 1966. This organization was accepted into the AFL-CIO in 1972 and changed its name to the _____ Union.

Exam Probability: **Low**

7. *Answer choices:*

(see index for correct answer)

- a. Kibbutz
- b. United Farm Workers
- c. Free tenant
- d. Rural tenancy

Guidance: level 1

:: Water law ::

The _____ is the primary federal law in the United States governing water pollution. Its objective is to restore and maintain the chemical, physical, and biological integrity of the nation's waters; recognizing the responsibilities of the states in addressing pollution and providing assistance to states to do so, including funding for publicly owned treatment works for the improvement of wastewater treatment; and maintaining the integrity of wetlands. It is one of the United States' first and most influential modern environmental laws. As with many other major U.S. federal environmental statutes, it is administered by the U.S. Environmental Protection Agency, in coordination with state governments. Its implementing regulations are codified at 40 C.F.R. Subchapters D, N, and O.

Exam Probability: **Medium**

8. *Answer choices:*

(see index for correct answer)

- a. Permanent water rights
- b. Clean Water Act
- c. Water quality law
- d. Water right

Guidance: level 1

:: Culture ::

_____ is a society which is characterized by individualism, which is the prioritization or emphasis, of the individual over the entire group. _____s are oriented around the self, being independent instead of identifying with a group mentality. They see each other as only loosely linked, and value personal goals over group interests. _____s tend to have a more diverse population and are characterized with emphasis on personal achievements, and a rational assessment of both the beneficial and detrimental aspects of relationships with others. _____s have such unique aspects of communication as being a low power-distance culture and having a low-context communication style. The United States, Australia, Great Britain, Canada, the Netherlands, and New Zealand have been identified as highly _____s.

Exam Probability: **High**

9. *Answer choices:*

(see index for correct answer)

- a. cultural framework
- b. Intracultural
- c. High-context
- d. Low-context

Guidance: level 1

:: Data management ::

_____ is a form of intellectual property that grants the creator of an original creative work an exclusive legal right to determine whether and under what conditions this original work may be copied and used by others, usually for a limited term of years. The exclusive rights are not absolute but limited by limitations and exceptions to _____ law, including fair use. A major limitation on _____ on ideas is that _____ protects only the original expression of ideas, and not the underlying ideas themselves.

Exam Probability: **High**

10. *Answer choices:*

(see index for correct answer)

- a. Data monetization
- b. Conference on Innovative Data Systems Research
- c. Long-running transaction
- d. Core Data

Guidance: level 1

:: Majority–minority relations ::

_____, also known as reservation in India and Nepal, positive discrimination / action in the United Kingdom, and employment equity in Canada and South Africa, is the policy of promoting the education and employment of members of groups that are known to have previously suffered from discrimination. Historically and internationally, support for _____ has sought to achieve goals such as bridging inequalities in employment and pay, increasing access to education, promoting diversity, and redressing apparent past wrongs, harms, or hindrances.

Exam Probability: **Low**

11. *Answer choices:*

(see index for correct answer)

- a. cultural dissonance
- b. positive discrimination
- c. Affirmative action

Guidance: level 1

:: Anti-competitive behaviour ::

_____ is a secret cooperation or deceitful agreement in order to deceive others, although not necessarily illegal, as a conspiracy. A secret agreement between two or more parties to limit open competition by deceiving, misleading, or defrauding others of their legal rights, or to obtain an objective forbidden by law typically by defrauding or gaining an unfair market advantage is an example of _____ . It is an agreement among firms or individuals to divide a market, set prices, limit production or limit opportunities. It can involve "unions, wage fixing, kickbacks, or misrepresenting the independence of the relationship between the colluding parties". In legal terms, all acts effected by _____ are considered void.

Exam Probability: **High**

12. *Answer choices:*

(see index for correct answer)

- a. Resale price maintenance
- b. Institute for Consumer Antitrust Studies
- c. Copperweld Corp. v. Independence Tube Corp.
- d. Killer bees

Guidance: level 1

:: ::

_____ generally refers to a focus on the needs or desires of one's self. A number of philosophical, psychological, and economic theories examine the role of _____ in motivating human action.

Exam Probability: **Low**

13. *Answer choices:*

(see index for correct answer)

- a. cultural
- b. Sarbanes-Oxley act of 2002
- c. Self-interest
- d. corporate values

Guidance: level 1

:: Industry ::

_____ is the manner in which a given entity has decided to address issues of energy development including energy production, distribution and consumption. The attributes of _____ may include legislation, international treaties, incentives to investment, guidelines for energy conservation, taxation and other public policy techniques. Energy is a core component of modern economies. A functioning economy requires not only labor and capital but also energy, for manufacturing processes, transportation, communication, agriculture, and more.

Exam Probability: **Low**

14. *Answer choices:*

(see index for correct answer)

- a. Chemical process
- b. Secondary sector of the economy
- c. Nostalgia industry
- d. Energy policy

Guidance: level 1

:: Labour relations ::

_____ is a field of study that can have different meanings depending on the context in which it is used. In an international context, it is a subfield of labor history that studies the human relations with regard to work – in its broadest sense – and how this connects to questions of social inequality. It explicitly encompasses unregulated, historical, and non-Western forms of labor. Here, _____ define "for or with whom one works and under what rules. These rules determine the type of work, type and amount of remuneration, working hours, degrees of physical and psychological strain, as well as the degree of freedom and autonomy associated with the work."

Exam Probability: **Medium**

15. *Answer choices:*

(see index for correct answer)

- a. Labor relations
- b. Global union federation
- c. Union shop
- d. Eurocadres

Guidance: level 1

:: Monopoly (economics) ::

The _____ of 1890 was a United States antitrust law that regulates competition among enterprises, which was passed by Congress under the presidency of Benjamin Harrison.

Exam Probability: **High**

16. *Answer choices:*

(see index for correct answer)

- a. History of monopoly
- b. Sherman Antitrust Act
- c. Concentration ratio
- d. Patent portfolio

Guidance: level 1

:: Fraud ::

In law, _____ is intentional deception to secure unfair or unlawful gain, or to deprive a victim of a legal right. _____ can violate civil law, a criminal law, or it may cause no loss of money, property or legal right but still be an element of another civil or criminal wrong. The purpose of _____ may be monetary gain or other benefits, for example by obtaining a passport, travel document, or driver's license, or mortgage _____, where the perpetrator may attempt to qualify for a mortgage by way of false statements.

Exam Probability: **Medium**

17. *Answer choices:*

(see index for correct answer)

- a. Subex
- b. Health care fraud
- c. Fraud
- d. Hitler Diaries

Guidance: level 1

:: Ethically disputed business practices ::

_____ is the trading of a public company's stock or other securities by individuals with access to nonpublic information about the company. In various countries, some kinds of trading based on insider information is illegal. This is because it is seen as unfair to other investors who do not have access to the information, as the investor with insider information could potentially make larger profits than a typical investor could make. The rules governing _____ are complex and vary significantly from country to country. The extent of enforcement also varies from one country to another. The definition of insider in one jurisdiction can be broad, and may cover not only insiders themselves but also any persons related to them, such as brokers, associates and even family members. A person who becomes aware of non-public information and trades on that basis may be guilty of a crime.

Exam Probability: **Low**

18. *Answer choices:*

(see index for correct answer)

- a. Suicide bidding
- b. Spamming
- c. Insider trading
- d. Copyright troll

Guidance: level 1

:: Financial regulatory authorities of the United States ::

The _____ is an agency of the United States government responsible for consumer protection in the financial sector. CFPB's jurisdiction includes banks, credit unions, securities firms, payday lenders, mortgage-servicing operations, foreclosure relief services, debt collectors and other financial companies operating in the United States.

Exam Probability: **Medium**

19. *Answer choices:*

(see index for correct answer)

- a. Securities Investor Protection Corporation
- b. Consumer Financial Protection Bureau
- c. Federal Deposit Insurance Corporation
- d. Farm Credit Administration

Guidance: level 1

:: Criminal law ::

_____ is the body of law that relates to crime. It proscribes conduct perceived as threatening, harmful, or otherwise endangering to the property, health, safety, and moral welfare of people inclusive of one's self. Most _____ is established by statute, which is to say that the laws are enacted by a legislature. _____ includes the punishment and rehabilitation of people who violate such laws. _____ varies according to jurisdiction, and differs from civil law, where emphasis is more on dispute resolution and victim compensation, rather than on punishment or rehabilitation. Criminal procedure is a formalized official activity that authenticates the fact of commission of a crime and authorizes punitive or rehabilitative treatment of the offender.

Exam Probability: **High**

20. *Answer choices:*

(see index for correct answer)

- a. Self-incrimination
- b. Criminal law
- c. Mala in se
- d. Mala prohibita

Guidance: level 1

:: ::

_____ is the practice of deliberately managing the spread of information between an individual or an organization and the public. _____ may include an organization or individual gaining exposure to their audiences using topics of public interest and news items that do not require direct payment. This differentiates it from advertising as a form of marketing communications. _____ is the idea of creating coverage for clients for free, rather than marketing or advertising. But now, advertising is also a part of greater PR Activities. An example of good _____ would be generating an article featuring a client, rather than paying for the client to be advertised next to the article. The aim of _____ is to inform the public, prospective customers, investors, partners, employees, and other stakeholders and ultimately persuade them to maintain a positive or favorable view about the organization, its leadership, products, or political decisions. _____ professionals typically work for PR and marketing firms, businesses and companies, government, and public officials as PIOs and nongovernmental organizations, and nonprofit organizations. Jobs central to _____ include account coordinator, account executive, account supervisor, and media relations manager.

Exam Probability: **Medium**

21. *Answer choices:*
(see index for correct answer)

- a. Public relations
- b. functional perspective
- c. co-culture
- d. imperative

Guidance: level 1

:: ::

Cannabis, also known as _____ among other names, is a psychoactive drug from the Cannabis plant used for medical or recreational purposes. The main psychoactive part of cannabis is tetrahydrocannabinol, one of 483 known compounds in the plant, including at least 65 other cannabinoids. Cannabis can be used by smoking, vaporizing, within food, or as an extract.

Exam Probability: **High**

22. *Answer choices:*

(see index for correct answer)

- a. Marijuana
- b. deep-level diversity
- c. co-culture
- d. functional perspective

Guidance: level 1

:: Writs ::

In common law, a writ of _____ is a writ whereby a private individual who assists a prosecution can receive all or part of any penalty imposed. Its name is an abbreviation of the Latin phrase _____ pro domino rege quam pro se ipso in hac parte sequitur, meaning "[he] who sues in this matter for the king as well as for himself."

Exam Probability: **Low**

23. *Answer choices:*

(see index for correct answer)

- a. Qui tam
- b. Writ of assistance

Guidance: level 1

:: Leadership ::

_____ is leadership that is directed by respect for ethical beliefs and values and for the dignity and rights of others. It is thus related to concepts such as trust, honesty, consideration, charisma, and fairness.

Exam Probability: **Medium**

24. *Answer choices:*

(see index for correct answer)

- a. Superleadership
- b. Evolutionary leadership theory
- c. Situational leadership
- d. Strategic leadership

Guidance: level 1

:: ::

_____ is the means to see, hear, or become aware of something or someone through our fundamental senses. The term _____ derives from the Latin word perceptio, and is the organization, identification, and interpretation of sensory information in order to represent and understand the presented information, or the environment.

Exam Probability: **High**

25. *Answer choices:*

(see index for correct answer)

- a. Perception
- b. process perspective
- c. corporate values
- d. deep-level diversity

Guidance: level 1

:: Minimum wage ::

A _____ is the lowest remuneration that employers can legally pay their workers—the price floor below which workers may not sell their labor. Most countries had introduced _____ legislation by the end of the 20th century.

Exam Probability: **Low**

26. *Answer choices:*

(see index for correct answer)

- a. Working poor
- b. Minimum Wage Fairness Act
- c. Guaranteed minimum income
- d. Minimum wage

Guidance: level 1

A _____ service is an online platform which people use to build social networks or social relationship with other people who share similar personal or career interests, activities, backgrounds or real-life connections.

Exam Probability: **Medium**

27. *Answer choices:*

(see index for correct answer)

- a. Social networking
- b. Sarbanes-Oxley act of 2002
- c. empathy
- d. information systems assessment

Guidance: level 1

:: ::

The Ethics & Compliance Initiative was formed in 2015 and consists of three nonprofit organizations: the Ethics Research Center, the Ethics & Compliance Association, and the Ethics & Compliance Certification Institute. Based in Arlington, Virginia, United States, ECI is devoted to the advancement of high ethical standards and practices in public and private institutions, and provides research about ethical standards, workplace integrity, and compliance practices and processes.

Exam Probability: **High**

28. *Answer choices:*

(see index for correct answer)

- a. Sarbanes-Oxley act of 2002
- b. Ethics Resource Center
- c. interpersonal communication
- d. hierarchical perspective

Guidance: level 1

:: Industrial ecology ::

_____ is a strategy for reducing the amount of waste created and released into the environment, particularly by industrial facilities, agriculture, or consumers. Many large corporations view P2 as a method of improving the efficiency and profitability of production processes by technology advancements. Legislative bodies have enacted P2 measures, such as the _____ Act of 1990 and the Clean Air Act Amendments of 1990 by the United States Congress.

Exam Probability: **Medium**

29. *Answer choices:*

(see index for correct answer)

- a. Eco-costs value ratio
- b. Thermoeconomics
- c. Pollution Prevention
- d. Kalundborg Eco-industrial Park

Guidance: level 1

_____ was a philosopher during the Classical period in Ancient Greece, the founder of the Lyceum and the Peripatetic school of philosophy and Aristotelian tradition. Along with his teacher Plato, he is considered the "Father of Western Philosophy". His writings cover many subjects – including physics, biology, zoology, metaphysics, logic, ethics, aesthetics, poetry, theatre, music, rhetoric, psychology, linguistics, economics, politics and government. _____ provided a complex synthesis of the various philosophies existing prior to him, and it was above all from his teachings that the West inherited its intellectual lexicon, as well as problems and methods of inquiry. As a result, his philosophy has exerted a unique influence on almost every form of knowledge in the West and it continues to be a subject of contemporary philosophical discussion.

Exam Probability: **Medium**

30. *Answer choices:*

(see index for correct answer)

- a. surface-level diversity
- b. levels of analysis
- c. imperative
- d. co-culture

Guidance: level 1

:: Business ethics ::

_____ is a type of harassment technique that relates to a sexual nature and the unwelcome or inappropriate promise of rewards in exchange for sexual favors. _____ includes a range of actions from mild transgressions to sexual abuse or assault. Harassment can occur in many different social settings such as the workplace, the home, school, churches, etc. Harassers or victims may be of any gender.

Exam Probability: **Low**

31. *Answer choices:*

(see index for correct answer)

- a. Moral hazard
- b. Fair value
- c. Sexual harassment
- d. Corporate Knights

Guidance: level 1

:: Natural gas ::

_____ is a naturally occurring hydrocarbon gas mixture consisting primarily of methane, but commonly including varying amounts of other higher alkanes, and sometimes a small percentage of carbon dioxide, nitrogen, hydrogen sulfide, or helium. It is formed when layers of decomposing plant and animal matter are exposed to intense heat and pressure under the surface of the Earth over millions of years. The energy that the plants originally obtained from the sun is stored in the form of chemical bonds in the gas.

Exam Probability: **Medium**

32. *Answer choices:*

(see index for correct answer)

- a. Sour gas
- b. Natural gas
- c. Petrochemistry
- d. Renewable natural gas

Guidance: level 1

:: ::

The American Recovery and Reinvestment Act of 2009, nicknamed the _____ , was a stimulus package enacted by the 111th U.S. Congress and signed into law by President Barack Obama in February 2009. Developed in response to the Great Recession, the ARRA's primary objective was to save existing jobs and create new ones as soon as possible. Other objectives were to provide temporary relief programs for those most affected by the recession and invest in infrastructure, education, health, and renewable energy.

Exam Probability: **Medium**

33. *Answer choices:*

(see index for correct answer)

- a. Sarbanes-Oxley act of 2002

- b. corporate values
- c. deep-level diversity
- d. Recovery Act

Guidance: level 1

:: International trade ::

_____ involves the transfer of goods or services from one person or entity to another, often in exchange for money. A system or network that allows _____ is called a market.

Exam Probability: **Medium**

34. *Answer choices:*

(see index for correct answer)

- a. Comparative advantage
- b. National Foreign Trade Council
- c. Kennedy Round
- d. Bill of lading

Guidance: level 1

:: ::

A _____ is an organization, usually a group of people or a company, authorized to act as a single entity and recognized as such in law. Early incorporated entities were established by charter. Most jurisdictions now allow the creation of new _____ s through registration.

Exam Probability: **Low**

35. *Answer choices:*

(see index for correct answer)

- a. hierarchical perspective
- b. interpersonal communication
- c. Corporation
- d. information systems assessment

Guidance: level 1

:: Progressive Era in the United States ::

The Clayton Antitrust Act of 1914, was a part of United States antitrust law with the goal of adding further substance to the U.S. antitrust law regime; the _____ sought to prevent anticompetitive practices in their incipiency. That regime started with the Sherman Antitrust Act of 1890, the first Federal law outlawing practices considered harmful to consumers. The _____ specified particular prohibited conduct, the three-level enforcement scheme, the exemptions, and the remedial measures.

Exam Probability: **Low**

36. *Answer choices:*

(see index for correct answer)

- a. Mann Act
- b. Clayton Antitrust Act
- c. Clayton Act

Guidance: level 1

:: Corporate crime ::

> _____ LLP, based in Chicago, was an American holding company. Formerly one of the "Big Five" accounting firms, the firm had provided auditing, tax, and consulting services to large corporations. By 2001, it had become one of the world's largest multinational companies.

Exam Probability: **High**

37. *Answer choices:*

(see index for correct answer)

- a. Arthur Andersen
- b. KPMG tax shelter fraud
- c. Walter Forbes
- d. State-corporate crime

Guidance: level 1

:: ::

A _____ is a problem offering two possibilities, neither of which is unambiguously acceptable or preferable. The possibilities are termed the horns of the _____, a clichéd usage, but distinguishing the _____ from other kinds of predicament as a matter of usage.

Exam Probability: **Medium**

38. *Answer choices:*

(see index for correct answer)

- a. process perspective
- b. personal values
- c. information systems assessment
- d. Dilemma

Guidance: level 1

:: Human resource management ::

_____ is the ethics of an organization, and it is how an organization responds to an internal or external stimulus. _____ is interdependent with the organizational culture. Although it is akin to both organizational behavior and industrial and organizational psychology as well as business ethics on the micro and macro levels, _____ is neither OB or I/O psychology, nor is it solely business ethics. _____ express the values of an organization to its employees and/or other entities irrespective of governmental and/or regulatory laws.

Exam Probability: **High**

39. *Answer choices:*

(see index for correct answer)

- a. Multiculturalism
- b. TPI-theory
- c. ABC Consultants
- d. Restructuring

Guidance: level 1

:: United States federal labor legislation ::

The _____ of 1988 is a United States federal law that generally prevents employers from using polygraph tests, either for pre-employment screening or during the course of employment, with certain exemptions.

Exam Probability: **Low**

40. *Answer choices:*

(see index for correct answer)

- a. Civil Rights Act of 1964
- b. Federal Employers Liability Act
- c. Erdman Act
- d. Employee Polygraph Protection Act

Guidance: level 1

:: ::

_____ is a cognitive process that elicits emotion and rational associations based on an individual's moral philosophy or value system. _____ stands in contrast to elicited emotion or thought due to associations based on immediate sensory perceptions and reflexive responses, as in sympathetic central nervous system responses. In common terms, _____ is often described as leading to feelings of remorse when a person commits an act that conflicts with their moral values. An individual's moral values and their dissonance with familial, social, cultural and historical interpretations of moral philosophy are considered in the examination of cultural relativity in both the practice and study of psychology. The extent to which _____ informs moral judgment before an action and whether such moral judgments are or should be based on reason has occasioned debate through much of modern history between theories of modern western philosophy in juxtaposition to the theories of romanticism and other reactionary movements after the end of the Middle Ages.

Exam Probability: **Medium**

41. *Answer choices:*

(see index for correct answer)

- a. surface-level diversity
- b. corporate values
- c. Sarbanes-Oxley act of 2002
- d. Conscience

Guidance: level 1

:: Commercial crimes ::

_____ is an agreement between participants on the same side in a market to buy or sell a product, service, or commodity only at a fixed price, or maintain the market conditions such that the price is maintained at a given level by controlling supply and demand.

Exam Probability: **Low**

42. *Answer choices:*

(see index for correct answer)

- a. Monopolization
- b. Cheque fraud
- c. Price fixing
- d. Embezzlement

Guidance: level 1

:: Organizational structure ::

An _____ defines how activities such as task allocation, coordination, and supervision are directed toward the achievement of organizational aims.

Exam Probability: **Medium**

43. *Answer choices:*

(see index for correct answer)

- a. Unorganisation
- b. Organization of the New York City Police Department
- c. Blessed Unrest
- d. Organizational structure

Guidance: level 1

:: Mortgage ::

In finance, _____ means making loans to people who may have difficulty maintaining the repayment schedule, sometimes reflecting setbacks, such as unemployment, divorce, medical emergencies, etc. Historically, subprime borrowers were defined as having FICO scores below 600, although "this has varied over time and circumstances."

Exam Probability: **High**

44. *Answer choices:*

(see index for correct answer)

- a. Subprime lending
- b. Mortgage equity withdrawal
- c. Primary servicer
- d. Repayment mortgage

Guidance: level 1

:: Environmental economics ::

____ is an institutional arrangement designed to help producers in developing countries achieve better trading conditions. Members of the ____ movement advocate the payment of higher prices to exporters, as well as improved social and environmental standards. The movement focuses in particular on commodities, or products which are typically exported from developing countries to developed countries, but also consumed in domestic markets most notably handicrafts, coffee, cocoa, wine, sugar, fresh fruit, chocolate, flowers and gold. The movement seeks to promote greater equity in international trading partnerships through dialogue, transparency, and respect. It promotes sustainable development by offering better trading conditions to, and securing the rights of, marginalized producers and workers in developing countries. ____ is grounded in three core beliefs; first, producers have the power to express unity with consumers. Secondly, the world trade practices that currently exist promote the unequal distribution of wealth between nations. Lastly, buying products from producers in developing countries at a fair price is a more efficient way of promoting sustainable development than traditional charity and aid.

Exam Probability: **Medium**

45. *Answer choices:*

(see index for correct answer)

- a. Resource intensity
- b. Fair trade
- c. RSEE
- d. Space Competitiveness Index

Guidance: level 1

:: Power (social and political) ::

_____ is a form of reverence gained by a leader who has strong interpersonal relationship skills. _____, as an aspect of personal power, becomes particularly important as organizational leadership becomes increasingly about collaboration and influence, rather than command and control.

Exam Probability: **Medium**

46. *Answer choices:*

(see index for correct answer)

- a. need for power
- b. Expert power
- c. Referent power

Guidance: level 1

:: Law ::

_____ is a body of law which defines the role, powers, and structure of different entities within a state, namely, the executive, the parliament or legislature, and the judiciary; as well as the basic rights of citizens and, in federal countries such as the United States and Canada, the relationship between the central government and state, provincial, or territorial governments.

Exam Probability: **Medium**

47. *Answer choices:*

(see index for correct answer)

- a. Comparative law
- b. Legal case

Guidance: level 1

:: Minimum wage ::

The _____ are working people whose incomes fall below a given poverty line due to lack of work hours and/or low wages. Largely because they are earning such low wages, the _____ face numerous obstacles that make it difficult for many of them to find and keep a job, save up money, and maintain a sense of self-worth.

Exam Probability: **High**

48. *Answer choices:*

(see index for correct answer)

- a. Minimum wage in Taiwan
- b. Working poor
- c. National Anti-Sweating League
- d. Minimum Wage Fairness Act

Guidance: level 1

:: ::

_____ in the United States is a federal and state program that helps with medical costs for some people with limited income and resources. _____ also offers benefits not normally covered by Medicare, including nursing home care and personal care services. The Health Insurance Association of America describes _____ as "a government insurance program for persons of all ages whose income and resources are insufficient to pay for health care." _____ is the largest source of funding for medical and health-related services for people with low income in the United States, providing free health insurance to 74 million low-income and disabled people as of 2017. It is a means-tested program that is jointly funded by the state and federal governments and managed by the states, with each state currently having broad leeway to determine who is eligible for its implementation of the program. States are not required to participate in the program, although all have since 1982. _____ recipients must be U.S. citizens or qualified non-citizens, and may include low-income adults, their children, and people with certain disabilities. Poverty alone does not necessarily qualify someone for _____ .

Exam Probability: **High**

49. *Answer choices:*

(see index for correct answer)

- a. functional perspective
- b. Character
- c. Medicaid
- d. deep-level diversity

Guidance: level 1

:: Pyramid and Ponzi schemes ::

_____ was an Italian swindler and con artist in the U.S. and Canada. His aliases include Charles Ponci, Carlo, and Charles P. Bianchi. Born and raised in Italy, he became known in the early 1920s as a swindler in North America for his money-making scheme. He promised clients a 50% profit within 45 days or 100% profit within 90 days, by buying discounted postal reply coupons in other countries and redeeming them at face value in the United States as a form of arbitrage. In reality, Ponzi was paying earlier investors using the investments of later investors. While this type of fraudulent investment scheme was not originally invented by Ponzi, it became so identified with him that it now is referred to as a "Ponzi scheme". His scheme ran for over a year before it collapsed, costing his "investors" $20 million.

Exam Probability: **Medium**

50. *Answer choices:*

(see index for correct answer)

- a. Donald Anthony Walker Young
- b. Young Living
- c. Earl Jones
- d. Stanley Chais

Guidance: level 1

:: Corporate scandals ::

Exxon Mobil Corporation, doing business as _____ , is an American multinational oil and gas corporation headquartered in Irving, Texas. It is the largest direct descendant of John D. Rockefeller's Standard Oil Company, and was formed on November 30, 1999 by the merger of Exxon and Mobil. _____ 's primary brands are Exxon, Mobil, Esso, and _____ Chemical.

Exam Probability: **High**

51. *Answer choices:*

(see index for correct answer)

- a. Carrian Group
- b. ExxonMobil
- c. Aluminium price-fixing conspiracy
- d. Pro Arts

Guidance: level 1

:: ::

The _____ is an American stock exchange located at 11 Wall Street, Lower Manhattan, New York City, New York. It is by far the world's largest stock exchange by market capitalization of its listed companies at US$30.1 trillion as of February 2018. The average daily trading value was approximately US$169 billion in 2013. The NYSE trading floor is located at 11 Wall Street and is composed of 21 rooms used for the facilitation of trading. A fifth trading room, located at 30 Broad Street, was closed in February 2007. The main building and the 11 Wall Street building were designated National Historic Landmarks in 1978.

Exam Probability: **Low**

52. *Answer choices:*

(see index for correct answer)

- a. levels of analysis
- b. imperative
- c. New York Stock Exchange
- d. open system

Guidance: level 1

:: ::

_____ is a region of India consisting of the Indian states of Bihar, Jharkhand, West Bengal, Odisha and also the union territory Andaman and Nicobar Islands. West Bengal's capital Kolkata is the largest city of this region. The Kolkata Metropolitan Area is the country's third largest.

Exam Probability: **Medium**

53. *Answer choices:*

(see index for correct answer)

- a. hierarchical perspective
- b. East India
- c. open system

- d. empathy

Guidance: level 1

:: ::

The _____ Group is a global financial investment management and insurance company headquartered in Des Moines, Iowa.

Exam Probability: **Medium**

54. *Answer choices:*

(see index for correct answer)

- a. Character
- b. empathy
- c. Principal Financial
- d. deep-level diversity

Guidance: level 1

:: Social philosophy ::

The _____ describes the unintended social benefits of an individual's self-interested actions. Adam Smith first introduced the concept in The Theory of Moral Sentiments, written in 1759, invoking it in reference to income distribution. In this work, however, the idea of the market is not discussed, and the word "capitalism" is never used.

Exam Probability: **Low**

55. *Answer choices:*

(see index for correct answer)

- a. Freedom to contract
- b. Societal attitudes towards abortion
- c. Invisible hand
- d. vacancy chain

Guidance: level 1

:: Timber industry ::

The _____ is an international non-profit, multi-stakeholder organization established in 1993 to promote responsible management of the world's forests. The FSC does this by setting standards on forest products, along with certifying and labeling them as eco-friendly.

Exam Probability: **High**

56. *Answer choices:*

(see index for correct answer)

- a. West Coast lumber trade
- b. Forest Stewardship Council
- c. Q-pit
- d. British timber trade

Guidance: level 1

:: Renewable energy ::

_____ is the conversion of energy from sunlight into electricity, either directly using photovoltaics, indirectly using concentrated _____, or a combination. Concentrated _____ systems use lenses or mirrors and tracking systems to focus a large area of sunlight into a small beam. Photovoltaic cells convert light into an electric current using the photovoltaic effect.

Exam Probability: **Medium**

57. *Answer choices:*

(see index for correct answer)

- a. Variable renewable energy
- b. Solar power
- c. Biomass Energy Centre
- d. Solar water heating

Guidance: level 1

:: Market-based policy instruments ::

> Cause marketing is defined as a type of corporate social responsibility, in which a company's promotional campaign has the dual purpose of increasing profitability while bettering society.

Exam Probability: **Medium**

58. *Answer choices:*

(see index for correct answer)

- a. Regional Clean Air Incentives Market
- b. Feebate
- c. Tax on trees
- d. Cause-related marketing

Guidance: level 1

:: Social responsibility ::

The United Nations Global Compact is a non-binding United Nations pact to encourage businesses worldwide to adopt sustainable and socially responsible policies, and to report on their implementation. The _____ is a principle-based framework for businesses, stating ten principles in the areas of human rights, labor, the environment and anti-corruption. Under the Global Compact, companies are brought together with UN agencies, labor groups and civil society. Cities can join the Global Compact through the Cities Programme.

Exam Probability: **High**

59. *Answer choices:*

(see index for correct answer)

- a. Enterprise 2020
- b. Stanley A. Deetz
- c. Collective impact
- d. Clann Credo

Guidance: level 1

Accounting

Accounting or accountancy is the measurement, processing, and communication of financial information about economic entities such as businesses and corporations. The modern field was established by the Italian mathematician Luca Pacioli in 1494. Accounting, which has been called the "language of business", measures the results of an organization's economic activities and conveys this information to a variety of users, including investors, creditors, management, and regulators.

:: SEC filings ::

_____ is a prescribed regulation under the US Securities Act of 1933 that lays out reporting requirements for various SEC filings used by public companies. Companies are also often called issuers , filers or registrants .

Exam Probability: **High**

1. *Answer choices:*

(see index for correct answer)

- a. Form S-4
- b. Schedule TO
- c. Schedule 13D
- d. Regulation S-K

Guidance: level 1

:: ::

Generally speaking, a _____ begins on the New Year's Day of the given calendar system and ends on the day before the following New Year's Day, and thus consists of a whole number of days. A year can also be measured by starting on any other named day of the calendar, and ending on the day before this named day in the following year. This may be termed a "year's time", but not a " _____ ". To reconcile the _____ with the astronomical cycle certain years contain extra days .

Exam Probability: **Medium**

2. *Answer choices:*

(see index for correct answer)

- a. hierarchical
- b. open system
- c. corporate values
- d. Calendar year

Guidance: level 1

:: Financial accounting ::

_____ refers to any one of several methods by which a company, for `financial accounting` or tax purposes, depreciates a fixed asset in such a way that the amount of depreciation taken each year is higher during the earlier years of an asset's life. For financial accounting purposes, _____ is expected to be much more productive during its early years, so that depreciation expense will more accurately represent how much of an asset's usefulness is being used up each year. For tax purposes, _____ provides a way of deferring corporate income taxes by reducing taxable income in current years, in exchange for increased taxable income in future years. This is a valuable tax incentive that encourages businesses to purchase new assets.

Exam Probability: **High**

3. *Answer choices:*

(see index for correct answer)

- a. Authorised capital

- b. Certified Public Accountants Association
- c. Exit rate
- d. Hidden asset

Guidance: level 1

:: ::

A _____ is a tax paid to a governing body for the sales of certain goods and services. Usually laws allow the seller to collect funds for the tax from the consumer at the point of purchase. When a tax on goods or services is paid to a governing body directly by a consumer, it is usually called a use tax. Often laws provide for the exemption of certain goods or services from sales and use tax.

Exam Probability: **Low**

4. *Answer choices:*

(see index for correct answer)

- a. process perspective
- b. Sarbanes-Oxley act of 2002
- c. levels of analysis
- d. personal values

Guidance: level 1

:: Accounting in the United States ::

The _____ is a private-sector, nonprofit corporation created by the Sarbanes–Oxley Act of 2002 to oversee the audits of public companies and other issuers in order to protect the interests of investors and further the public interest in the preparation of informative, accurate and independent audit reports. The PCAOB also oversees the audits of broker-dealers, including compliance reports filed pursuant to federal securities laws, to promote investor protection. All PCAOB rules and standards must be approved by the U.S. Securities and Exchange Commission.

Exam Probability: **Medium**

5. *Answer choices:*
(see index for correct answer)

- a. Public Company Accounting Oversight Board
- b. Uniform Certified Public Accountant Examination
- c. Comprehensive Performance Assessment
- d. Financial Accounting Foundation

Guidance: level 1

:: ::

The U.S. _____ is an independent agency of the United States federal government. The SEC holds primary responsibility for enforcing the federal securities laws, proposing securities rules, and regulating the securities industry, the nation's stock and options exchanges, and other activities and organizations, including the electronic securities markets in the United States.

Exam Probability: **Low**

6. *Answer choices:*

(see index for correct answer)

- a. interpersonal communication
- b. Securities and Exchange Commission
- c. surface-level diversity
- d. similarity-attraction theory

Guidance: level 1

:: Accounting in the United States ::

_____ refers to a Memorandum of Understanding signed in September 2002 between the Financial Accounting Standards Board , the US standard setter, and the International Accounting Standards Board . The agreement is so called as it was reached in Norwalk.

Exam Probability: **High**

7. Answer choices:

(see index for correct answer)

- a. Norwalk Agreement
- b. International Qualification Examination
- c. National Association of State Boards of Accountancy
- d. Accounting Today

Guidance: level 1

:: Financial statements ::

> A Statement of changes in equity and similarly the statement of changes in owner's equity for a sole trader, statement of changes in partners' equity for a partnership, statement of changes in Shareholders' equity for a Company or statement of changes in Taxpayers' equity for Government financial statements is one of the four basic financial statements.

Exam Probability: **High**

8. Answer choices:

(see index for correct answer)

- a. Government financial statements
- b. Statements on auditing standards
- c. Clean surplus accounting
- d. Emphasis of matter

Guidance: level 1

:: ::

_____ science is the application of science to criminal and civil laws, mainly—on the criminal side—during criminal investigation, as governed by the legal standards of admissible evidence and criminal procedure.

Exam Probability: **High**

9. *Answer choices:*

(see index for correct answer)

- a. Sarbanes-Oxley act of 2002
- b. personal values
- c. hierarchical perspective
- d. Character

Guidance: level 1

:: Types of accounting ::

Various _____ systems are used by various public sector entities. In the United States, for instance, there are two levels of government which follow different accounting standards set forth by independent, private sector boards. At the federal level, the Federal Accounting Standards Advisory Board sets forth the accounting standards to follow. Similarly, there is the _____ Standards Board for state and local level government.

Exam Probability: **High**

10. *Answer choices:*

(see index for correct answer)

- a. Personal environmental impact accounting
- b. Sustainability accounting
- c. Governmental accounting

Guidance: level 1

:: Financial ratios ::

The _____ or dividend-price ratio of a share is the dividend per share, divided by the price per share. It is also a company's total annual dividend payments divided by its market capitalization, assuming the number of shares is constant. It is often expressed as a percentage.

Exam Probability: **Low**

11. *Answer choices:*

(see index for correct answer)

- a. PB ratio
- b. Dividend yield
- c. Market-to-book
- d. Information ratio

Guidance: level 1

:: Generally Accepted Accounting Principles ::

> The _____ principle is a cornerstone of accrual accounting together with the matching principle. They both determine the accounting period in which revenues and expenses are recognized. According to the principle, revenues are recognized when they are realized or realizable, and are earned, no matter when cash is received. In cash accounting – in contrast – revenues are recognized when cash is received no matter when goods or services are sold.

Exam Probability: **Medium**

12. *Answer choices:*

(see index for correct answer)

- a. net realisable value
- b. Petty cash
- c. Revenue recognition
- d. Gross profit

Guidance: level 1

:: Basic financial concepts ::

In finance, maturity or _____ refers to the final payment date of a loan or other financial instrument, at which point the principal is due to be paid.

Exam Probability: **Medium**

13. *Answer choices:*

(see index for correct answer)

- a. Maturity date
- b. Forward guidance
- c. Tax shield
- d. Leverage cycle

Guidance: level 1

:: Generally Accepted Accounting Principles ::

The first published description of the process is found in Luca Pacioli's 1494 work Summa de arithmetica, in the section titled Particularis de Computis et Scripturis. Although he did not use the term, he essentially prescribed a technique similar to a post-closing _____ .

Exam Probability: **High**

14. *Answer choices:*

(see index for correct answer)

- a. Fin 48
- b. Trial balance
- c. Cost principle
- d. Treasury stock

Guidance: level 1

:: Actuarial science ::

The _____ is the greater benefit of receiving money now rather than an identical sum later. It is founded on time preference.

Exam Probability: **High**

15. *Answer choices:*

(see index for correct answer)

- a. Actuarial notation
- b. Medical underwriting
- c. Catastrophe modeling
- d. Force of mortality

Guidance: level 1

:: ::

_____ , also known as internet banking, is an electronic payment system that enables customers of a bank or other financial institution to conduct a range of financial transactions through the financial institution's website. The _____ system will typically connect to or be part of the core banking system operated by a bank and is in contrast to branch banking which was the traditional way customers accessed banking services.

Exam Probability: **High**

16. *Answer choices:*

(see index for correct answer)

- a. Online banking
- b. Character
- c. cultural
- d. interpersonal communication

Guidance: level 1

:: International Financial Reporting Standards ::

_____, usually called IFRS, are standards issued by the IFRS Foundation and the International Accounting Standards Board to provide a common global language for business affairs so that company accounts are understandable and comparable across international boundaries. They are a consequence of growing international shareholding and trade and are particularly important for companies that have dealings in several countries. They are progressively replacing the many different national accounting standards. They are the rules to be followed by accountants to maintain books of accounts which are comparable, understandable, reliable and relevant as per the users internal or external. IFRS, with the exception of IAS 29 Financial Reporting in Hyperinflationary Economies and IFRIC 7 Applying the Restatement Approach under IAS 29, are authorized in terms of the historical cost paradigm. IAS 29 and IFRIC 7 are authorized in terms of the units of constant purchasing power paradigm.IAS 2 is related to inventories in this standard we talk about the stock its production process etcIFRS began as an attempt to harmonize accounting across the European Union but the value of harmonization quickly made the concept attractive around the world. However, it has been debated whether or not de facto harmonization has occurred. Standards that were issued by IASC are still within use today and go by the name International Accounting Standards , while standards issued by IASB are called IFRS. IAS were issued between 1973 and 2001 by the Board of the International Accounting Standards Committee . On 1 April 2001, the new International Accounting Standards Board took over from the IASC the responsibility for setting International Accounting Standards. During its first meeting the new Board adopted existing IAS and Standing Interpretations Committee standards . The IASB has continued to develop standards calling the new standards " _____ ".

Exam Probability: **High**

17. *Answer choices:*

(see index for correct answer)

- a. IAS 16

- b. IAS 7
- c. International Public Sector Accounting Standards
- d. International Financial Reporting Standards

Guidance: level 1

:: Management accounting ::

_____ is the process of reviewing and analyzing a company's financial statements to make better economic decisions to earn income in future. These statements include the income statement, balance sheet, statement of cash flows, notes to accounts and a statement of changes in equity . _____ is a method or process involving specific techniques for evaluating risks, performance, financial health, and future prospects of an organization.

Exam Probability: **Medium**

18. *Answer choices:*

(see index for correct answer)

- a. Factory overhead
- b. Pre-determined overhead rate
- c. Construction accounting
- d. Notional profit

Guidance: level 1

:: Financial regulatory authorities of the United States ::

The _____ is the revenue service of the United States federal government. The government agency is a bureau of the Department of the Treasury, and is under the immediate direction of the Commissioner of Internal Revenue, who is appointed to a five-year term by the President of the United States. The IRS is responsible for collecting taxes and administering the Internal Revenue Code, the main body of federal statutory tax law of the United States. The duties of the IRS include providing tax assistance to taxpayers and pursuing and resolving instances of erroneous or fraudulent tax filings. The IRS has also overseen various benefits programs, and enforces portions of the Affordable Care Act.

Exam Probability: **High**

19. *Answer choices:*
(see index for correct answer)

- a. National Credit Union Administration
- b. Internal Revenue Service
- c. National Futures Association
- d. Consumer Financial Protection Bureau

Guidance: level 1

:: Budgets ::

A _____ is a financial plan for a defined period, often one year. It may also include planned sales volumes and revenues, resource quantities, costs and expenses, assets, liabilities and cash flows. Companies, governments, families and other organizations use it to express strategic plans of activities or events in measurable terms.

Exam Probability: **High**

20. *Answer choices:*

(see index for correct answer)

- a. Budget
- b. Performance-based budgeting
- c. Envelope system
- d. Budgeted cost of work scheduled

Guidance: level 1

:: Banking ::

A _____ is a financial institution that accepts deposits from the public and creates credit. Lending activities can be performed either directly or indirectly through capital markets. Due to their importance in the financial stability of a country, _____ s are highly regulated in most countries. Most nations have institutionalized a system known as fractional reserve _____ ing under which _____ s hold liquid assets equal to only a portion of their current liabilities. In addition to other regulations intended to ensure liquidity, _____ s are generally subject to minimum capital requirements based on an international set of capital standards, known as the Basel Accords.

Exam Probability: **High**

21. *Answer choices:*

(see index for correct answer)

- a. Excess reserves
- b. Soft probe
- c. Bank
- d. International Bank of Azerbaijan-Georgia

Guidance: level 1

:: Stock market ::

_____ is a form of stock which may have any combination of features not possessed by common stock including properties of both an equity and a debt instrument, and is generally considered a hybrid instrument. _____ s are senior to common stock, but subordinate to bonds in terms of claim and may have priority over common stock in the payment of dividends and upon liquidation. Terms of the _____ are described in the issuing company's articles of association or articles of incorporation.

Exam Probability: **High**

22. *Answer choices:*

(see index for correct answer)

- a. Relative valuation
- b. Preferred stock
- c. NorCom
- d. Super-majority amendment

Guidance: level 1

:: Inventory ::

Costs are associated with particular goods using one of the several formulas, including specific identification, first-in first-out, or average cost. Costs include all costs of purchase, costs of conversion and other costs that are incurred in bringing the inventories to their present location and condition. Costs of goods made by the businesses include material, labor, and allocated overhead. The costs of those goods which are not yet sold are deferred as costs of inventory until the inventory is sold or written down in value.

Exam Probability: **Medium**

23. *Answer choices:*

(see index for correct answer)

- a. Order fulfillment
- b. Phantom inventory
- c. Stock control
- d. Cost of goods sold

Guidance: level 1

:: Generally Accepted Accounting Principles ::

The term _____ is most often used to describe a practice or document that is provided as a courtesy or satisfies minimum requirements, conforms to a norm or doctrine, tends to be performed perfunctorily or is considered a formality.

Exam Probability: **Low**

24. *Answer choices:*

(see index for correct answer)

- a. Paid in capital
- b. Revenue recognition
- c. Liability

- d. Pro forma

Guidance: level 1

:: Legal terms ::

_____ or _____ interest, in law, is anything that functions contrary to a party`s interest. This word should not be confused with averse.

Exam Probability: **High**

25. *Answer choices:*
(see index for correct answer)

- a. Adverse
- b. Factual basis
- c. Adverse party
- d. Empty chair

Guidance: level 1

:: Management accounting ::

A _____ is a cost that differs between alternatives being considered. In order for a cost to be a _____ it must be.

Exam Probability: **Low**

26. *Answer choices:*

(see index for correct answer)

- a. Relevant cost
- b. Management control system
- c. Spend management
- d. Extended cost

Guidance: level 1

:: Fraud ::

In law, _____ is intentional deception to secure unfair or unlawful gain, or to deprive a victim of a legal right. _____ can violate civil law, a criminal law, or it may cause no loss of money, property or legal right but still be an element of another civil or criminal wrong. The purpose of _____ may be monetary gain or other benefits, for example by obtaining a passport, travel document, or driver's license, or mortgage _____, where the perpetrator may attempt to qualify for a mortgage by way of false statements.

Exam Probability: **Low**

27. *Answer choices:*

(see index for correct answer)

- a. Fraud
- b. Wine fraud
- c. Regummed stamp
- d. Workers Resistance

Guidance: level 1

:: United States Generally Accepted Accounting Principles ::

In a companies' financial reporting, _____ "includes all changes in equity during a period except those resulting from investments by owners and distributions to owners". Because that use excludes the effects of changing ownership interest, an economic measure of _____ is necessary for financial analysis from the shareholders' point of view

Exam Probability: **Low**

28. *Answer choices:*

(see index for correct answer)

- a. Available for sale
- b. Impaired asset
- c. FIN 46
- d. Comprehensive income

Guidance: level 1

:: Management accounting ::

The _____ is a professional membership organization headquartered in Montvale, New Jersey, United States, operating in four global regions: The Americas, Asia/Pacific, Europe, and Middle East/India.

Exam Probability: **Low**

29. *Answer choices:*

(see index for correct answer)

- a. Variance
- b. Notional profit
- c. Institute of Management Accountants
- d. Management control system

Guidance: level 1

:: Valuation (finance) ::

The _____ is one of three major groups of methodologies, called valuation approaches, used by appraisers. It is particularly common in commercial real estate appraisal and in business appraisal. The fundamental math is similar to the methods used for financial valuation, securities analysis, or bond pricing. However, there are some significant and important modifications when used in real estate or business valuation.

Exam Probability: **High**

30. *Answer choices:*

(see index for correct answer)

- a. Income approach
- b. Diminution in value
- c. Accretion/dilution analysis
- d. International Valuation Standards Council

Guidance: level 1

:: Pricing ::

_____ is the difference between a lower selling price and a higher purchase price, resulting in a financial loss for the seller.

Exam Probability: **High**

31. *Answer choices:*

(see index for correct answer)

- a. Express pricing
- b. Capital loss
- c. Base period price
- d. Rational pricing

Guidance: level 1

:: Financial ratios ::

A _____ or accounting ratio is a relative magnitude of two selected numerical values taken from an enterprise's financial statements. Often used in accounting, there are many standard ratios used to try to evaluate the overall financial condition of a corporation or other organization. _____ s may be used by managers within a firm, by current and potential shareholders of a firm, and by a firm's creditors. Financial analysts use _____ s to compare the strengths and weaknesses in various companies. If shares in a company are traded in a financial market, the market price of the shares is used in certain _____ s.

Exam Probability: **Medium**

32. *Answer choices:*

(see index for correct answer)

- a. Average collection period
- b. Cash flow return on investment
- c. Debt-to-income ratio

- d. Debt-to-GDP ratio

Guidance: level 1

:: Legal terms ::

An _____ is an action which is inaccurate or incorrect. In some usages, an _____ is synonymous with a mistake. In statistics, "_____" refers to the difference between the value which has been computed and the correct value. An _____ could result in failure or in a deviation from the intended performance or behaviour.

Exam Probability: **Low**

33. *Answer choices:*
(see index for correct answer)

- a. Antragsdelikt
- b. Excuse
- c. Cross-examination
- d. Error

Guidance: level 1

:: Generally Accepted Accounting Principles ::

An _____ or profit and loss account is one of the financial statements of a company and shows the company's revenues and expenses during a particular period.

Exam Probability: **High**

34. *Answer choices:*

(see index for correct answer)

- a. Chinese accounting standards
- b. Depreciation
- c. Deferral
- d. Net profit

Guidance: level 1

:: Inventory ::

_____ is the amount of inventory a company has in stock at the end of its fiscal year. It is closely related with _____ cost, which is the amount of money spent to get these goods in stock. It should be calculated at the lower of cost or market.

Exam Probability: **High**

35. *Answer choices:*

(see index for correct answer)

- a. Stock obsolescence
- b. Ending inventory
- c. Average cost method
- d. Stock control

Guidance: level 1

:: International accounting organizations ::

The _____ is the global organization for the accountancy profession. Founded in 1977, IFAC has more than 175 members and associates in more than 130 countries and jurisdictions, representing nearly 3 million accountants employed in public practice, industry and commerce, government, and academe. The organization supports the development, adoption and implementation of international standards for accounting education, ethics, and the public sector as well as audit and assurance. It supports four independent standard-setting boards, which establish international standards on ethics, auditing and assurance, accounting education, and public sector accounting. It also issues guidance to encourage high quality performance by professional accountants in business and small and medium accounting practices.

Exam Probability: **Medium**

36. *Answer choices:*
(see index for correct answer)

- a. Confederation of Asian and Pacific Accountants
- b. International Federation of Accountants

- c. International Auditing and Assurance Standards Board
- d. International Accounting Education Standards Board

Guidance: level 1

:: ::

In the field of analysis of algorithms in computer science, the _____ is a method of amortized analysis based on accounting. The _____ often gives a more intuitive account of the amortized cost of an operation than either aggregate analysis or the potential method. Note, however, that this does not guarantee such analysis will be immediately obvious; often, choosing the correct parameters for the _____ requires as much knowledge of the problem and the complexity bounds one is attempting to prove as the other two methods.

Exam Probability: **High**

37. *Answer choices:*

(see index for correct answer)

- a. surface-level diversity
- b. Accounting method
- c. co-culture
- d. personal values

Guidance: level 1

:: Management accounting ::

_____ are costs that are not directly accountable to a cost object. _____ may be either fixed or variable. _____ include administration, personnel and security costs. These are those costs which are not directly related to production. Some _____ may be overhead. But some overhead costs can be directly attributed to a project and are direct costs.

Exam Probability: **High**

38. *Answer choices:*

(see index for correct answer)

- a. Environmental full-cost accounting
- b. Indirect costs
- c. Operating profit margin
- d. Corporate travel management

Guidance: level 1

:: Business ::

The seller, or the provider of the goods or services, completes a sale in response to an acquisition, appropriation, requisition or a direct interaction with the buyer at the point of sale. There is a passing of title of the item, and the settlement of a price, in which agreement is reached on a price for which transfer of ownership of the item will occur. The seller, not the purchaser typically executes the sale and it may be completed prior to the obligation of payment. In the case of indirect interaction, a person who sells goods or service on behalf of the owner is known as a _____ man or _____ woman or _____ person, but this often refers to someone selling goods in a store/shop, in which case other terms are also common, including _____ clerk, shop assistant, and retail clerk.

Exam Probability: **Low**

39. *Answer choices:*

(see index for correct answer)

- a. Intangible asset finance
- b. Shriram Properties
- c. Winklevoss Capital Management
- d. Sales

Guidance: level 1

:: United States Generally Accepted Accounting Principles ::

In the United States, a _____ is one of the five governmental fund types established by GAAP. It is classified as a restricted true endowment fund for governments and non-profit organizations. Put simply, a _____ may be used to generate and disburse money to those entitled to receive payments by qualification or agreement, as in the case of Alaska citizens or residents that satisfy the rules for payment from their _____ from State oil revenues. It was first introduced through GASB Statement 34. The name of the fund comes from the purpose of the fund: a sum of equity used to permanently generate payments to maintain some financial obligation. Also, a fund can only be classified as a _____ if the money is used to report the status of a restricted financial resource. The resource is restricted in the sense that only earnings from the resource are used and not the principal. For example, a fund can be classified as a _____ if it is being used to pay for accounting services for a perpetual endowment of a government-run cemetery or financial endowments towards a government-run library.

Exam Probability: **High**

40. *Answer choices:*

(see index for correct answer)

- a. GASB 45
- b. Permanent fund
- c. Comprehensive income
- d. FIN 46

Guidance: level 1

:: Financial ratios ::

_____ or asset turns is a financial ratio that measures the efficiency of a company's use of its assets in generating sales revenue or sales income to the company.

Exam Probability: **Low**

41. *Answer choices:*

(see index for correct answer)

- a. stock turnover
- b. Retention rate
- c. Envy ratio
- d. Equity ratio

Guidance: level 1

:: ::

The _____ is a private, non-profit organization standard-setting body whose primary purpose is to establish and improve Generally Accepted Accounting Principles within the United States in the public's interest. The Securities and Exchange Commission designated the FASB as the organization responsible for setting accounting standards for public companies in the US. The FASB replaced the American Institute of Certified Public Accountants' Accounting Principles Board on July 1, 1973.

Exam Probability: **High**

42. Answer choices:

(see index for correct answer)

- a. cultural
- b. deep-level diversity
- c. Financial Accounting Standards Board
- d. Character

Guidance: level 1

:: Finance ::

In accounting, _____ is the portion of a subsidiary corporation's stock that is not owned by the parent corporation. The magnitude of the _____ in the subsidiary company is generally less than 50% of outstanding shares, or the corporation would generally cease to be a subsidiary of the parent.

Exam Probability: **Medium**

43. Answer choices:

(see index for correct answer)

- a. Regulatory News Service
- b. Offshore bank
- c. Minority interest
- d. Rollover

Guidance: level 1

:: ::

An _____ is a systematic and independent examination of books, accounts, statutory records, documents and vouchers of an organization to ascertain how far the financial statements as well as non-financial disclosures present a true and fair view of the concern. It also attempts to ensure that the books of accounts are properly maintained by the concern as required by law. _____ ing has become such a ubiquitous phenomenon in the corporate and the public sector that academics started identifying an " _____ Society". The _____ or perceives and recognises the propositions before them for examination, obtains evidence, evaluates the same and formulates an opinion on the basis of his judgement which is communicated through their _____ ing report.

Exam Probability: **Low**

44. *Answer choices:*

(see index for correct answer)

- a. deep-level diversity
- b. cultural
- c. process perspective
- d. interpersonal communication

Guidance: level 1

:: Taxation ::

_____ is a type of tax law that allows a person to give assets to his or her spouse with reduced or no tax imposed upon the transfer. Some _____ laws even apply to transfers made postmortem. The right to receive property conveys ownership for tax purposes. A decree of divorce transfers the right to that property by reason of the marriage and is also a transfer within a marriage. It makes no difference whether the property itself or equivalent compensation is transferred before, or after the decree dissolves the marriage. There is no U.S. estate and gift tax on transfers of any amount between spouses, whether during their lifetime or at death. There is an important exceptions for non-citizens. The U.S. federal Estate and gift tax _____ is only available if the surviving spouse is a U.S. citizen. For a surviving spouse who is not a U.S. citizen a bequest through a Qualified Domestic Trust defers estate tax until principal is distributed by the trustee, a U.S. citizen or corporation who also withholds the estate tax. Income on principal distributed to the surviving spouse is taxed as individual income. If the surviving spouse becomes a U.S. citizen, principal remaining in a Qualifying Domestic Trust may then be distributed without further tax.

Exam Probability: **Medium**

45. *Answer choices:*

(see index for correct answer)

- a. Income tax and gambling losses
- b. Marital deduction
- c. Kharaj
- d. Severance tax

Guidance: level 1

:: Competition (economics) ::

In taxation and accounting, _____ refers to the rules and methods for pricing transactions within and between enterprises under common ownership or control. Because of the potential for cross-border controlled transactions to distort taxable income, tax authorities in many countries can adjust intragroup transfer prices that differ from what would have been charged by unrelated enterprises dealing at arm's length. The OECD and World Bank recommend intragroup pricing rules based on the arm's-length principle, and 19 of the 20 members of the G20 have adopted similar measures through bilateral treaties and domestic legislation, regulations, or administrative practice. Countries with _____ legislation generally follow the OECD _____ Guidelines for Multinational Enterprises and Tax Administrations in most respects, although their rules can differ on some important details.

Exam Probability: **Low**

46. *Answer choices:*
(see index for correct answer)

- a. Self-competition
- b. Leapfrogging
- c. Category killer
- d. Transfer pricing

Guidance: level 1

:: Income taxes ::

An _____ is a tax imposed on individuals or entities that varies with respective income or profits. _____ generally is computed as the product of a tax rate times taxable income. Taxation rates may vary by type or characteristics of the taxpayer.

Exam Probability: **Low**

47. *Answer choices:*

(see index for correct answer)

- a. Rouanet Law
- b. Lifetime income tax
- c. Illinois Fair Tax
- d. Portland Arts Tax

Guidance: level 1

:: Accounting terminology ::

In accounting/accountancy, _____ are journal entries usually made at the end of an accounting period to allocate income and expenditure to the period in which they actually occurred. The revenue recognition principle is the basis of making _____ that pertain to unearned and accrued revenues under accrual-basis accounting. They are sometimes called Balance Day adjustments because they are made on balance day.

Exam Probability: **Low**

48. Answer choices:

(see index for correct answer)

- a. Adjusting entries
- b. Double-entry accounting
- c. General ledger
- d. Statement of financial position

Guidance: level 1

:: Generally Accepted Accounting Principles ::

_____ is, in accrual accounting, money received for goods or services which have not yet been delivered. According to the revenue recognition principle, it is recorded as a liability until delivery is made, at which time it is converted into revenue.

Exam Probability: **Low**

49. Answer choices:

(see index for correct answer)

- a. Net profit
- b. Cost pool
- c. Operating income before depreciation and amortization
- d. Deferred income

Guidance: level 1

:: ::

_____ is the consumption and saving opportunity gained by an entity within a specified timeframe, which is generally expressed in monetary terms. For households and individuals, "_____ is the sum of all the wages, salaries, profits, interest payments, rents, and other forms of earnings received in a given period of time."

Exam Probability: **Medium**

50. *Answer choices:*

(see index for correct answer)

- a. Income
- b. process perspective
- c. hierarchical
- d. corporate values

Guidance: level 1

:: Employment classifications ::

Generally, tax authorities will view a person as self-employed if the person chooses to be recognized as such, or is generating income such that the person is required to file a tax return under legislation in the relevant jurisdiction. In the real world, the critical issue for the taxing authorities is not that the person is trading but is whether the person is profitable and hence potentially taxable. In other words, the activity of trading is likely to be ignored if no profit is present, so occasional and hobby- or enthusiast-based economic activity is generally ignored by authorities.

Exam Probability: **Low**

51. *Answer choices:*

(see index for correct answer)

- a. Casual employment
- b. Freelancer
- c. Self-employment
- d. Temporary work

Guidance: level 1

:: Manufacturing ::

_____ costs are all manufacturing costs that are related to the cost object but cannot be traced to that cost object in an economically feasible way.

Exam Probability: **High**

52. *Answer choices:*

(see index for correct answer)

- a. Manufacturing overhead
- b. Nanofoundry
- c. Advanced planning and scheduling
- d. ISA-88

Guidance: level 1

:: Stock market ::

A _____, equity market or share market is the aggregation of buyers and sellers of stocks, which represent ownership claims on businesses; these may include securities listed on a public stock exchange, as well as stock that is only traded privately. Examples of the latter include shares of private companies which are sold to investors through equity crowdfunding platforms. Stock exchanges list shares of common equity as well as other security types, e.g. corporate bonds and convertible bonds.

Exam Probability: **Low**

53. *Answer choices:*

(see index for correct answer)

- a. Intermarket sweep order
- b. Common stock
- c. Yellow strip

- d. Stock Market

Guidance: level 1

:: Management accounting ::

_____ is a method of identifying and evaluating activities that a business performs, using activity-based costing to carry out a value chain analysis or a re-engineering initiative to improve strategic and operational decisions in an organization.

Exam Probability: **Low**

54. *Answer choices:*

(see index for correct answer)

- a. Responsibility center
- b. Notional profit
- c. Revenue center
- d. Construction accounting

Guidance: level 1

:: Accounting terminology ::

Accounts are typically defined by an identifier and a caption or header and are coded by account type. In computerized accounting systems with computable quantity accounting, the accounts can have a quantity measure definition.

Exam Probability: **High**

55. *Answer choices:*

(see index for correct answer)

- a. Adjusting entries
- b. managerial accounting
- c. profit and loss statement
- d. Chart of accounts

Guidance: level 1

:: Credit cards ::

The _____ Company, also known as Amex, is an American multinational financial services corporation headquartered in Three World Financial Center in New York City. The company was founded in 1850 and is one of the 30 components of the Dow Jones Industrial Average. The company is best known for its charge card, credit card, and traveler's cheque businesses.

Exam Probability: **High**

56. *Answer choices:*

(see index for correct answer)

- a. Credit CARD Act of 2009
- b. TaiwanMoney Card
- c. Smiley v. Citibank
- d. Cashplus

Guidance: level 1

:: Economic globalization ::

_____ is an agreement in which one company hires another company to be responsible for a planned or existing activity that is or could be done internally, and sometimes involves transferring employees and assets from one firm to another.

Exam Probability: **Low**

57. *Answer choices:*

(see index for correct answer)

- a. global financial
- b. reshoring

Guidance: level 1

:: Insurance terms ::

A _____ in the broadest sense is a natural person or other legal entity who receives money or other benefits from a benefactor. For example, the _____ of a life insurance policy is the person who receives the payment of the amount of insurance after the death of the insured.

Exam Probability: **High**

58. *Answer choices:*

(see index for correct answer)

- a. replacement cost
- b. Beneficiary
- c. Subrogation
- d. Co-insurance

Guidance: level 1

:: Generally Accepted Accounting Principles ::

_____ is all a person's receipts and gains from all sources, before any deductions. The adjective "gross", as opposed to "net", generally qualifies a word referring to an amount, value, weight, number, or the like, specifying that necessary deductions have not been taken into account.

Exam Probability: **High**

59. *Answer choices:*

(see index for correct answer)

- a. Construction in progress
- b. Gross income
- c. Goodwill
- d. Reserve

Guidance: level 1

INDEX: Correct Answers

Foundations of Business

1. d: Payment

2. a: Ownership

3. d: Investment

4. d: Target market

5. a: Risk

6. b: Free trade

7. c: Market value

8. d: Competition

9. a: Industrial Revolution

10. a: Budget

11. d: Question

12. : Cash

13. : Dividend

14. c: Audience

15. : Human resources

16. c: Threat

17. : Currency

18. a: Affirmative action

19. d: Percentage

20. : Risk management

21. a: Social security

22. b: Capital market

23. : Focus group

24. c: Joint venture

25. : Labor relations

26. : Venture capital

27. a: Accounts receivable

28. d: Property

29. b: Sexual harassment

30. d: Publicity

31. c: Accounting

32. d: Negotiation

33. c: Case study

34. : Industry

35. c: Policy

36. d: Marketing mix

37. c: Scheduling

38. c: Purchasing

39. a: Retail

40. c: Sharing

41. c: Bias

42. b: System

43. : Balance sheet

44. d: Project management

45. d: Dimension

46. b: Internal control

47. d: Marketing

48. : Crisis

49. d: Interview

50. : Project

51. d: Productivity

52. a: Land

53. c: Bribery

54. : Partnership

55. d: Pattern

56. : Management system

57. b: Inventory

58. b: Gross domestic product

59. : Perception

Management

1. : Schedule

2. c: Inventory control

3. : Management system

4. a: Intranet

5. c: Bounded rationality

6. a: Ownership

7. : Entrepreneur

8. d: Choice

9. a: Research and development

10. c: Office

11. b: Task force

12. c: Self-assessment

13. a: Social capital

14. b: Project manager

15. d: Transactional leadership

16. d: Logistics

17. a: Kaizen

18. : Revenue

19. d: Theory X

20. a: Organizational learning

21. b: Proactive

22. a: Incentive

23. c: Executive officer

24. c: SWOT analysis

25. c: Export

26. : Industrial Revolution

27. a: European Union

28. a: Productivity

29. b: Dilemma

30. : Risk management

31. a: Project team

32. c: Decentralization

33. a: Information

34. a: International trade

35. b: Contingency theory

36. c: Bias

37. a: Procurement

38. c: Statistic

39. c: Learning organization

40. d: Environmental scanning

41. d: Quality circle

42. b: Governance

43. b: Quality assurance

44. b: Performance appraisal

45. c: Business plan

46. b: Strategic alliance

47. a: Customer

48. c: Entrepreneurship

49. d: Small business

50. c: Business process

51. c: Synergy

52. c: Resource management

53. d: Business model

54. b: Strategic management

55. : Sexual harassment

56. b: Pension

57. d: Project

58. d: Profit sharing

59. : Absenteeism

Business law

1. : Stock

2. c: Copyright

3. : Firm offer

4. d: Enron

5. a: Federal government

6. : Option contract

7. b: Contract law

8. : Public policy

9. a: Testimony

10. : Consumer Good

11. : Relevant market

12. a: Financial privacy

13. b: Duty of care

14. d: Cause of action

15. c: Resource

16. a: Bankruptcy

17. d: Property

18. a: Income

19. b: Clayton Act

20. a: Independent contractor

21. d: Statute

22. a: Common carrier

23. b: Aid

24. : Lease

25. b: Affirmative action

26. c: Undue influence

27. d: Advertisement

28. : Mirror image rule

29. d: Employment law

30. c: Shares

31. d: Warehouse

32. : Tangible

33. a: Forgery

34. : Personnel

35. d: Offeror

36. : Deed

37. b: Purchasing

38. : Injunction

39. a: Revocation

40. a: Mediation

41. c: Auction

42. d: Uniform Commercial Code

43. b: Duress

44. c: Disclaimer

45. a: Fee simple

46. c: Limited liability

47. : Res ipsa

48. b: Misrepresentation

49. d: Inventory

50. : Private law

51. a: Revenue

52. b: Management

53. d: Sherman Act

54. : Garnishment

55. d: Corporation

56. : Eminent domain

57. : Authority

58. d: Certiorari

59. d: Warranty

Finance

1. : Credit

2. a: Fixed asset

3. b: Break-even

4. b: Cost accounting

5. a: Risk assessment

6. b: Opportunity cost

7. : Future value

8. b: Derivative

9. b: Capital asset pricing model

10. a: Debenture

11. d: Chart of accounts

12. d: Economy

13. c: Adjusting entries

14. a: Asset

15. a: Shareholder

16. b: Financial instrument

17. : Citigroup

18. : Indenture

19. d: Par value

20. c: Market price

21. a: Cost of goods sold

22. d: Managerial accounting

23. : Source document

24. : Enron

25. b: Bad debt

26. a: Patent

27. b: Stock price

28. : Fraud

29. c: Demand

30. c: Shares

31. b: Industry

32. a: Debt

33. a: Operating Income

34. b: Manufacturing cost

35. c: General ledger

36. b: Rate risk

37. c: Sales

38. c: Financial market

39. a: Time value of money

40. b: Commercial paper

41. a: Standard deviation

42. b: Working capital

43. d: Total cost

44. b: Incentive

45. d: Net profit

46. c: Saving

47. : Presentation

48. a: Buyer

49. : Government bond

50. a: Need

51. d: Convertible bond

52. b: Policy

53. d: Value Line

54. d: Net present value

55. c: Inflation

56. d: Return on investment

57. c: Credit card

58. : Subsidiary ledger

59. b: Accrued liabilities

Human resource management

1. b: Employee engagement

2. c: Total Quality Management

3. a: Local union

4. d: Workforce

5. b: Occupational Information Network

6. : Onboarding

7. c: Executive search

8. b: Unemployment benefits

9. a: Restructuring

10. b: Locus of control

11. a: Social contract

12. a: Paid time off

13. d: Vertical integration

14. b: Distance learning

15. a: Nearshoring

16. c: Employee surveys

17. a: National Association of Colleges and Employers

18. : Recession

19. d: Strategy map

20. a: Cost of living

21. c: Outplacement

22. d: Bottom line

23. : Overlearning

24. c: Piece rate

25. a: Sexual harassment

26. b: Workforce management

27. b: Ownership

28. d: Service Employees International Union

29. b: Employee stock

30. c: Tacit knowledge

31. b: Strategic management

32. a: Scientific management

33. c: Asset

34. a: Layoff

35. c: Glass ceiling

36. a: Reinforcement

37. : Wage

38. b: Empowerment

39. c: Realistic job preview

40. : Construct validity

41. d: McDonnell Douglas Corp. v. Green

42. b: Profession

43. a: Total Reward

44. a: Vesting

45. b: Employee Free Choice Act

46. c: Meeting

47. a: Family violence

48. : National Labor Relations Act

49. a: Action learning

50. a: Trainee

51. b: Scanlon plan

52. b: Foreign worker

53. b: Drug test

54. b: Organizational structure

55. b: E-HRM

56. d: Centralization

57. a: Living wage

58. : Retraining

59. a: Agency shop

Information systems

1. b: Data aggregator

2. d: Software as a service

3. : User interface

4. c: Data integrity

5. b: Consumer-to-business

6. : Yelp

7. b: Mass customization

8. d: Expert system

9. d: Backbone network

10. d: ICANN

11. a: Cybersquatting

12. a: Payment system

13. : Zynga

14. : Data center

15. c: Content management system

16. c: Service-oriented architecture

17. a: Automated teller machine

18. a: Information overload

19. a: Botnet

20. a: Questionnaire

21. a: Word

22. d: Market share

23. : Viral marketing

24. a: Data element

25. b: Netflix

26. b: Web server

27. b: Government-to-government

28. : Information management

29. b: Edge computing

30. c: Peer production

31. c: Electronic data interchange

32. d: Click-through

33. : Security controls

34. d: Click fraud

35. c: Code

36. a: Critical success factor

37. b: Gmail

38. d: Data file

39. b: Geocoding

40. c: Authentication

41. b: Chart

42. b: Accessibility

43. d: Social network

44. d: Computer security

45. d: Transport Layer Security

46. d: Database management system

47. a: Social shopping

48. b: Outsourcing

49. d: Global Positioning System

50. a: Enterprise search

51. b: Click-through rate

52. c: Pop-up ad

53. : PeopleSoft

54. a: Information governance

55. c: Enterprise information system

56. c: Information technology

57. b: Debit card

58. d: Porter five forces analysis

59. d: Information flow

Marketing

1. : Value proposition

2. a: Disintermediation

3. d: Social network

4. : Warranty

5. a: Public

6. c: Merchant

7. b: Cost-plus pricing

8. b: Infomercial

9. c: Global marketing

10. : Committee

11. d: Complexity

12. b: Direct selling

13. : Brainstorming

14. a: Feedback

15. d: Consumer Protection

16. a: Leadership

17. : Resource

18. b: Concept testing

19. a: Telemarketing

20. a: Star

21. c: Competitive intelligence

22. c: Department store

23. c: Monopoly

24. c: Personnel

25. b: Strategy

26. a: Trademark

27. b: Shares

28. a: Goal

29. a: Social media

30. c: Brand

31. d: Performance

32. d: Credit

33. d: Competitive advantage

34. c: Marketing plan

35. c: Reinforcement

36. c: Need

37. c: Public relations

38. d: Preference

39. a: Direct mail

40. a: Argument

41. a: Merchandising

42. d: Early adopter

43. : Presentation

44. : Market development

45. : Price

46. b: Marketing channel

47. d: Regulation

48. d: Advertisement

49. c: Aid

50. c: Penetration pricing

51. c: Green marketing

52. b: Sponsorship

53. d: Evolution

54. b: Cognitive dissonance

55. c: Adoption

56. d: Innovation

57. c: Raw material

58. : Services marketing

59. c: Advertising

Manufacturing

1. c: Opportunity cost

2. b: Electronic data interchange

3. d: Quality audit

4. a: Planning

5. a: New product development

6. b: Toshiba

7. d: Steel

8. : Procurement

9. c: DMAIC

10. a: Virtual team

11. b: Project manager

12. : Accreditation

13. b: Heat transfer

14. d: Purchase order

15. : Manufacturing

16. a: Management process

17. b: Transaction cost

18. c: Customer

19. : Estimation

20. b: Lead

21. a: Control limits

22. d: Purchasing manager

23. a: Goal

24. d: Natural resource

25. d: Statistical process control

26. : Total cost of ownership

27. d: Initiative

28. a: Design of experiments

29. c: Concurrent engineering

30. a: Rolling Wave planning

31. d: Information management

32. : E-commerce

33. b: Supply chain

34. : Capacity planning

35. d: Acceptance sampling

36. b: Process capability

37. d: Project team

38. d: Ishikawa diagram

39. c: Property

40. c: Quality management

41. d: Quality assurance

42. a: American Society for Quality

43. d: Process flow diagram

44. c: Durability

45. b: Extended enterprise

46. d: Raw material

47. a: Resource

48. b: Technical support

49. b: Throughput

50. b: Quality policy

51. c: Economies of scope

52. : Waste

53. : Purchasing process

54. : Heat treating

55. : Reverse auction

56. d: Minitab

57. : Licensed production

58. : Quality function deployment

59. a: Control chart

Commerce

1. b: Contribution margin

2. : Staff position

3. c: Consignee

4. d: Webvan

5. a: Procurement

6. c: Initiative

7. a: Variable cost

8. a: Market structure

9. : Raw material

10. a: Asset

11. a: Wage

12. : Credit

13. c: Quality assurance

14. b: Committee

15. b: Customer service

16. b: Negotiation

17. a: Frequency

18. d: Product line

19. d: Insurance

20. b: Hospitality

21. d: Federal government

22. d: Human resources

23. d: Planning

24. d: Audit

25. d: Real estate

26. : Online advertising

27. c: Organization chart

28. b: Mining

29. d: Amazon Payments

30. c: Exchange rate

31. : Building

32. d: Appeal

33. b: Microsoft

34. c: Electronic funds transfer

35. c: Standardization

36. : Commerce

37. c: Board of directors

38. : Transaction cost

39. : Productivity

40. b: Jurisdiction

41. d: Pension

42. a: Wholesale

43. a: Deregulation

44. d: GeoCities

45. b: Customs

46. d: British Airways

47. d: Complaint

48. : Evaluation

49. a: Fraud

50. b: Economy

51. b: Merger

52. a: Joint venture

53. d: Chief executive officer

54. b: Drawback

55. b: Consultant

56. a: Freight forwarder

57. b: Inflation

58. d: Logistics Management

59. c: Anticipation

Business ethics

1. a: Federal Trade Commission

2. : Pure Food and Drug Act

3. c: Corporate citizenship

4. c: Fair Trade Certified

5. : Skill

6. c: Pollution

7. b: United Farm Workers

8. b: Clean Water Act

9. : Individualistic culture

10. : Copyright

11. c: Affirmative action

12. : Collusion

13. c: Self-interest

14. d: Energy policy

15. a: Labor relations

16. b: Sherman Antitrust Act

17. c: Fraud

18. c: Insider trading

19. b: Consumer Financial Protection Bureau

20. b: Criminal law

21. a: Public relations

22. a: Marijuana

23. a: Qui tam

24. : Ethical leadership

25. a: Perception

26. d: Minimum wage

27. a: Social networking

28. b: Ethics Resource Center

29. c: Pollution Prevention

30. : Aristotle

31. c: Sexual harassment

32. b: Natural gas

33. d: Recovery Act

34. : Trade

35. c: Corporation

36. c: Clayton Act

37. a: Arthur Andersen

38. d: Dilemma

39. : Organizational ethics

40. d: Employee Polygraph Protection Act

41. d: Conscience

42. c: Price fixing

43. d: Organizational structure

44. a: Subprime lending

45. b: Fair trade

46. c: Referent power

47. c: Constitutional law

48. b: Working poor

49. c: Medicaid

50. : Charles Ponzi

51. b: ExxonMobil

52. c: New York Stock Exchange

53. b: East India

54. c: Principal Financial

55. c: Invisible hand

56. b: Forest Stewardship Council

57. b: Solar power

58. d: Cause-related marketing

59. : UN Global Compact

Accounting

1. d: Regulation S-K

2. d: Calendar year

3. : Accelerated depreciation

4. : Sales tax

5. a: Public Company Accounting Oversight Board

6. b: Securities and Exchange Commission

7. a: Norwalk Agreement

8. : Statement of retained earnings

9. : Forensic

10. c: Governmental accounting

11. b: Dividend yield

12. c: Revenue recognition

13. a: Maturity date

14. b: Trial balance

15. : Time value of money

16. a: Online banking

17. d: International Financial Reporting Standards

18. : Financial statement analysis

19. b: Internal Revenue Service

20. a: Budget

21. c: Bank

22. b: Preferred stock

23. d: Cost of goods sold

24. d: Pro forma

25. a: Adverse

26. a: Relevant cost

27. a: Fraud

28. d: Comprehensive income

29. c: Institute of Management Accountants

30. a: Income approach

31. b: Capital loss

32. : Financial ratio

33. d: Error

34. : Income statement

35. b: Ending inventory

36. b: International Federation of Accountants

37. b: Accounting method

38. b: Indirect costs

39. d: Sales

40. b: Permanent fund

41. : Asset turnover

42. c: Financial Accounting Standards Board

43. c: Minority interest

44. : Audit

45. b: Marital deduction

46. d: Transfer pricing

47. : Income tax

48. a: Adjusting entries

49. d: Deferred income

50. a: Income

51. c: Self-employment

52. a: Manufacturing overhead

53. d: Stock Market

54. : Activity-based management

55. d: Chart of accounts

56. : American Express

57. c: Outsourcing

58. b: Beneficiary

59. b: Gross income

CPSIA information can be obtained
at www.ICGtesting.com
Printed in the USA
LVHW031226301019
635717LV00006B/559/P